IN THE
LEADERSHIP
MODE

IN THE
LEADERSHIP
MODE

CONCEPTS, PRACTICES, AND TOOLS
FOR A DIFFERENT LEADERSHIP

DON DUNOON

Foreword by
Iva Wilson
Retired President, Philips Display Components
First President, Society for Organizational Learning (SoL)

ACKNOWLEDGEMENTS

Hundreds of people have contributed to this book and I am deeply grateful to them, even though the vast majority are unknown to me at this time. These are the participants in my workshops and seminars over almost a decade and a half whose observations, questions, ideas, and critiques have stimulated, challenged, and sharpened the thinking that has resulted in this book.

Dr Tony Donovan, my *Organisational Behaviour* teacher at the University of New South Wales in the late 1980s and early 1990s, sparked my initial interest in the relationship between leadership and learning. Now retired, Tony was a great teacher. His classes at UNSW were inspiring, especially his course *Human Potentialities*. Tony introduced me to many of the authors, frameworks, and concepts that have contributed to the development of my own approach to leadership. And, over the years, he has generously provided advice, counsel, and support. He also offered confronting—but necessary—feedback on some early chapter drafts.

I have been privileged to be assisted by two people who are authors in this area in their own right. Dr. Iva Wilson and Dr. JoAnne O'Brien-Levin (then Wyer) wrote, with Bert Frydman, *The Power of Collaborative Leadership: Lessons for the Learning Organization* (Butterworth Heinemann, 2000).

Iva, who has kindly contributed the Foreword, is a retired President of Philips Display Components, was the first President of the Society for Organizational Learning (SoL), and is now an executive coach and consultant. Over nearly two years in the writing process, I have been most fortunate to have Iva as a mentor and advisor. Iva graciously assisted me in thinking through some key concepts, particularly with respect to the leadership-management relationship. The combination of her top-level business experience and organizational learning know-how, together with the encouragement and support she has offered, have been most important in helping me to pull the book together.

JoAnne, as the editor of this book, brought a unique combination of subject matter expertise and superb editing skills to the role. JoAnne's appreciation of the intent and core concepts of the book, her deep knowledge of the fields of leadership and organizational learning, together with her writing skills and attention to detail, resulted in major improvements to the unfolding and expression of ideas. Beyond that, she was able to contribute to the development of some of the key concepts. And this was all done in a most responsive, easy-to-work-with style. Five "in" words come to mind to describe JoAnne's contribution: intelligent, insightful, incisive, inventive—and invaluable.

The writings of many authors have helped shape my thinking about the ideas presented here, and I am indebted to them: in particular; Chris Argyris, Peter Block, David Bohm, Arthur Deikman, Wilfred Drath, Michael Fullan, W. Timothy Gallwey, Peter Gronn, Ronald Heifetz, William Isaacs, John Kotter, Linda Lambert, Ellen Langer, Gareth Morgan, Robert Quinn, Joseph Rost, Edgar Schein, Donald Schön, Peter Senge, and William Torbert. While the names are in alphabetical order, it is a happy coincidence that the most influential individual appears first.

Several clients over the years have provided encouragement and helpful input. Particular thanks go to Don Challen, Dr Brian Jones, Julie Thompson, and Ross Woodward.

Ingo Voss and Linda Maclean as the book design team were creative, responsive, and showed a wonderful ability to capture just what I wanted. I am very grateful to them.

I am deeply appreciative for the "critical friendship" of Christopher Szaday, Tony Dolk, Robert Dolk, Carl Jefferys, Wendy Dyson, Deborah Trevan-Catling, Rodney Gray, Greg Masters, and Andrew O'Keefe.

David Noble most generously shared his story of discovering the Wollemi Pine, which opens Chapter 1.

Thanks go also to John Elsom and the staff at Questacon, Australia's National Science and Technology Centre in Canberra, for their help on the Chapter 3 story, featuring the Curve Ball ride.

During the lengthy writing process, I very much valued the camaraderie of the staff at my "writing headquarters," Everywhere Internet/Gloria Jeans in Sydney.

Finally, thanks with love go to my immediate family—wife Jennifer and children Bridget and Liam—for their patience and support as I struggled to "wrestle the book to the floor." Yes, kids, the book is finally finished!

CONTENTS

Foreword   ix

Introduction   1

PART ONE Foundations

Chapter 1   *Three Vines in the Forest of Leadership*   13

Chapter 2   *Leadership from a Learning Perspective*   27

Chapter 3   *The Roots of Leadership-Mode Action*   53

Chapter 4   *Reinterpreting the Leadership-Management Relationship*   75

Chapter 5   *Active Choice and the Leadership Mode*   93

PART TWO The ARIES Framework—Practices and Tools

Preamble to Part Two   113

Chapter 6   *Attending*   117

Chapter 7   *Reflecting*   131

Chapter 8   *Inquiring*   147

Chapter 9   *Expressing*   167

Chapter 10   *Synthesizing*   183

Epilogue   197

Appendix   *More Untangling of the Vines of Leadership*   207

Notes   211

About the Author   223

Index   225

FOREWORD

Iva Wilson

Retired President, Philips Display Components
First President, Society for Organizational Learning (SoL)

Out of the blue, one day in October of 2006, an Australian who said he was writing a book on leadership contacted me. He said he had discovered my own book *The Power of Collaborative Leadership: Lessons for the Learning Organization*. I co-authored this book with JoAnne O'Brien-Levin (formerly Wyer) and Bert Frydman. The caller said he thought that he and I shared some common ground, and he was wondering whether I would be willing to take a look at what he had written so far and give him feedback. The caller was Don Dunoon, the author of this book.

In this first call, Don described to me the general thrust of his book. He told me that his approach to leadership, which he has been developing and testing for years, challenged some basic premises. Namely, he questioned the prevailing assumption that leadership can only be done by people whom others see as leaders, by virtue of their personal characteristics or qualities. He also challenged other commonly-held ideas: that leadership is the province of only those in authority; that leadership is based on influence; and that it is a waste of time to tease out any distinction between leadership and management.

Don talked about leadership as grounded in learning (rather than influence), and as something very distinct from management.

As to my own background, I had been involved with Learning Organization concepts since the early 1990s. I had worked closely with Peter Senge, first as the president of a company committed to weaving Organizational Learning tools into the fabric of the organization in order to deal more effectively with business issues, and later as the president of the Society of Organizational Learning, which emerged out of the Organizational Learning Center of MIT. Because of the resonance with my own background, I was greatly intrigued by what Don said. The fact that I had also co-authored a book on leadership based on Organizational Learning tools further underscored my interest in Don's work.

This is how our relationship began. With time, I had the opportunity to read the material in his book as he was developing it. I gave him my commentary, and discussed with him some potential implications of his work.

Having read many books on leadership I can say that Don's book is different in many ways. He has set out to think about leadership as a process and has introduced in this book a new concept of leadership that is distinctive and, importantly, separate from management. He has identified a new "species" of leadership, which he terms learning-centered leadership, and talks about this form of leadership as being expressed through specific, in-the-moment interventions. When people make these interventions, they are acting "in the leadership mode." Don makes a distinction between actions we take in the leadership mode and those we take when we are in what he calls the "management mode." He argues that leadership-mode action is important because the management mode is inadequate for helping people face and overcome the contentious problems that confound most organizations. His argument is that in most organizations the management mode dominates, and this dominance hampers efforts to deal with such problems. Through various "case stories" he illustrates the need for one mode as opposed to the other.

In spite of the fact that many scholars and other authors talk about learning as a process that improves one's leadership, the characterization of leadership Don introduces is novel. I have not seen anything like it in any other book on leadership. Reading Don's book truly opened my eyes relative to my own leadership style, particularly with respect to the ways in which I went about my work as president of Philips Display Components. While I was introducing the tools and methods of Organizational Learning into the organization I was certain that I had opened the doors for others in the company to, as Don puts it, practice learning-centered leadership. Only after reading Don's book did I realize the mistakes I made as I attempted to walk this new path. I am strongly recommending this book to all those who are serious about making positive and lasting changes in their way of leading.

In this book Don also introduces a set of practices and tools to help practitioners apply the new concepts. The overall framework goes by the name ARIES, which is an acronym for each of the learning-leadership practices: attending, reflecting, inquiring, expressing, and synthesizing. At one level, Don sees these as practices; by working with them, people can progressively develop their capability, for performing learning-centered leadership work. At another level, ARIES is a set of pragmatic tools that we can use to help us deal with contentious problems.

Laying the groundwork for a new, groundbreaking view of leadership—as well as providing practitioners with a toolkit—is no small task. The book must cover a lot of ground, so there is quite a bit of material. To make it easier for the reader, the book is divided into two parts: Part 1 lays out the argument for a new view of leadership, and so is more conceptual. Part 2 introduces the ARIES practices and tools, and shows their practical application. As Don points out in the book's introduction, the reader can choose what to focus on depending on his or her interests. I would personally suggest that those who are interested in a new way of defining leadership should spend a lot of time reading and reflecting on Part 1. Those in organizations needing change would benefit most from examining the practices and tools in Part 2, and thinking about how they might use them to regenerate leadership based on Don's definitions.

As a leader myself, and also as an individual who has studied and written a book on leadership, I found reading both parts to be beneficial, though I was drawn more to Part 2. In any case, throughout the book Don has pointed out how to best use the material for one's benefit. He has also supplied summaries at the end of each chapter. The summaries describe very well the material dealt with in each chapter in an abridged form. If the reader is interested in acquiring an overview before delving in, this is a good way to start.

In summary, I believe this book will add a substantial amount of new knowledge to the field of leadership. This new knowledge is important and necessary if we are to improve upon the current state of leadership in organizations, and to make them more successful in the future.

July 2008

INTRODUCTION

Outlines of a Usefully Different Leadership

Bernardo, a mid-level executive in a components distribution business, wants his company to be more innovative, a view apparently shared by many employees. Despite the company's internal and external communications referring to its "commitment to innovation," a recent survey has revealed that this is not the reality many employees see. Bernardo is thinking of raising with top executives the gap between the company's claims and employee perceptions—but he is hesitant. "I don't know that they want to deal with this issue," he says. "In the past I definitely wouldn't have spoken up, as I haven't seen myself as a leader. These days I don't dwell on the leader question. I'm more concerned with building my intervention skills."

Alice, a high school assistant principal, is seeking to bring about a change in the school's teaching and learning culture, to better enable the learning needs of all students to be met. She has long regarded herself as a capable leader. "I've usually been able to set a direction," she says, "and influence and motivate others to come with me. But it's not working now. Some of the teachers openly oppose the new direction. These people are stuck in a time warp. And I have to deal with this on top of the pressures involved in overseeing the day-to-day running of the school."

Bernardo and Alice are both dealing with what I am calling "contentious problems." These are essentially problems that can be viewed from different perspectives: there is no single answer or solution to be revealed. Such problems have a Janus-like (two-headed) character. To gain a sense of this image, you might imagine an ancient statue, a statue with one head facing to your left and one head to your right.

The left-facing head represents the more overt, explicit aspects of a contentious problem, meaning the things that are tangible, documented, or observable. With Alice's school change problem, some of the explicit aspects are the arguments—perhaps expressed with passion and intensity—that Alice and the teachers are putting forward, and the "evidence" each side is drawing on to support those arguments. Switching to Bernardo's innovation problem, explicit aspects here include the actual results from the employee survey and stated company values and policies relating to innovation.

The right-facing head of the statue represents those aspects of a contentious problem that are more subtle, covert, or implicit. We can think of this head as covered with a veil or a shroud—the "head of hidden intelligence." It stands for what is in people's hearts and minds about the problem but which has not been made explicit. In Bernardo's innovation case, it appears the gap between the company's stated commitment to innovation and the survey results has not been discussed openly yet. Because the topic appears to have been avoided, we might well imagine that at least some members of the executive group have privately-held thoughts and feelings on this matter. In Alice's case, it is also likely that much is unspoken. Alice probably has in mind strategies about how she intends to achieve change that she has not yet shared. Equally, the teachers may have assumptions, concerns, and fears that they have not given voice to—or perhaps have not even recognized themselves.

Commonly, in dealing with contentious problems, we allow ourselves to be preoccupied with the left-sided head. We focus on the more tangible, concrete aspects of the problem. We argue about the "facts" and those more solid aspects as if the other head did not exist. The veil remains firmly in place. Yet, if we can lift that veil somewhat, we potentially tap into huge resources that could be helpful in dealing with the problem: deep but implicit assumptions; unvoiced concerns and feelings; and knowledge that people hold, but keep to themselves. Most likely the teachers in Alice's school—or the employees in Bernardo's company—would have much to contribute to working through contentious problems in their respective organizations, but their contribution often goes unsolicited.

A critical challenge for leadership is to draw out these latent mental resources, so that they may be examined, interpreted, and integrated—allowing that some contention may remain—to achieve joint understandings about present realities and preferred futures, and to generate energy for change. In effect, this requires tapping into and working with the intelligence reflected by both heads of the statue. But, our dominant views of leadership hold us back.

Why We Need a Different View of Leadership

Conventional approaches to leadership are of limited usefulness in dealing with contentious problems. This is because the most widely held assumptions underpinning these approaches are outdated, at best. Four of the most prevalent assumptions are:

1. Leadership is equivalent to leaders.
2. Leadership is exclusively the function of those in positions of considerable authority.
3. Leadership is based in influence processes.
4. Little is to be gained by trying to differentiate leadership and management.

These assumptions are not necessarily without some foundation.[1] The problem is that uncritical reliance upon them distorts our understanding of leadership and limits the possibilities we can see. Ultimately, this diminishes the potential for leadership to achieve results—particularly with respect to contentious problems. For example:

Leadership is Equivalent to Leaders Leadership and leaders are commonly treated as largely interchangeable terms: leaders perform leadership, and leadership is performed by leaders. We attach leadership to some people, who—because of their perceived personal qualities or attributes—are regarded as leaders. A consequence is that the potential leadership contribution of "non-leaders" or "followers" is denied. Consider this example: a small, specialist financial advisory company had four directors. Three of the four said to the fourth, who was quieter and more reserved than the others, "We don't see you as a leader." Yet, depending on how we frame our understanding of leadership, that fourth director might be able to make a significant contribution, even if he does not fit conventional images (or, more strictly, his colleagues' images) of a leader. Focusing on the "who" of leadership distracts us from the "what." As long as we focus on which *people* are leaders or not, we can be blinded from looking at the *processes* of leadership, in terms of the kinds of actions that will help us deal most productively with contentious problems.

Leadership is Exclusively the Function of those in Positions of Considerable Authority One consequence of this assumption is that the actions of top executives—for instance, in strategy-making, policy review and performance monitoring—can be taken as representing leadership, without any critical appraisal of what those actions involve. Yet, the people in the highest-ranking roles are often remote from the issues, and may have little appreciation of the contentious matters. People who are closer to the action may have a better appreciation of specific aspects of the problem but, insofar as they have lesser or little authority, they tend not to see leadership contributions as theirs to make. The intention here is not to discount the importance of leadership at the top, but to foster fresh thinking and action in relation to leadership at *all* levels of the hierarchy.

Leadership is Primarily an Influence Process This notion underpins "transformational leadership," currently a dominant paradigm. Ideally, the transformational leader assesses the problem to be dealt with, develops a vision representing the problem overcome, and communicates the vision so as to inspire and enthuse others to pursue the vision. Undoubtedly, some people demonstrate transformational qualities and there are numerous success stories. But often the promise remains unfulfilled, as Alice is experiencing in her efforts to lead change in the school.

The transformational leader may be unable to gauge accurately what others think and feel, but do not openly state about the problem. Perhaps "followers" are not convinced of either the vision's desirability or that it can be achieved. They may remain silent about their reservations so as to appear loyal and committed. Transformational leadership approaches have little to offer in dealing with the hidden dimension of contentious problems—what people are potentially aware of but do not talk about—other than processes for better persuading others to go along with the leader's view.

Little is to be Gained from Trying to Separate Leadership and Management This fourth assumption reflects the confusion implicit in the other assumptions. If we neglect to differentiate leadership and management, we may believe we are exercising leadership when we are actually undertaking management actions, all the while wondering why we are making little progress.

A key proposition in this book is that management processes are *distinctly different* from leadership processes, with that distinction being not sufficiently well understood. This confusion hinders the resolution of contentious problems. I contend that most actions taken in relation to contentious problems are made in the management mode, even though the language of leadership is frequently invoked.

Management processes are important and useful with contentious problems in particular kinds of circumstances, such as when the need is to contain or limit the problem or to be able to demonstrate that action is being taken. As well, management and leadership processes can beneficially complement one another in dealing with such problems. Where management processes are not well suited, however, is in drawing out and examining the differing perceptions surrounding contentious problems. For that, we need leadership.

A Usefully Different Perspective

Dealing with contentious problems productively requires leadership of a distinct kind: leadership that is grounded in continuous learning. This kind of leadership is process-focused and highly relational. Why? Overcoming contentious problems requires nurturing the ability of groups to candidly evaluate their current realities, to come to a shared assessment, and then to create a shared vision of a desired future. In so doing, we harness collective energy, which is the only way to bring about—and sustain—the deep changes that these problems signify.

To that end, this book puts forward a new vision of leadership, with the following defining characteristics:

- Instead of focusing on the leader as a person, this distinct form accentuates leadership *processes*. These processes involve group members in assessing current realities, clarifying a common purpose and vision, and harnessing energy to bring the vision into being. This work takes place over time, through individuals taking certain kinds of actions—we shall use the term, "interventions"—which contribute to the group's leadership work. To intentionally undertake such interventions is to act "in the leadership mode."

- Rather than tying leadership to authority, our distinct form of leadership treats authority as only a background factor, not as a defining feature. An implication is that, in a group setting, anyone in the group can potentially make leadership interventions.

- In place of reliance on influence processes, the emphasis in this type of leadership is on *learning* processes. Learning here refers to processes of joint sense-making, in which people think together to formulate integrated understandings—while also remaining open to reviewing and, if necessary, changing, their own assumptions and conclusions. Reflecting the importance of learning, I refer to this as *learning-centered leadership* (sometimes abbreviating it to *learning-leadership*).

- In preference to setting aside the relationship between leadership and management as unhelpful or too difficult, learning-centered leadership is positioned specifically in relation to management action. Choices between leadership and management interventions are a central concern in this view of leadership. This reflects that, in most organizations, management processes dominate—notwithstanding that leadership is a much talked-about topic.

Fortunately, this form of leadership is not just a theoretical construct. It has highly practical application and is being practiced by some. But this form is neither well known, nor well established. This state of affairs reflects the dominance of those outdated assumptions about leaders, authority, influence, and the leadership-management relationship. As long as we look at leadership through the lens of these assumptions, our newly identified form remains largely invisible. Envisioning this form requires setting these assumptions to one side. This is not a matter of rejecting the assumptions altogether. But, insofar as we wish to study or apply the alternative form, we must step clear of these long-held beliefs.

Practical Benefits

What might be the practical benefits of approaching our understanding of leadership from such a different direction?

- We increase the potential of gaining contributions to leadership work from many people who, like Bernardo, do not see themselves as fitting the mold of a conventional leader, or do not occupy positions of elevated authority. Potentially, leadership activity draws upon more of the talent that exists within a group or organization.

- We increase the potential for bringing to the surface, scrutinizing, and integrating more of what stakeholders can potentially contribute, but which now remains implicit or hidden. Applying learning-centered leadership processes might, for instance, enable Alice to work with the teachers to build a joint understanding of the problem and a common vision for overcoming it. In so doing, they would elicit energy for change.

- We make better, more informed choices about how to act. If we have a clear concept of the leadership-management distinction, we are better positioned to choose the intervention option that best fits particular situations. Understanding leadership and management as distinct forms of activity assists us to intentionally interweave the two forms to good effect—as well as to assess the relative attention we give to each over time, and to act onwhat we find.

All of these are key to working effectively with contentious problems, as this book will make clear.

The Book's Purpose

This book has three purposes:

- To bring to light a view of leadership grounded in processes of joint and individual learning rather than influence (or authority), and which is distinct from management processes;

- To articulate and demonstrate the attitudes and practices which can help us bring this view of leadership into the mainstream; and

- To equip individual readers with frameworks and tools for use in developing their own capability in learning-centered leadership.

The concepts, practices and tools herein are discussed in relation to leadership in organizational settings, including business, governmental agencies, and schools. As to the kinds of problems for which the processes described here may be useful, they include:

- Change-related issues characterized by contending viewpoints between stakeholders or apparent resistance to change;

- Situations in which one needs to confront people in higher-ranking roles about difficult issues;

- Instances of poor group or individual performance where there appears to be an attitudinal dimension; and

- Problems within and between groups and organizations.

Some might ask, what is really new here? After all, other writers on leadership have discussed, variously, the preoccupation with the leader in the leadership literature, the confusion between leadership and authority, leadership as an influence process, and the leadership–management relationship. The distinctive edge in this book is to frame a conventional view of leadership as grounded in particular assumptions regarding each and all four of these elements, and to put forward an alternative form that springs from a different set of premises, together with a set of frameworks and tools to support people in enacting this different form.

Overview of IN THE LEADERSHIP MODE

PART ONE Foundations

The five chapters of Part 1 outline the essential concepts that characterize this distinct form of leadership, and set it apart from a management orientation. Like the footings of a house, these concepts are the essential foundational building blocks.

Chapter 1 looks at the prevailing contemporary thinking about leadership and leaders, and the authority and influence processes that tend to characterize that thinking. Clarifying our understanding of some of the most widely-held images surrounding leadership will assist in preparing the ground for our exploratory work in chapters 2 to 5, and help demonstrate why a fundamentally distinct approach to thinking about leadership is needed.

The focus of Chapter 2 is on leadership as grounded in learning. With the aid of the story of Bernardo's experience, we delve into the processes of assessing current realities in relation to a contentious problem, clarifying a preferred future, and harnessing energy for deep-reaching change. We examine the kinds of interventions that individuals can make to contribute to the group's joint leadership work.

Chapter 3 utilizes another in-depth story, this time involving Alice, to explore three core concepts that underpin learning-centered leadership, including the specific leadership-mode interventions made by individuals. The concepts are relational working, mindful working, and practice-basis.

The notion that leadership and management are distinct forms of action is the subject of Chapter 4. We move beyond unhelpful notions of leaders being in some ways different from managers to instead look at how the *processes* of leadership and management differ, and explore why the differences matter. We introduce the concept of the management mode, and see that while both the leadership mode and the management mode are necessary, in most organizational settings it is the latter that is dominant. While the management-mode dominance raises some problematic implications, recasting the leadership-management relationship opens up scope for complementary action.

"Active choice and leadership mode," Chapter 5, deals with the inevitability that leadership in the form presented here brings with it risks and difficulties, as well as opportunities. Weighing up the potential benefits and consequences and deciding whether and how to intervene require the application of conscious, active choice. Through case examples we examine the exercise of choice in light of underlying cultural forces and challenging behaviors. A set of guidelines to support leadership-mode action is offered.

PART TWO The ARIES Framework—Practices and Tools

Five practices for making the leadership mode operational are introduced in Part 2 under the banner of ARIES: Attending, Reflecting, Inquiring, Expressing, and Synthesizing, with one chapter on each. We can extend our house construction analogy to Part 2. These chapters might be thought of as akin to the walls, flooring, and roof of our structure; they provide essential frameworks and support to help nurture the practice of this new form of leadership. The practices described represent counterpoints to the management-mode-oriented behavior patterns that dominate in most organizations. The chapters also include tools to assist practitioners in giving effect to this distinct leadership form.

Chapter 6 explores the important practice of attending, which goes beyond mere listening to denote paying attention to the richness of the present moment. Through examining a story of a local government change effort, we look at the need to differentiate between observation and inference, and the practicalities of doing so.

Reflecting, in Chapter 7, refers to practices that help us interpret, both individually and jointly, what is perceived. We introduce a tool, the Reflection Matrix, for making sense of multiple perspectives and discuss the process of reflecting in the moment.

Chapter 8, Inquiring, looks into the use of questioning processes to enable us to become more informed about the viewpoints of others, including their underlying thoughts, feelings, and assumptions. Far from being a purely technical process, inquiring involves dealing with issues of defensiveness and threat, implying a need to be aware of one's impact on others from moment to moment. The chapter includes a framework of question types. Examples illustrate how to use these different types of questions to bring forth what deeply matters to others in relation to a particular subject.

Expressing one's views so as to foster learning by all involved is the subject of Chapter 9. It is a challenge to speak out about what is deeply important to us while also recognizing that our views are not "the truth," but only a part of a larger picture. This chapter introduces a framework that many of my workshop participants have found helpful in enabling them to speak out on matters they had previously found too difficult.

Chapter 10 discusses the practice of synthesizing as a key practice for advancing group learning. Interventions are described that can help connect and perhaps reinterpret or integrate diverse perspectives. A second aspect of synthesizing involves identifying core challenges that need to be reckoned with in the process of moving towards a preferred future.

The Epilogue reviews the main themes of the book and canvasses some aspects relating to the development of learning-centered leadership capability—for individuals and also for organizations and larger groups.

Throughout the book, stories and examples have been incorporated to illustrate opportunities for action, and challenges faced in the leadership mode. These illustrations variously reflect challenges for senior executives, middle managers, and experienced operational personnel in a range of settings. These instances are adapted from my own consulting and teaching experience and from discussions with participants in the many workshops and seminars I have conducted over more than a decade.

The stories and examples have been selected and shaped to support and draw out particular ideas, themes, and possibilities. The intention is to "bring to life" ways of seeing and practicing learning-centered leadership that, for the most part, exist only as potentialities and opportunities. (This form is emerging and largely obscured from view, due to conventional assumptions.) The illustrations do not purport to represent matters of fact, portray actual people or events, or prove that the concepts, practices, and tools offered are effective in application. Reflecting and reinforcing their fictional nature, the stories are referred to in the text as "case stories." That said, hundreds of workshop participants have found that the concepts, practices, and tools offer powerful new means for thinking about and practicing leadership. In addition, while the book focuses mainly on workplace applications, many have reported finding these resources useful in applications outside the workplace, such as in sporting, family, or community activities.

This is obviously not a short book, and I recognize that many people skim books on leadership and management rather than read them from cover to cover. So what advice can I give to help you gain the most from the book?

If your interest is primarily in tools and their application, then it is likely that you will be most interested in Part 2. If this is the case, you might begin by reading the summary at the end of each chapter in Part 1. Then, dip into those chapters that most interest you before going on to read Part 2 more closely. Part 1 does set up the frameworks for the rest of the book, so I encourage you not to skip through it too quickly. Moreover, chapters 2, 3, and 5 include case stories that deal with efforts to apply learning-centered leadership.

If your interests lie more with conceptual approaches to the subject of leadership, you are likely to find the chapters of Part 1 to be of most relevance. However, the tools and frameworks in Part 2 represent applications of the concepts, so you may find those of interest as well.

Let the exploration commence!

PART ONE

FOUNDATIONS

ONE

Three Vines in the Forest of Leadership

" Living fossils from the time of dinosaurs": This was how *The New York Times* reported David Noble's 1994 discovery of the tree that became known as the Wollemi Pine, named after the national park in which it was found.[1] While exploring a remote and largely inaccessible forest about 100 miles from Sydney, Noble noticed an unusual-looking tree. As a park ranger, Noble was familiar with most of the local flora. What caught his attention first about this tree was that some of its leaves sprouted directly from the trunk. This was uncommon among Australian trees. He also noticed that the leaves were compound, like fern fronds, with many leaflets. Again, this was out of the ordinary among Australian trees. In addition, the tree's bark was unusual; it had "bubbly" effects, according to Noble, "almost like someone had sprayed the tree with chocolate crackles or coco pops."

Noble decided to take a cutting and went home to consult his botanical books, expecting to find the tree listed. It was not. The possibility began to dawn on him that he had discovered a tree not previously known. Noble then took the cutting into his work at the National Parks and Wildlife Service, where the significance of his find soon became apparent.[2] Based on fossil records, trees of this type were thought to have become extinct about two million years ago.[3] Since its discovery, the tree has been the subject of extensive scientific research and is now grown all over the world. Especially intriguing is the fact that such a tree could stand undiscovered in a forest so close to a major metropolitan center.

Now picture, if you will, a different kind of "forest," a forest populated with the literature and ideas about leadership generated over the past fifty years. As you might imagine, it is a dense wood with some very tall timbers and bushy undergrowth, comprised of many books, frameworks, tools, and concepts. There have been books on servant leadership, transformational leadership, ethical leadership, intelligent leadership, and just about every other variety imaginable. With countless assessment and development tools and how-to-do-it manuals also out there, it is a thickly wooded forest indeed.

Yet, in a secluded corner in a deep gorge, almost obscured by tangled vines and undergrowth, grows a rarely seen and largely untapped "species" of leadership. Many hikers have ventured close by, but few have found their way into this space. This different leadership species involves people working together to inquire into present realities, to develop common understandings about what they want to achieve—allowing that contention may still exist—and to marshal energy to make their preferred futures eventuate. Such learning-centered leadership is based on a recognition that perhaps the deepest expression of leadership occurs when practitioners "learn their way through" deep-seated problems, where they discover how to frame them differently, and thus can bring into being new ways of dealing with them.

Gaining access to that species of leadership hidden in the gorge is challenging. It requires that we pull back the vines that obscure the entrance. Each of these vines represents a major supposition that, in turn, defines our conventional thinking about leadership: leadership as identified with leaders,[4] leadership as identified with authority, and leadership as involving influence processes. (A fourth vine, which we shall pull back in Chapter 4, is the traditional assumption that leadership and management cannot be meaningfully or beneficially separated.) These metaphorical vines, depicted in Figure 1.1, are firmly wrapped around most of the well-established frameworks in our forest of leadership.

FIGURE 1.1 Revealing the Hidden Gorge of Leadership

Leadership as identified with Leaders

Leadership as identified with Authority

Leadership as identified with Influence

Gaining access to the gorge requires untangling the vines that obstruct the entrance

To open up to the novel perspective on leadership that is the subject of this book, we first need to develop some perspective on contemporary mainstream ideas on the subject. Otherwise, we risk viewing the new ideas through the lenses of established mindsets. In the following sections we pull back the vines and briefly critique the conventional intertwining of leadership with leaders, authority, and influence.

Noticing a Preoccupation with Leaders

If you pick up a book on leadership while browsing in a bookstore, it is probable that the book will use the term "leader" liberally, as if the two terms were interchangeable, and that it is self-evident that leadership is what leaders do. The idea that these terms are often jumbled together is not new. In his book, *Leadership for the Twenty First Century*, Joseph Rost traced the development of theories of leadership during the past hundred years, focusing particularly on how definitions of leadership had changed over time. One common thread he noticed was a tendency by leadership scholars to fail to differentiate the terms "leadership" and "leader."[5]

The premise that leadership and leaders are one and the same is deeply ingrained—and it serves to limit, to confine, our thinking about leadership. Mixing up the terms leadership and leader results in a blurring of categories: the processes of leadership are discussed in the same breath with leader attributes, leader behaviors, or leader development. That leaders are a built-in feature of the leadership package is a given. It becomes difficult to conceive of leadership without leaders figuring centrally.

I see this haziness of thought regarding leaders and leadership repeatedly in the workshops I run. Sometimes I invite participants to prepare a "mind map" (or concept map) illustrating the ideas they believe are critical to understanding the *processes* of leadership. I ask them to leave aside considerations of the qualities and attributes of leaders. Yet, the discussion usually turns quickly to individual characteristics such as integrity, intelligence, or courage.

Our historical tendency to conflate leadership and leaders has important implications. For one, it perpetuates our acceptance of the view that leadership is the province of the exceptional, or at least special, few. A consequence is that we deny the possibility that others can contribute significantly and productively to leadership. The cost is to greatly underestimate the potential of the many; to diminish the insight, wisdom, experience, and energy that ordinary people—as well as extraordinary people who do not fit a leader mold—can bring to tackling contentious problems.[6]

With this understanding as a backdrop, our attention in coming chapters will be on leadership *processes*, especially those that can help us deal effectively with contentious problems in order to achieve change. This is not meant to deny, or detract from, the work of people who are regarded as leaders, or to say that ideas about leaders are without value. It is to say that our consideration of leadership processes will be clearer, sharper, and more strongly grounded if we differentiate the work of leadership from a discussion about leaders.

There is another, equally important reason for setting aside the assumption that leadership necessarily involves leaders. Doing so allows us to re-examine the relationship between leadership and management practices (the subject of Chapter 4). With a clearer understanding of each of these forms of action, and how they can beneficially fit together, we enhance our capacity for dealing with vexing problems—as we shall see later. If, however, we still have notions of leaders front-of-mind, we risk being caught up in fruitless comparisons between leaders and managers. We would miss seeing the potential, lying largely untapped in our hidden gorge, that leadership-oriented actions hold for dealing with contentious problems, as distinct from management-oriented actions.

Moving aside the vine of the leader, which partly obscures the entrance to the hidden gorge, is a bit threatening, for a variety of reasons. If we personally regard ourselves as leaders, where does a concept of leadership without leaders leave us? What is our role? How can we make a difference, particularly in helping the groups in which we are involved deal with difficult problems? If, on the other hand, we look to others to provide leadership, we may also feel uncertain. Who can we rely on? In the absence of a leader, who will inspire or guide us? Are we destined to wander aimlessly, without direction or effective decision-making?

A focus on leaders is comforting. It makes life simpler. We can pin our hopes and aspirations on these individuals; we can also project our fears and anxieties onto them. When things are going well, we have someone to depend on. When they are not, we have someone to blame. Focusing on leaders also absolves us of the need to contemplate our own personal contribution—or lack of it—to leadership. Just as it can be reassuring for us, personally, to depend on others for leadership, it can also be affirming for the leaders concerned. The belief that others need or depend on us can be a major driver of self-esteem. And it is not just leaders and those who look to them for guidance who benefit from the entanglement of leaders and leadership. The interests of a great many consulting companies, academic researchers, and leadership development programs are aligned in continuing our identification of leadership with leaders.

For all of these reasons, letting go of the presumed equivalence between leaders and leadership is not easy to do. It requires that we take some risk. It asks us to be willing to challenge our own and others' presuppositions, and to embrace some uncertainty—arguably characteristics of leadership itself. But untangling leaders from leadership is just the first step on the journey. Both terms are closely bound up with ideas about authority.

Leadership and Authority

The Entwining of Leadership and Authority

It is common usage for the terms leader and leadership to refer to people in the most high-ranking formal roles. This is so across the board, in business, politics, or the professions. When we hear of a "leadership threat" to a political leader we presume this signifies a challenge to the individual's holding of a particular office. Profiles in popular business and management magazines frequently describe how CEO "business leaders" have turned around, transformed, or reinvented their organizations—usually with little reference to the deeper complexities and problems presumably encountered, let alone to the efforts of other people. Such usage reinforces the entrenched images of leaders being mainly people at the top and leadership being what they, and they alone, do.[7]

This attachment of leadership to authority, particularly as it applies in the workplace, was made plain to me at a conference on leadership development. Virtually all the presentations, questions, and discussion focused on the development of individual leaders, especially on so-called "emerging leaders." It seemed taken as given that we were talking about people in executive positions, whether they held them now, or were likely to sometime in the future.

The language we regularly use in the workplace underpins and maintains these conventional images. The term "leadership position" commonly refers to a role with high-level decision-making authority, while "leadership team" generally refers only to top executive groups. Groups looking after operational areas, in contrast, are more likely to be referred to as "management teams."

I once suggested to an executive team that their middle-level managers might do better at handling change-related issues if they were exposed to some leadership development activities. The CEO leaned across the table towards me. "Not leadership development," he remarked forcefully, "management development," as if to scuttle the idea of any connection between leadership and middle managers. That term was apparently reserved for those at the top.

It seems that the presumed equivalence between leadership and formal authority is as strong as ever. Never mind that Philip Selznick debunked the link as long ago as 1957. As he put it, "Leadership is not equivalent to office-holding or high prestige or authority or decision-making ... If this view is correct ... it means that only some (and sometimes none) of the activities of decision-makers are leadership activities."[8]

The association between leadership and positions of formal authority does not begin in the workplace. It is socialized into most of us from an early age. If you doubt this, try asking at your local school about leadership opportunities for students. Many schools proudly tout the openings they offer for "student leaders" on student representative councils as well as on sporting teams, debating groups, and the like. Such roles may not carry much, if any, authority. These roles may provide the fortunate occupants with valuable experiences. Yet, they also help shape and reinforce the popular concept that leadership has to do with formal roles and authority.

Consequences of Identifying Leadership with Authority

A viewpoint of leadership-equals-leaders-equals-authority encourages the contribution of those in the higher echelons of organizations to be taken largely as given, with other considerations regarding leadership in the workplace flowing from that starting point. Such a viewpoint contributes to closing down our perceptions. We just do not tend to see the possibilities for leadership contributions by people further down the hierarchy. A consequence can be the reinforcement of existing power and status relationships, and a reduction in the potential for achieving genuine dispersal of leadership.

The kinds of problems that result from our confusing leadership and authority were illustrated for me when I worked with an executive team on questions of culture in their organization. Although the executive team members referred to themselves as "the leadership team," the signs of much actual leadership happening were few. While on a teambuilding retreat with the executive team and managers at the next level down, it emerged that the top team was seen by the other managers as having difficulty in making decisions and as not sufficiently involving the manager group. The managers complained that they were consulted mainly on matters of minor importance, while the top team kept the more significant questions within their group.

In discussions, it became apparent that the top team believed they needed to handle the important issues themselves. Not only that, they also needed to be perceived as doing so, and doing so well. "We're the leadership group," said one member. "We can't make mistakes—or be seen to be making them." Interestingly, two of the executive members confided to me later that the concern with being seen to make the "right" decisions often impeded their making any decisions at all.

Authority bestows upon people, within limits, the scope and legitimacy to act in particular ways, such as to determine priorities, make decisions, and allocate resources. Possessing authority effectively entitles those in the higher levels of organizations to have their views take precedence over those of lower-ranked colleagues. Like the executive team in the example, people in the higher reaches are thought of as "the leadership." They tend to have the power to determine what issues are talked about, the terms of the conversation, and who gets to participate. As a consequence, the weight attached to the views of top-ranking people can be more a function of their role, status, and power than of any quality of thought or insight reflected in those views.

In addition, those at the top have an incentive to assert their views strongly, and defend them vigorously. If you regard your leadership as a function of your authority, then a challenge to your views is a challenge to your authority. And that is threatening. Most people in strongly hierarchical organizations understand this implicitly: to question the views of someone up the line is a potentially "career-limiting move." What often happens is that people in the lower ranks are encouraged to suppress their views, while the views of their higher-ranking colleagues go unchallenged. Under such circumstances, any constructive examination of the differences of view that characterize contentious problems tends to be thwarted—to the detriment of the organization as a whole.

Setting Aside the Identification of Leadership with Authority

If we want to think afresh about leadership processes for dealing productively with contentious problems, then we need to set aside the vine, or assumption, of leadership as identified with authority, just as we did with the vine of leadership as identified with the leader.

As with leadership and leaders, our effort to differentiate leadership from authority is not to deny the importance of authority in organizations. This book does not argue for doing away with hierarchy, or for creating flat organizations. Instead, the approach advanced here treats authority as a contextual, background factor rather than as a determinant. In this approach, people at potentially any level in an organization can undertake or contribute to leadership; they do not have to have formal authority to do so.[9] At the same time, their position in the hierarchy will have a bearing on the scope of the leadership they exercise. For example, a member of an operational team might make leadership interventions regarding her team's work and its relations with other groups. In ordinary circumstances we would not expect that team member to take leadership action with respect to corporate direction—though, of course, that may be possible and desirable in some situations.

As with the "leader vine," pulling back the vine that represents leadership identified with authority tends to prompt wariness. Some of high rank might see suggestions to recast the leadership-authority connection as an attempt to diminish their leadership role. This is not the intention here. We can still recognize an association between leadership and authority; we can still grant that people at the top of the pyramid arguably should, and often do, perform a great deal of leadership work. We just need to avoid the presumption of a causal link; that is, assuming that what CEOs and other high-ranking people do as a direct expression of their elevated role is *necessarily* leadership.

There is another concern that we need to acknowledge. As long as leadership is vested in authority, it can seem to be controlled, stabilized. But to loosen the attachment—and especially to suggest that potentially just about anyone can contribute at some level to leadership—sparks threat. One fear is of "loose cannon" or maverick leaders pursuing their own agendas. As one executive put it, "I have fifty-one sections under me. And I don't want fifty-one leaders." Fifty-one individuals running around seeking to develop their own visions could be a troubling prospect; the old adage of too many cooks spoiling the broth comes to mind. Yet, when we focus on leadership processes rather than leaders as individuals and role occupants, such concerns tend to fall away. Fifty-one people—many who may not consider themselves leaders—being involved in joint leadership work could be quite exciting.

The benefit of setting aside the identification of leadership with authority (as with the identification of leadership with leaders), is that it further enables us to put the spotlight on the processes of leadership that are so key to working effectively with contentious problems. But clarifying the view requires that we deal with another vine obstructing the entrance to our hidden gorge: the assumption that leadership is based in influence processes.

Considering Leadership as Influence-based

"Leadership ultimately involves an ability to define the reality of others." This stark assessment was offered in 1986 by Gareth Morgan in his much-lauded book *Images of Organization*.[10] If we zoom forward to 2002, we get a similar—though more muted—appraisal from the noted observer of the leadership literature, Gary Yukl:

> " Most definitions of leadership reflect the assumption that it involves a process whereby intentional influence is exerted by one person over other people to guide, structure and facilitate activities and relationships in a group or organization."[11,12]

Influence, of course, can be exerted in a variety of ways, from coercion, to logical persuasion, to appeals based on the explicit or implicit promise of rewards for doing what the person exercising influence wants. In the more practitioner-oriented leadership literature over the past twenty years, one particular type of influence has been a recurring theme: articulating and communicating an inspiring vision in ways that motivate people to "buy-in" to the vision. The term *transformational leadership* is sometimes used to describe such approaches.[13]

Influence and Transformation

Consider this point of view, from a high-ranking chemical company executive, on leadership as grounded in formulating and communicating a vision:

"Leaders have visions. They analyze the situation either consciously or subconsciously and then develop a vision of where they want to go. The thing which separates an outstanding leader from others is the ability to see further. The successful leader is one who sees over the horizon, beyond where most people see. One of the key elements of leadership is to develop a sense of where you want to go that's beyond the scope of other people.

"The second element of leadership is to communicate that vision and to inspire one's followers towards common purpose. Unless you can communicate to your followers or the people with whom you are charged with leading, you cannot expect them to go in the direction that you want them to go. It's that sense of communicating with people and inspiring them that gives that sense of common purpose.

"It's not sufficient just to communicate in a clinical way. You have to work on people so they feel inspired and they are part of a winning team which is going in that direction. Strong leadership does point people in a common direction. There is common purpose and enthusiasm. Without it you have people pulling in all sorts of directions and that gives rise to wasted effort and frustration."[14]

This executive's ideas reflect a view of leadership that has become somewhat conventional wisdom since the 1980s. While the subject of transformational leadership has many variants, the common elements involve the individual leader clarifying and communicating a direction and seeking, in various ways, to persuade others to commit to that direction.[15]

One of the more prominent books in this area is *The Leadership Challenge*, by Kouzes and Posner.[16] Here is what these authors say about the leader as having a vision:

" … You must first clarify your own visions of the future before you can enlist others in a shared vision … before you can inspire others, you have to be inspired yourself."[17]

" One of the most important practices of leadership is giving life and work a sense of meaning and purpose by offering an exciting vision."[18]

Once the leader "has" the vision, it then must be communicated in ways that will bring others on board. How is this done? Engaging the support of others, in this view, essentially involves appealing to their interests and needs.

Kouzes and Posner again:

" It's about enrolling others so they can see how their own interests and aspirations are aligned with the vision and can thereby become mobilized to commit their individual energies to its realization."[19]

From this perspective, the essential process is as follows: The leader clarifies and articulates a preferred vision of the future, tunes in to the needs and aspirations of followers, and then—through influence—enables them to see how their needs can be met by signing-on with that vision.

The specifics of Kouzes and Posner's framework are not what is most important here. What is important is that it is illustrative of a broader school of thinking concerning leadership and transformation. It is a school of thought that sets great store in the ability to influence. But are there limits to Kouzes and Posner-style transformational leadership? Where does this view of leadership potentially become problematic? (Note that in this discussion, the focus is on leaders working towards change for honorable purposes. We leave aside the question of leaders simply serving their own interests.[20])

Hazards of Transformational Leadership

An image comes to mind of an attractive natural rock pool on the seashore where people are swimming and playing. The view beneath the surface is obscured by a combination of surf washing into the pool and strands of kelp swirling to and fro. A few swimmers dive in, apparently unaware of the dangers posed by rocky outcrops just below the water's surface. The area needs a sign to warn visitors of the dangers of diving. In a similar vein, the waters of transformational leadership may appear inviting. Diving in, though, can also be perilous.

Consider the example of Georgia, a general manager acknowledged by her peers and those who report to her as a visionary leader—far-sighted, imaginative, and inspiring. The feedback from a survey of people with whom she worked confirmed to Georgia that she was seen as setting an exciting direction, stirring colleagues to want to succeed, and challenging them intellectually. Along with the glowing accounts, however, came signs of unease. It was not that people disagreed with her vision, or thought that she had misjudged where the organization needed to head. The problem was she had effectively left others behind.[21] Team members made comments in the feedback such as, "We're overwhelmed," "I can't keep up—she's got so many ideas," and "I'm finding it hard enough to cope with today's work without worrying about the future." The perception was that Georgia was strong on thinking about where the group needed to be, but disconnected from people's current experience. The more she talked up the future, the more they felt uncomfortable—a mixture perhaps of being inspired by her vision, overwhelmed by the challenges of achieving it, and feeling guilty for not being able to meet her expectations. Apparently, Georgia responded to the lack of evident action in support of the vision with further attempts to fire-up her staff. And so the pattern went.

No one had told Georgia about the effect she was having on people. Perhaps this was because colleagues were concerned about appearing less committed to the vision and change than she was. Maybe they were worried about how she might react. Whatever the reasons, her experience illustrates a significant risk: leaders who apply transformational methods, such as those prescribed by Kouzes and Posner, run the risk of not gaining authentic feedback from their "followers.'"

A related danger is that these leaders may gain compliance, but not genuine commitment to realizing the vision. People may nod their heads at the right times and do what is required—but that does not mean they are genuinely "sold" on the vision. They may go through the motions in order to gain approval, or avoid sanction. It can be difficult for a leader to tell whether people are truly enthused by the vision, or just doing what they believe the leader wants.

In Georgia's case, her vision for the future was not at issue. But imagine a scenario where some of the leader's constituents have significant disagreement with aspects of the vision. In such cases, a hazard is that colleagues may be reluctant to give voice to those disagreements for fear of incurring the leader's displeasure. So, the leader may miss out on feedback that might otherwise point to a need to modify the vision.

Another possibility is that people resent the leaders' efforts to "sell" them the vision, and see this behavior as disingenuous or manipulative. Again, such perceptions are likely to be at odds with the leader's desire to foster commitment. An example comes from an agricultural research organization that, some years ago, attempted to market to its research scientists an organizational vision for cutting-edge research in support of sustainable farming. In its communications to the scientists, the organization emphasized the benefits to them of the new direction. However, at the time, the scientists did not see a sufficient connection between their own research aspirations and the declared future direction. Consequently, they resisted what they saw as the organization's efforts to impose the vision on them. Had they been involved in co-creating the vision, the outcome may have been different.

A fundamental drawback with transformational leadership, in the sense of a leader "having" and communicating a vision so as to inspire others, is that it lacks any mechanism for the mutual testing of perceptions surrounding the vision. For example, followers may wonder: To what extent is the leader genuinely disclosing her thoughts, as distinct from putting what may be a weak or difficult idea in the best possible light? The leader is also hamstrung in this regard. If the leader were to express any reservations she might hold about the vision, she runs the risk of undercutting the "inspirational" component. The leader is also left to wonder: How fully and candidly are followers revealing any concerns they may have? What essential feedback am I missing?

Again, there is no way, within the transformational perspective, for this to be meaningfully established. The authority relationship between leader and follower implies a structural bias; followers tend to suppress or distort some or all of their concerns. Just because everyone says they "support change" does not mean that they are really committed to the leader's preferred path. Rather than encouraging conversations in which the interested parties express what they deeply think and feel, transformational leadership encourages leaders and followers to "operate on" each other to further their respective intentions.

This not to deny the fact that some individuals might be aptly described as truly transformational leaders. No doubt there are people who demonstrate particular farsightedness in their thinking, who are able to give voice to compelling images of a preferred future, and who seem to be capable of motivating others to strive towards the vision. How desirable the vision might be in any particular case is, of course, another matter. Nevertheless, while transformational leaders may, in some instances, succeed in bringing new visions to life, this must be regarded as a problematic enterprise.

Dominant though they may be, conceptions of leadership as grounded in leaders, authority, and influence represent one broad way of framing our understanding of leadership, not the only way. It is time to open up the possibility of conceiving of leadership in a fundamentally different way.

Establishing a Clearer Line of Sight

We have suggested that the field of leadership is like a forest ensnared with vines, with the vines obscuring the entrance to a largely unexplored gorge containing a distinctive variety of leadership.

The vines we have examined in this chapter are the identification of leadership with leaders, authority, and influence. Pulling clear these vines is necessary to gain access to the gorge so we can appreciate this little known species. (And our view will not be fully clear until Chapter 4, when we disentangle the last vine, which concerns the relationship between leadership and management.)

Disentangling the "leader vine" enables us to focus on the work of leadership as process, rather than investing some people with leadership, but not others.

What emerges, then, is the possibility of more people—many of whose personal style might not fit traditional images of the leader—being able to contribute to leadership work. Holding clear the "authority vine"—by thinking of it as a background or contextual factor, rather than as a central feature of leadership—creates scope for greater contributions by people who hold little if any formal authority. Pulling back the "influence vine" opens up the possibility of leadership as situated in learning, with people jointly making sense of contentious problems, while being open to reformulating their own views in the process.

Now that we have done some work towards untangling these aspects of a conventional leadership paradigm, we need to continue to hold them back so that we may perceive our new variety as clearly as possible. The line of reasoning is not that conventional concepts are without value; just that moving them aside can reveal a variety of leadership that otherwise is blocked from view. We do not need to destroy the vines that block our path, or to reject established concepts of leadership. Instead, we need to notice and contemplate them, and then—with some critical assessment—put them to one side. Accordingly, you will find few references to leaders, authority (in relation to leadership), or influence-based approaches in the remainder of the book, except in discussions about more conventional approaches to the subject.

As our line of sight into the adjoining gorge becomes clearer, we should be better able to distinguish the features that characterize leadership grounded in learning processes. That is our task in the next chapter.

See the Appendix, "More untangling of the vines of leadership," for additional discussion:

- *"When executives decide on contentious matters"—suggests that thinking of executive "calls" on difficult matters as acts of leadership can inhibit our appreciation of a learning-based form of leadership, such as we examine in Chapter 2.*

- *"Distributed leadership: a cautionary tale" —questions the oft-made assertion that this form represents a break from leader and authority-based conceptions of leadership.*

- *"Leadership as mutual influence" —considers whether the prospect of multiple leaders in a group exercising influence overcomes the limitations of transformational leadership.*

Chapter Summary

Drawing on the 1994 discovery of the Wollemi Pine, a species thought to have become extinct two million years ago, we invoked the image of leadership as a forest representing the diversity of books, frameworks, and other materials generated over the past half century. Most of the forest is ensnared with "vines" representing conventional assumptions about leadership. These assumptions include the idea that leadership is the province of leaders, that leadership involves the exercise of authority, and that leadership is essentially an influence process. (Another vine concerning the relationship between leadership and management is discussed in Chapter 4.) Although most of the forest is covered with these vines, nearby—but difficult to see— is a gorge where a different form of leadership grows.

This chapter explored some ways in which these vines (assumptions) constrict our contemporary concepts of leadership. We looked at how the terms leadership and leader tend to be used interchangeably, making it difficult to conceive of a concept of leadership without leaders figuring centrally. As well, we discussed how the common confusion between leadership and formal authority limits our thinking about possible leadership contributions from those not in the upper levels of their organizations. One common theme, which we examined with reference to Kouzes and Posner's book, *The Leadership Challenge*, is the notion of the leader having, and communicating, a vision that inspires others. We considered some of the difficulties common to a transformational approach, including the possibility that the leader may not receive critical feedback from those he or she is trying to influence.

The aim is not to do away with conventional perspectives, but to notice and contemplate them, and to offer some critical appraisal, particularly in terms of how such perspectives constrain our ability to work with contentious problems. Understanding these current realities—and then setting them aside—will enable us to see more clearly our alternative, a learning-centered perspective on leadership.

Questions for Reflection

1.1 To what degree does your own concept of leadership concentrate on "leaders," in the sense of individuals with particular attributes, styles, or roles? In what ways, if any, might your concept of leadership be different if you put thoughts about leaders to one side?

1.2 To what extent is leadership identified with authority in your own organization (or one that you have experience with)? What implications might flow from regarding authority as a contextual, background factor for leadership in that organization?

1.3 How important are influence-based processes in your own concept of leadership? What limitations, if any, do you see regarding the usefulness of influence-based approaches?

Chapter
TWO

Leadership from a Learning Perspective

Bernardo felt slightly apprehensive as he entered the room for his company's monthly Corporate Strategic Group (CSG, as it was known locally) meeting. The CSG was intended as a forum on the bigger questions facing this components distribution business. The group comprised the top twenty-five or so executives, including members of the top team and the next level down, Bernardo's level. Bernardo had tended to take a back-seat in these discussions but he was determined that today would be different: he would pitch some ideas about innovation to get his colleagues thinking and talking about what was really going on. Bernardo is about to try his hand at intervening in the leadership mode.

To appreciate our alternative approach to leadership, it will help to immerse ourselves in a specific situation. Drawing on the experience of Bernardo and his colleagues, we shall view some of the practicalities of enacting leadership from a learning perspective. The case story will also be used to examine and illuminate some key concepts relating to learning-centered leadership.[1] This will give us a view that is free of the "vines"—meaning the emphases on leaders, authority, and influence—that entangle conventional perspectives, as we saw in Chapter 1.

Opening up this different view requires that we introduce several concepts that underpin a learning perspective. These are previewed below.

- Whereas transformational leadership emphasizes leaders influencing followers, learning-centered leadership emphasizes processes of joint sense making by those with an interest in a contentious problem.

- Critical to learning-centered leadership is a *relational* orientation, in which we give precedence to processes of joint thinking and action over task achievement, and hold our own views open to scrutiny. A relational orientation is critical if implicit aspects of the contentious problem are to be explored in relative safety.

- To fully comprehend them, the processes of learning-centered leadership in dealing with the contentious problem need to be viewed, in effect, through two "lenses." One lens enables a "higher-level" or "stepped-back" view, focusing on processes as they unfold over a period. The second lens gives a "close-up" view of the same processes, focusing on specific actions at points in time.

- The higher-level view puts emphasis on the need for group members to establish current realities, clarify preferred futures (purpose and vision), and harness energy for deep-reaching change, in relation to the contentious problem.

- The close-up view accentuates actions—interventions—by individuals at specific moments in time. These learning-centered leadership interventions, which must be made relationally, may be as small as asking a question, or putting forward one's own views concerning the contentious problem.

- When we make learning-centered leadership interventions, we can say that we are "in the leadership mode." (This term takes on greater significance when we get to Chapter 4, which discusses the distinction between the leadership and management modes, as well as how they relate.)

Remember, we are departing in substantial ways from established conceptions of leadership. So, it is to be expected that the territory we are exploring in this chapter may seem unfamiliar. For now I ask that you "hold" any such uncertainty about the concepts and proceed on the prospect that greater clarity will emerge as you go through the book.

We begin our discussion by examining the centrality of "learning" in learning-centered leadership, with its focus on processes for the social construction of meanings and its relational orientation. Next, we consider why it is helpful to view learning-centered leadership through two lenses; we explore how this bi-focal investigation enables a higher-level view of processes unfolding over time, and a close-up view of specific actions that occur in the moment. After a brief outline of the benefits of a learning-centered approach, the case story is presented. We see Bernardo, with support from one of his colleagues, intervening to help the Corporate Strategic Group move toward a shared understanding of a previously contentious problem.

We utilize the case story to survey the elements of our higher-level view—establishing current realities, identifying preferred futures (purpose and vision), and harnessing energy for deep-reaching change. Interwoven with this discussion—and following it—we consider the kinds of individual actions (interventions) that assist a group to move towards desired change. It is when we make these learning-centered leadership interventions that we act "in the leadership mode." The chapter concludes with a review of the essential differences between learning-centered leadership and the transformational variety.

Learning and a Relational Orientation

In contrast to dominant views of leadership that tend to focus on individual leaders, formal authority, and influence, the emphasis here is on *learning processes*. Where there are contentious issues, learning is essential if the group is to move through the contention to construct common meanings—and to recognize and acknowledge the areas of residual difference as well.

When a group begins to face a contentious problem, we can expect there to be a level of confusion, messiness, and tension. (For our purposes, a group is defined as any collection of two or more people attempting to work through a contentious problem.[2]) There is neither a shared sense of the nature of the problem nor a clear image of what might constitute a preferred future. People may, in fact, be talking about quite different problems, as well as using language differently—possibly reflecting dissimilar professional paradigms as well as variation in life experiences and values. *Learning* here refers to the means by which the group and the individuals within it make sense of the matters in contention. Learning in this context involves group members in seeking to draw out, make explicit, and then integrate the various meanings attached to the problem, as a basis for action. The group is building, or constructing, common meaning from the particular perspectives of stakeholders. In academic circles, this form of learning has been termed "constructivist."[3]

A learning effort begins when a group commences initial efforts to grapple with the problem. We can think of learning as occurring at any point along the way where members recognize that their own understandings share commonalities with those of other group members.[4] There may well be difficulties and ongoing tensions, but a sense emerges in the group that members are finding common ground, that they are making sense of the problem together. Possibly, the group may come to a shared understanding that differs in key respects from the ways in which *any* of the individual members had previously formulated the problem. (And we shall see signs of such an outcome in the case story that we consider shortly.)

Such learning, with people "making-meaning" together, is an essentially social enterprise. The shared meaning comes from efforts to combine people's various ways of seeing. Learning, in this form, is far removed from the conventional notion of people passively *receiving* knowledge or guidance from an expert or leader. Instead, the group is participating in *creating* knowledge; in particular, it is creating knowledge that is specific to its own circumstances.

Working through contentious problems in this way involves people putting forward their personal experience and worldviews—including some of their most basic assumptions, values, and beliefs—and allowing these to be processed by the group. Learning occurs, both for individuals and for the group as a whole, only insofar as group members are able to incorporate elements of other perspectives into their own. Necessarily, if the group is to find common ground regarding current reality and vision, some individuals will need to let go or modify their previous conceptions of the problem.

The notion of "letting go" implies an element of threat and defensiveness. And, as we shall see, threat and defensiveness are primary considerations in learning-centered leadership—especially since we are seeking to draw out and apply implicit or hidden intelligence that may be relevant to the problem. We do not seek to avoid threat and the prospect of defensive reactions, but nor do we intentionally act in ways likely to provoke them. In order to process the different ways of conceiving of a problem, people must have a degree of safety.

In addition, to facilitate learning, the processes of thinking and acting to-gether must be valued, and put ahead of direct task achievement. This is necessary to create the environment that enables the hidden intelligence, resident wisdom, and experience relevant to the problem to come to light. This is not to say that outcomes do not matter; they do. But there is a confidence that better outcomes emerge from joint work when the quality of interactions truly matters, rather than when tasks are the sole and primary focus.

A hallmark of learning-leadership activity, then, is what might be termed a "relational stance." Adopting a relational stance implies being receptive to the perspectives of others. This is more than a matter of listening politely; it entails paying attention at a deep level and being willing to reflect on our own views and assumptions in the process—as well as allowing these to be reviewed by oth-ers. Since we are dealing with contentious problems, for which—by definition—there are no singular answers, we must keep open the possibility that *any contribu-tion by any group member* can be a source of intelligence for the group.

Maintaining such as stance is indeed difficult, as we shall see in more detail in Chapter 3. Still, if we do not demonstrate receptiveness to others' views as well as the capacity to reflect on our own, the prospects for joint inquiry into the implicit domain—what people think and feel but find difficult to talk about—are likely to be negligible.

In sum, the view here is that contentious problems require leadership grounded in processes of joint and individual learning rather than influence (or authority), and that these learning processes must be conducted in a highly relational manner.

Viewing Learning-centered Leadership Work Through Two Lenses

Now that we have put aside (in Chapter 1) the identification of leadership with leaders, authority, and influence, we have removed the more obvious options for tackling a contentious problem. We have put to one side, as not helpful to learn-ing, the possibility of someone in a formal authority role exercising leadership, derived from their authority, to make a decision as to a best course. Similarly, we have set aside the possibility of a transformational leader—whether in a role of formal authority or not—articulating and communicating a vision of the problem to be overcome, and mobilizing people around that vision.

How can we think of a learning-based approach to leadership as being helpful to a group in finding its way through the disarray? To answer this question, we need to view leadership processes at two levels: a higher, or stepped-back, level, and at a close-up level. Hence the idea of looking through two lenses: one lens reveals the higher-level processes that need to unfold over a period, concerning establishing current realities, clarifying a preferred future and harnessing energy for deep-reaching change. The second lens focuses on *the same processes*, but in a close-up, immediate sense, emphasizing actions taken by individuals at specific points in time.

Let us look briefly at learning-centered leadership through each of these lenses. Later, we shall expand these views in the light of the case story involving Bernardo.

Firstly, with respect to the higher-level view: Why does a group need to establish current realities, clarify a preferred future (purpose and vision), and harness energy for deep-reaching change?

We have said that when a group first engages with a contentious problem, there will commonly be a range of interpretations and perhaps accompanying feelings of confusion, messiness, and tension. Establishing a shared sense of what is presently real is difficult but essential. If this does not happen, group members are likely to continue interpreting the problem through their various individual perceptual filters. The group might "agree" on strategies for dealing with the problem, but if group members continue to construct the problem differently in their own minds, then any strategies or solutions will be based not on a well-grounded problem definition, but on an incomplete or partial—possibly superficial—appraisal. So, at best, the solution is likely to deal only with some aspects of the problem, or just symptoms. And, insofar as group members are acting from different framings of the problem, their actions in responding to it are likely to "pull in different directions," rather than representing aligned effort.

Developing clarity of purpose and vision is also critical if the group is to maximize its ability to overcome a contentious problem, rather than merely "stumble towards" its future. *Purpose* represents the outcomes the group is trying to achieve. If a sense of purpose is not well established, the group may find itself jumping to define and pursue strategies without being clear as to what results those strategies are designed to bring about. *Vision* stands for what the desired outcomes will "look like" when achieved. In the absence of a clear, coherent, and unifying vision, a group may lack a strong focus for its efforts, with energy and effort dissipating as the group reacts to current circumstances.

A group must generate energy if it is to develop and sustain the momentum necessary to move from the messiness of the present to the realization of its vision over a period of time. Yet, energy does not come from a leader "motivating" and "inspiring" people. Nor is "harnessing energy" a separate phase in the learning-leadership process. Energy for change is generated when group members jointly discover meaning about topics that are important to them, find ways to construct a joint vision, and work together towards achieving it.

From a learning-leadership perspective, the achievement of a desired vision always implies deep-reaching change. This is change not just at the "surface" level, as with modifications to structures or systems, but change that reaches down, to the implicit level of deeper mindsets and attitudes. The need for such change reflects that contentious problems are, by definition, interpreted differently by group members; yet, the group needs to find its way to a shared sense of current reality and vision to overcome the problem. Therefore, if a group is to move from the messiness of the present to the realization of a shared vision, one or more of the constituents will need to experience a shift in their perspectives. This is in addition to any concrete changes that are required.

In our higher-level view, we have emphasized that the group needs to establish current realities, build a shared sense of the future, and harness energy for deep-reaching change. But how does this work actually get done? To see, we need to look through our second lens, which focuses on interventions made in a particular moment.

Individuals contribute to the group's learning-leadership work by making specific, in-the-moment interventions. These interventions usually involve acts of speaking—such as asking a question to encourage deeper thinking on an issue, or expressing a viewpoint, non-dogmatically, to contribute towards the development of shared meaning. To qualify as learning-centered leadership interventions, such interventions must be made relationally. Essentially, this means that interventions must be made in ways that allow for the possibility of other interpretations. These specific actions represent the "nitty-gritty" work of learning-centered leadership. When we make such interventions intentionally we can be said to be acting "in the leadership mode."

The actual work of making learning-centered leadership interventions may be done by only one or two people in a group.[5] In the case story in this chapter, we will see it is mainly Bernardo who is undertaking the interventions, with some support from a colleague. Yet, Bernardo does not consider himself to be a "leader." Learning-leadership interventions can come from anyone (or any number of people) in the group, not only those who might be conventionally regarded as leaders. Achieving substantial change may take a great many such specific acts over an extended period.

The term learning-centered leadership encompasses both the higher-level view of the processes over time (concerning establishing current realities, clarifying preferred futures and harnessing energy for change), and the close-up view of specific interventions made at a point in time. The two lenses on learning-centered leadership do not reveal different processes, but two aspects of the same thing. Both are essential. As with sight in general, one eye affords us a view, but looking through both—sometimes more with one eye, sometimes the other—affords a greater sense of depth or perspective. We need to look through both lenses to truly appreciate this form of leadership. Transformational leadership, in contrast, tends to reflect a single lens approach, locating leadership in one or more individual leaders.

What are the benefits of our learning-based form of leadership? Why should we pursue such an approach? This chapter will illustrate two key benefits (with a third area of benefit to be dealt with in Chapter 4, in relation to the leadership-management relationship).

- One benefit is that it opens up the possibility that a wider range of people can contribute to the work of leadership. Even those who do not regard themselves as leaders can contribute—providing they are prepared to practice—by undertaking learning-leadership interventions. Because potentially any person in a group can contribute specific, relational interventions, we stand to increase the pool of talent undertaking leadership work. That implies more intelligence, experience and insight being applied to contentious problems.

- The second, related, benefit is that we can potentially bring a greater *depth* of knowledge and insight to bear on contentious problems. In specifically engaging with the implicit or hidden domain of assumptions, interests, feelings, and knowledge, this form of leadership seeks to draw forth, examine, and integrate the mental resources that people hold in relation to the problem, but might not otherwise volunteer. The prospect is that our consideration of the problem will be enriched inasmuch as we can gain access to, and apply, some of this hidden intelligence.

Before moving into the case story let me acknowledge some authors whose writings have played a part in shaping my own thinking on the ideas presented in this chapter.

Peter Senge introduced the terms *current reality* and *shared vision* in his book, *The Fifth Discipline*, and the presentation here—particularly in relation to visioning processes—draws heavily on his work.[6] The concept of leaning-centered leadership interventions as actions in the present moment is partly inspired by a concept, "action inquiry," developed by Bill Torbert and his associates.[7] The discussion in this chapter (and others) on dealing with defensiveness and threat in examining the hidden or implicit aspects of contentious problems is informed by the writings of Chris Argyris and Donald Schön.[8] I acknowledge, too, that others including Ronald Heifetz,[9] Linda Lambert,[10] and Wilfred Drath[11] have explored learning-oriented approaches to leadership. I have learned from each of them.

We first heard of Bernardo, the central character in the case story featured in this chapter, in the book's Introduction. Here we follow Bernardo's efforts to raise with his executive colleagues an important but previously undiscussed issue concerning innovation.

CASE STORY Lifting the Corporate Game on Innovation

TREADING WARILY AT THE CORPORATE STRATEGIC GROUP Bernardo nodded to two colleagues as he made his way to his seat. Looking around the room, he noticed mostly glum expressions on the faces of the seven or eight Corporate Strategic Group (CSG) members who had already arrived for the meeting. He wondered if they shared his ambivalence about the CSG. Sometimes the discussions were interesting, but often they wandered around or were hijacked by people pushing particular agendas. On occasion, some top executives, and especially George, the chief operating officer, would aggressively attack those whose ideas they disagreed with.

As part of a leadership development program he had participated in recently, Bernardo had received feedback from his team members and colleagues about his leadership and management effectiveness. One of the messages was that others saw him as needing to be more forthright in expressing his thoughts and ideas to more senior executives. Bernardo accepted that this assessment was valid. He saw his hesitance in speaking up as partly a reflection of his naturally reserved character. Another factor—particularly in relation to the CSG—was his wariness about getting into a public disagreement with top executives, and possibly coming off second best. Since receiving the feedback, Bernardo had been consciously practicing putting his views forward. So far, he had managed to do this without serious incident, including when he disagreed publicly with the CEO regarding the analysis of an issue concerning a corporate project with which Bernardo was involved.

GETTING THE GROUP'S ATTENTION Today, Bernardo was keen to get the CSG's attention, even if this meant taking some risks. Partly, he was motivated by his personal feedback results, partly by a passion he held for innovation. In particular, he wanted the group to face up to an apparent contradiction between the organization's stated value of encouraging innovation and the results of a recent employee survey. The survey showed that only about one-third of respondents had agreed with statements such as "New ideas are welcomed," and "I feel encouraged to question accepted ways of doing things." The results in some other areas, such as communication and learning and development, were just as bleak. The CSG had discussed these latter results in some depth and developed improvement strategies. But for some reason—Bernardo was not quite sure why—the innovation findings had been effectively sidestepped. No one had raised them since, and Bernardo was convinced this was not an oversight.

In one of several conversations with CSG members prior to today's session, Bernardo had established that Linda, the deputy general manager, supported his intentions and would back him up in the meeting. Feedback from other CSG members had been generally positive, though a couple had said, "You are brave in raising this issue," or words to that effect. (Bernardo's own boss had been away for some time with ill health.) Bernardo had also arranged with the convener that he would speak towards the end of the meeting, in the "Other Business" section. As well, he did some preparation for his pitch using a framework from the leadership program.[12]

When he received the nod from the convener, Bernardo rose to his feet, a slight shiver running down his spine.

BERNARDO MAKES HIS PITCH Though conscious of the need to be brief and avoid excessive detail, Bernardo began by offering some context for his remarks. Specifically, he referred to the importance of innovation if the organization intended to stay ahead of its competitors. He said his purpose in raising the issue was to encourage the CSG to look directly at the employee survey results concerning innovation, as a step towards building a more innovative organization. He mentioned his own wish—and that of colleagues with whom he had spoken—to work in an environment that supported creativity and new ways of doing business.

Bernardo then spoke about what innovation meant to him in the company's context—mainly emphasizing process improvement and new ways of engaging with customers—and about the apparent disconnection between the survey results and the company's stated intention to foster innovation as reflected in its "principles for success" statement. As to possible reasons for the disconnection, Bernardo suggested that everyone was "so caught up in getting our daily business done, that innovation just falls off the radar." He also said that he sensed a belief among some staff that putting innovative proposals forward could be a career-limiting move. As an example, he referred to one proposed innovation which, it was rumored among staff, a top executive had dismissed with the words, "Who came up with this ridiculous idea?"

Bernardo was careful to try to make his assumptions explicit and contestable. He stated that he assumed that CSG members really wanted the company to be innovative, and that this group, including top-team members, was open to looking at ways to encourage new thinking and action.

Speaking up on this matter had been difficult for Bernardo, and he said as much to the group, adding that he felt he was sticking his neck out in drawing the group's attention to the previously undiscussed survey findings. He acknowledged that when the CSG first discussed the survey results, he was amongst those who did not speak up on the innovation findings.

He briefly sketched his personal vision: a company culture in which generating, developing, and testing new ways of working was established practice. Bernardo concluded by inviting CSG members to respond, particularly on the question of the apparent disparity between the stated value of innovation and the survey results.

DEALING WITH CONTENTION: MULTIPLE VIEWS ON THE INNOVATION PROBLEM At first the room was silent. Then, in quick succession, three top-team members jumped in to argue against Bernardo's interpretation of the survey results. Marilyn, the head of corporate strategy, said that many employees clearly did not appreciate how much innovation was actually occurring. She added, "I think we need to do better at communicating what we're already doing." A second executive remarked, "Yes, it's true that the results on innovation were disappointing—but so were the results on some other items. I suspect this is more a matter of generalized employee grumbling." George, the operations chief, chimed in, "The real problem is people thinking that innovation only refers to major change; they're not considering all the smaller improvements that are happening around the place."

Bernardo explained later that he felt like dropping the whole matter then and there. His reluctance to speak out previously in executive forums had stemmed from a worry about having his ideas shot down by top-group members, yet this was precisely what seemed to be happening.

Then Linda, the deputy general manager, piped up. "Initially, I also thought the problem was that our people weren't acknowledging all the innovation that has been taking place. Now, I admit I'm not so sure. In addition, I couldn't help noticing how strongly some of us reacted to, and disagreed with, Bernardo's observations. It's as if we're trying to protect the self-image of our organization as doing innovation well. But now, I'm wondering how much that image reflects reality."

For a few moments Linda's words hung there. No one responded. Then, Al, the CEO, took the discussion in a new direction. "I'm sure we all agree we need to be innovative to succeed. But, perhaps we're not doing all we can to get innovation moving. What we need is to get our heads around some strategies for making it happen. We need to figure out what *actions* will help."

George, the operations chief, spoke up in a tone that Bernardo thought conveyed his customary agitation. Tapping his fingers on the table, he said, "I'm with Al. The danger is that all this talk about innovation is just a distraction from the main game of consistently delivering results for customers. Yes, we do need to improve our systems, and we're doing that, but what we don't need is to turn this into a talkfest about innovation. Obviously, the staff think we need to be more innovative, so let's demonstrate that we're doing something by getting a couple of strategies in place."

John, the corporate human resources head and one of Bernardo's second-tier executive peers, suggested that what the organization needed to encourage innovation was a better reward system. "In the company I last worked for, people had a financial incentive to come up with useful new ideas—and they did; it was really successful."

Linda, the deputy general manager, then asked John what led him to believe a reward system for innovation was a priority in their company's context. But, before John could reply, Gina, another second-tier executive, jumped in and argued that the company should identify some benchmarks by finding out what strategies had helped other companies boost innovation.

Bernardo sensed that the session was about to fall into a common pattern for the CSG: becoming so focused on solutions that the underlying issues were left largely undealt with. He thought to himself, "Do I let go now, or give it one last shot?" Deciding on the latter course, he took a deep breath. "I appreciate that we may need to get some action going, but I'm concerned that it might be premature to focus on strategies just yet. On the other hand, I certainly don't want to turn this into a talkfest, or see us distracted from business imperatives. My worry is if we are too hasty in moving to identify strategies, we might come up with solutions to the wrong problem. I think as a group we need to get a clearer understanding of the nature of the challenges involved in stimulating innovation first."

"I think Bernardo's got a point here," said Linda, the deputy general manager. "We need to get a handle on what employees are thinking before we rush into coming up with strategies. If we don't handle this exercise well, we could end up compounding the problem that the survey results revealed."

Again, the room fell silent. After waiting for a few moments, Bernardo said, "I think it might be worth diving more deeply into some of the territory we've covered. We've heard numerous thoughts about why the survey innovation results were out of line with our stated value of innovation." Bernardo then reviewed those reasons, among them that the company was not communicating sufficiently well about actual innovations, and that people were using the term innovation to mean different things.

Bernardo added, "We have lots of ideas about what might be leading to a lack of innovation, but we don't have much information that would help us assess the merits of these various ideas, or evaluate other possible explanations. It seems to me that, if we're serious about this topic—and I think we should be—we need to do some further work to find out what people really think about innovation, and perhaps about the obstacles to making it happen."

After some further discussion, it was agreed that Bernardo, Linda, and two others would undertake a project over the coming weeks, involving the use of focus groups, to gain deeper insight into staff perceptions regarding innovation.

Later that day Bernardo ran into one of his CSG colleagues at a café. "You took a risk in raising that issue," the colleague said. "But it went well. And you livened up an otherwise dull meeting. Congratulations."

POSTSCRIPT: AT THE CSG EIGHT WEEKS LATER Bernardo, Linda, and their colleagues were invited to report back on the findings of the focus group project. The assembled group appeared curious to find out the reasons for employees not seeing the company as very innovative. The most important finding was not among those discussed at the last meeting. It was that employees believed that top management would not listen carefully to new ideas, no matter how well thought-out those ideas were. A fear of having one's ideas criticized appeared to be a key contributing factor, along with a belief—as had been suggested at the CSG—that employees generally associate innovation with far-reaching changes.

The CSG members listened quietly as the small group reported their findings. As they announced their conclusions, some nodded as if to indicate agreement. Others said things like, "Yes, this makes sense to me." One or two rolled their eyes or mumbled as if to suggest they were not convinced. But, overall, it seemed to Bernardo that most of the CSG members were recognizing a strong grain of truth in what the small group reported back. In fact, there appeared to be a buzz of optimism in the room; it was as if they had succeeded in cracking open at least part of the problem.

In that meeting, the CSG decided to set up some additional small work groups to further the work on innovation. Each group would consist of a combination of staff and CSG members, and would be asked to consider some specific questions. For example, one group would inquire into what actions the company could take to help build the staff's confidence that new ideas would be listened to, and seriously considered.

As Bernardo gathered his papers at the end of the meeting, George—the operations head of whom Bernardo was somewhat wary—wandered over. "I was a bit rough on you last time," he said. "I was distracted by some urgent pressures. You're right to be pushing innovation; we do need to lift our game in this area."

In the chapter's introduction we introduced the idea of looking at learning-centered leadership through two lenses. One is focused on the higher-level view, emphasizing the need for group members, over a period of time, to establish a shared understanding of current realities with respect to a contentious problem, clarify preferred futures (purpose and vision), and harness energy for deep-reaching change. The second lens provides a close-up view; it emphasizes the specific interventions made by individuals at certain points in time in order to further the work of learning-centered leadership.

We shall now look at each of the higher-level learning-centered leadership processes in more detail. We will draw on examples from the case story to illustrate the specific kinds of intervention that this work entails. We will be utilizing both lenses to help deepen in our appreciation of learning-centered leadership.

Jointly Establishing Current Realities

We have seen that making progress on overcoming contentious problems involves finding common meaning from different, perhaps contradictory, constructions of reality. Yet, making such progress implies threat and tension. A desire to mitigate the discomfort can prompt the group to leap to action. Sometimes, this is manifest in people trying to impose their own interpretations and solutions. Often, the solutions put in place only address the symptoms, with the deeper issues being sidestepped by, for instance, calling in a consultant or other outside party. But without a clear understanding of the issue, these actions run the risk of being "quick fixes": they address only symptoms, not the underlying issue.

In light of this, our new view of leadership takes as starting propositions:

- That gaining a grounded definition of the problem by the group is essential if the underlying issues are to be dealt with, and merely symptomatic fixes avoided;

- That all perspectives can potentially contribute to the group's understanding of the problem;

- That relevant perspectives can be partly or completely hidden as a reflection of defensive behavior patterns in organizations and groups; and

- That a primary leadership challenge for individuals within a group is to intervene in ways that assist the group to achieve a shared understanding of—and, potentially, a creative synthesis of—their present realities.

An image of an iceberg can help us understand what it means to establish current realities in relation to a contentious problem. (The iceberg metaphor is adapted from an organizational development text by French and Bell.[13])

FIGURE 2.1 Explicit and Implicit Dimensions of a Problem

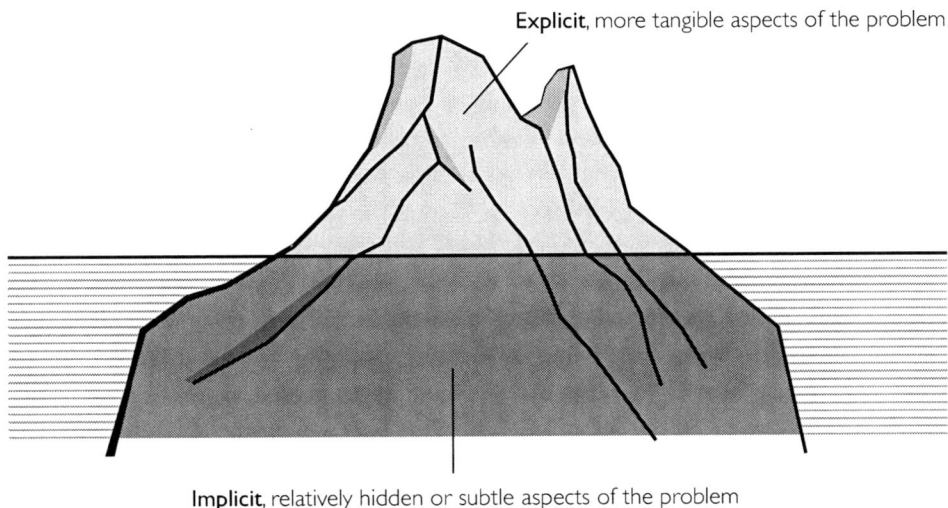

Explicit, more tangible aspects of the problem

Implicit, relatively hidden or subtle aspects of the problem

The part of the iceberg that is above the waterline represents the explicit aspects of a contentious problem. These are the aspects that are tangible, documented, or potentially observable by all stakeholders. In relation to our case story, examples would include policies about innovation, data about numbers of innovations proposed and developed, frameworks used in other organizations for fostering originality, documentation of systems and processes such as incentive or suggestion schemes, and findings from the employee survey as to which employee groups responded most favorably and unfavorably on innovation. Actual words spoken—such as those of the Corporate Strategic Group members in their discussion—can also be regarded as being in the explicit domain. Similarly, we can consider gestures, facial expressions, and body movements to be in the explicit realm, as they are observable by others (recognizing there will be differences in perception and interpretation).

Just as individuals viewing an iceberg from a boat in icy waters would be prone to directing their attention to different features, people are likely to do the same with respect to the explicit aspects of a contentious problem. We all exercise subjectivity in the choice of "facts" we pay attention to, and in the meaning and amount of emphasis we give them. (In fact, this is often the source of the contention.) Therefore, it makes sense not to regard the explicit side of a contentious problem as completely objective.

Where contentious problems are concerned, the challenge is to get the richest possible data set on the table for the group to work with. And, just as with an iceberg, a vast amount of the available information sits below the surface, out of view. This hidden information represents a largely untapped resource that can enrich the group's ability to address the contentious issue productively, and lay the groundwork for positive change. Consequently, it makes sense to delve below the waterline.

Delving Below the Waterline

The hidden or below-the-waterline level of the iceberg represents the more subtle or implicit aspects of a problem or issue. Here, if we are able to "drill-down," we get into the territory of what people may have in their awareness—but perhaps only partially formed—that may be very relevant to the issue at hand but which, for whatever reason, they have not stated, documented, or otherwise made explicit.

We return to the innovation story to illustrate this. Prior to Bernardo speaking up, the survey results concerning innovation and any related implications for the company were not being addressed. Judging by the remarks about Bernardo being "brave" to raise the issue, it appears that at least some CSG members were aware of the issue. Yet, CSG members had essentially acted as if the issue did not exist. In effect, though the survey results were explicit, this entire issue sat beneath the waterline, in the implicit or hidden domain.

Beneath the waterline lies the realm of hidden assumptions, unspecified interests, unprocessed feelings, and untapped knowledge. All of these are potential resources for group learning. If effectively brought to the surface, these hidden aspects add to the data set. As more of the hidden realm surfaces, the group can begin to assemble the data into an increasingly clear, more textured, and ultimately more accurate sense of the issue. When this occurs, viable, well-formed paths forward are more likely to emerge.

Again, let us return to our innovation story. Once Bernardo had made his presentation, the responses of other members indicated some divergent assumptions about the nature of the problem the group faced. One member, Marilyn, the strategy head, appeared to see the issue as being more about communications than innovation. Other CSG members offered explanations that the speakers apparently assumed represented the "true" reasons for the poor employee survey results on innovation. For example, one theorized that employees applied the term innovation only to more substantial changes, but not to minor improvements. Another assumed that the results reflected "generalized employee grumbling."

Practicing learning-centered leadership involves working with others to reveal some of this concealed material and to bring it out into the open, so that it can be sifted, interpreted, and integrated with more tangible (above-the-waterline) resources. This is crucial to enabling the group to reach a more grounded and shared comprehension of what is real. Disagreement between stakeholders may remain but, even then, there is a prospect of greater clarity as to where the differences of view lie.

Good questions are one key to working effectively with the implicit domain. Skilled inquiry can help surface hidden assumptions, unspecified interests, unprocessed—or unexpressed—feelings, and untapped knowledge. We might inquire, for instance, what *interest* the CEO, Al, was serving when he redirected the discussion away from a question about the group's self-image as innovative. Perhaps Al was concerned to maintain the stability of the CSG and avoid any risk of volatility that could accompany discussion of such a potentially sensitive topic. Similarly, when George tapped his fingers as he cautioned against a "talkfest" on innovation, we might ponder—and perhaps ask him—what *feeling* this action indicated. Was his remark a pointer to suppressed frustration, annoyance, and/or anger about these perceived distractions from core business operations? We might also consider how the group's ability to deal with contention could be enhanced if such hidden concerns could be brought to light.

The knowledge that employees hold about possible improvements represents another potential, but currently concealed, resource for the Corporate Strategic Group and the company. Various employees may have ideas for innovations—based on their knowledge of the business and their work in it—which they have not put forward, for reasons reflected in the focus group findings, including that employees believe their ideas will not be paid sufficient attention. Again, questions are key to mining this dormant resource.

Jointly establishing current realities involves engaging with both the explicit and hidden sides of contentious problems. From the examples we have looked at, it appears obvious that gaining access to more of this concealed intelligence is not without some risk. The work of probing the hidden domain can be expected to give rise to threat and defensiveness. Therefore, doing so can seem difficult, scary even. We need to openly acknowledge that there is risk, but also assert that this is not an insurmountable barrier to learning-leadership action; there are actionable ways to reduce the hazards in delving below the iceberg's surface, and to make joint exploration safer.

Key to propagating this new form of leadership is the challenge of learning how to reduce, or at least contain, the level of threat involved in accessing the implicit domain. In coming chapters—especially in Part 2—we shall see how to develop our intervention skills so as to generate richer understandings of what is real while also reducing the risk of hostile actions by others towards us.

Clarifying a Preferred Future—Sound Purpose and Shared Vision

Clarifying purpose and vision entails people inquiring into the futures that others aspire to, expressing their own preferences non-dogmatically, and creating new syntheses from diverging viewpoints. This requires drawing forth and learning more about what people are thinking and feeling, but perhaps have not fully clarified in their own minds or voiced to others.

Establishing Sound Purpose

A sense of purpose gives a group (or organization) direction, and helps to reconcile contention. One way of framing purpose is as service, as setting out not to act solely on the basis of self-interest, but to make a positive difference for others, to make the world a better place in some respect, even if in a modest way. In his book, *Stewardship,* Peter Block gives voice to this notion when he enjoins us to "commit and to find cause. To commit to something outside of ourselves. To be part of creating something we care about so we can endure the sacrifice, risk, and adventure that commitment entails. This is the deeper meaning of service."[14]

As Block makes clear, thinking of purpose as being about service invites us to center our attention on the difference we are striving to make: In what way will others be better off as a result of our efforts? How far are we prepared to go to in order to achieve those results? These are difficult questions—for both individuals and groups—and they are all too often stepped around. Instead of engaging with them, it can be tempting to focus on strategies and "solutions" without sufficient attention to nailing down how these measures will make a difference for others. We saw this in the innovation case, when George suggested that the CSG should "demonstrate that we're doing something by getting a couple of strategies in place." Who will benefit and in what ways from these proposed actions? This was not made explicit.

A challenge of learning-leadership is to be clear about our intentions regarding a particular problem, both in terns of the results we seek to achieve immediately, and those that require a longer time frame. This applies to both individuals and groups. If we do not clarify our purpose or intentions—and do not openly declare them—we are more likely to act out of narrow self-interest than from a sense of a wider good. One way to check our intentions is to apply what the late, renowned management and leadership author, Peter Drucker, called the "mirror test."[15] That is, we need to be able to look ourselves in the eye in the morning and state our purpose without a twinge of conscience.

As well as clarifying our intentions to ourselves, a learning stance on leadership calls for us to strive to communicate those intentions authentically to others. In the innovation story, Bernardo declared an immediate intention of getting the CSG to face up to the disconnection between the survey results on innovation and the company's statements on the subject. He said that his eventual aim was to contribute to the company becoming more innovative so that it could both retain its competitive strengths and be a satisfying place to work. Resurfacing an issue that the top executives had previously dodged could be expected to generate considerable threat, and therefore it could be quite risky. Yet, Bernardo was able to frame his pitch in ways that were likely to diminish that threat. For instance, he expressed his ideas provisionally and invited responses to them; he also declared his own assumptions and feelings about the matter.

Inasmuch as we mask or misrepresent our true purposes, we are likely to foster suspicion and mistrust more than learning, as others try to figure out our "real agenda." Practicing learning-leadership requires that we strive to articulate our intentions genuinely, in ways that make them explicit, and thereby contestable by others. A proposition underpinning this book is that words can be found to express just about whatever we need to say in a manner that is true to what we believe, and which invites engagement with others.[16]

Developing Shared Vision

While hundreds of books extol the worth of vision, the mere mention of the word can set employees' eyes rolling. To many, vision is synonymous with bland corporate statements, such as the goal of being "number one in our industry," or "the best customer service provider." The idea of "shared vision" can sometimes mean little more than the CEO giving a speech about his or her vision of the organization's future to employees and other stakeholders. Yet, when vision is approached more in process terms—in the sense of building a genuinely shared image of a preferred future that is compelling, strategically sensible, and achievable—it can have great power.

Unfortunately, the power of visioning is not often realized. It is when we become preoccupied with the "vision" as a final document or product that many problems come about. Our efforts frequently get derailed when we direct our attention mainly to what is above the waterline, rather than also thinking about what lies beneath.

Vision needs to be allowed to emerge over time, reflecting a synthesis of the distinctive contributions of stakeholders, rather than being grabbed and bolted down like a business objective in a planning exercise. When Bernardo in the innovation case made his pitch to the CSG, he spoke about what a more innovative company might be like for him and for others with whom he had spoken. At that time, though, some of his CSG colleagues had interpretations of the innovation problem that were different from Bernardo's. Others may not have been convinced that this was an issue that they needed to attend to at all. At the point where we left the story, a sense of vision was, if anything, only beginning to emerge. Drawing out a clear sense of vision is difficult when so much cloudiness exists about current reality. This is not to say that current reality needs to be established first; rather, that questions of current reality and vision may need to be sorted out in parallel, as part of an iterative process.

There is no doubting that visioning is difficult work, with many potential challenges. You may find, for example, that your efforts to build vision with colleagues and stakeholders are complicated by the actions of others who are seeking to impose their own visions from above. In contrast, it may be that you are seeking to develop a vision for your own group in the absence of a vision for the wider organization. Sometimes, stakeholders can seem to have a limited capacity for visioning, and so will express a vision that sounds more like a projection of the present: "What will our business plan need to look like in three years time?"

In any of these situations it can be tempting to conclude that vision-building is just too hard. The default is just to focus on the present, and let the future take care of itself—which puts the future at risk. If, on the other hand, you wish to have some say in shaping your future, then the challenge is to engage with others to find out more about the futures they aspire to, and to share with them what you envision. If doing this work in the larger environment beyond your own unit seems too difficult, then perhaps focus your visioning efforts locally, on matters over which you have more control, such as a particular project or aspect of the work.

Vision-building processes can be likened to the proverbial candle in the wind. The flame is easily blown out. Yet, when that flame is well protected, visioning efforts can illuminate brightly a preferred path ahead.

Returning to our case story, Bernardo and the Corporate Strategic Group have achieved greater clarity about their current reality vis-à-vis innovation. Now, they are poised to take the process further by developing a shared vision in relation to the innovation problem. There are no guaranteed prescriptions for how to build a shared vision. However, Part 2 of this book describes a set of leadership practices that are designed to assist individuals to intervene productively, and thus contribute to collective vision-building efforts. These practices include:

Attending	Paying attention to the aspirations and ideals that colleagues and stakeholders express for the future
Reflecting	Contemplating the meanings implicit in people's expressions of what a preferred future could be like
Inquiring	Asking questions to draw forth the vision that others see and the thoughts and feelings beneath their stated words
Expressing	Putting forward our own thoughts and feelings about the future in ways that are contestable, and which help us remain open to considering other views
Synthesizing	Weaving together differing interpretations (including our own) to frame a vision that speaks to those interpretations, yet perhaps also reframes them.

Harnessing Energy for Deep-Reaching Change

Although the prospect of change makes most of us uncomfortable, change is actually the norm in most organizations. Products and services, organizational structures, role definitions, accountabilities, reporting lines, business systems and processes—all these are subject to constant revision and change. All of these changes have one thing in common; they deal with relatively surface-level phenomena. Obviously, much organizational change is of this broad type, with restructuring being a particular favorite of many executives and boards.

Contentious issues, however, signify a need for change at deeper levels: in underlying assumptions, mindsets, and patterns of thinking and interaction. In many cases, changes to structures and other explicit-level aspects are likely to be necessary as well. Yet, unless some shift occurs in the perceptions and assumptions of at least some key stakeholders, there will be little real movement on the issue. Substantial progress is likely to remain elusive.

With our innovation story, something of a shift in the thinking among CSG members seems to have occurred between Bernardo's initial raising of the issue and the further discussion some weeks later, when the CSG established small groups to pursue the matter further. This shift was not achieved without difficulties, reflecting the complexities involved when change efforts engage with underlying mindsets and perceptions. Of course, bringing about substantial change with respect to innovation will require continued learning and action on the part of the CSG and its members as well as by other employees.

A further challenge for the CSG and other employees would be to embed and apply what was learned from the innovation issue over time so as to better develop the company's capacity to deal productively with other thorny problems. Looked at in this way, learning-centered leadership potentially becomes not only a matter of achieving deep-reaching change in relation to a particular contentious problem, but a continuing quest to better learn and act on a whole range of problems.

One necessary ingredient for achieving deep-reaching change—implicit (if not explicit) in most models of leadership—is energy and enthusiasm. Conventional transformational leadership models usually emphasize the leader as the primary source of the passion and "oomph" needed to propel change. These models point to factors such as the leader's belief and commitment to their cause, their ability to tap into the aspirations and concerns of followers, and their resilience in the face of setbacks.[17] But, in contrast to models of transformational leadership, the energy required for deep-reaching change does not—indeed, cannot—come from a leader "doing things" to people, i.e., motivating, inspiring, or aligning them. In our alternative view, the energy for change comes from people being involved in processes they regard as important and worthwhile. These processes include clarifying current realities and vision-building. They include thinking through questions of how the vision is to be achieved, developing and testing strategies, reflecting on progress, and initiating further action. As learning-leadership specialist, Linda Lambert observes, motivation in this field is self-generating.[18] It is in thinking and acting together that the spark is generated. In brief, the view here is that talking candidly, sharing aspirations, and acting jointly to bring a desired future into being is intrinsically energizing and motivating.

People being involved in the work of change, in the sense meant here, is different in quality and kind from the way many so-called "employee engagement" programs approach it. It is not a matter of simply inviting employees' input on changes, or of keeping employees inspired or informed. It is also distinct from the form of involvement in evidence in many initiatives, such as diversity programs, that are designed to attract and retain valued employees. As valuable as such actions and initiatives might be, they usually do not demonstrate the quality of involvement referred to here. The kind of involvement we speak about is manifest when those involved:

• Experience the processes as genuine and meaningful;

• Have confidence that their contributions are valued;

- Are able to exercise leadership themselves;

- Have reasonable access to support and assistance; and

- Are confident their work is actually contributing to change.

These are criteria for meaningful involvement; they reflect the kinds of factors that are fundamentally important to people in organizational settings. These are conditions that will generate the energy and enthusiasm required for deep-reaching change.

It is important to acknowledge that establishing these conditions in modern, high-pressured workplaces is a leadership challenge in itself—and it is no easy task. It is likely that some people will be skeptical, or even cynical, about the prospects for real change, perhaps believing they have "seen it all before" or re-member "when that idea was tried last time." In addition, and especially in today's business environment, people can feel overwhelmed by the day-to-day demands, and perceive they have little time, scope, or backing to contribute to change. The leadership challenge is to recognize such difficulties, to notice how they manifest, and to seek—jointly with those concerned—to inquire into and understand the principal apprehensions. Such efforts often enable a reframing of the problem, which opens up new possible avenues for action.

The Essence of Leadership-Mode Interventions

Learning-centered leadership is manifest, or expressed, through what we have referred to as leadership-mode interventions. These are actions taken relationally—such as Bernardo's speaking up on the survey results concerning innovation—towards the work of establishing current realities, clarifying preferred futures, and harnessing energy. When people undertake such interventions we can say that they are functioning "in the leadership mode."

Here is a more precise definition of leadership-mode interventions (which are variously referred to in the book as learning-centered leadership interventions or actions, and learning-leadership interventions or actions):

To act "in the leadership mode" is to intervene in a relational manner toward building shared meaning in a context of efforts to enable deep-reaching change with a contentious problem.

"Shared meaning" refers to the joint sense-making or meaning-making involved in establishing current realities, clarifying preferred futures, and harness-ing energy for change. This work, as we have seen, entails the construction of meanings from multiple perspectives, appreciating that any concept of a single true reality is illusory. Shared meaning does not necessarily mean that everyone holds the same understanding of all facets of an issue. Contention can remain, but those involved tend to recognize some important aspects on which they agree.

Any member (or members) of a group can undertake leadership-mode interventions, and the group can be as small as two people.[19] What counts is that the group is considering a contentious problem and at least one member is striving to achieve deep-reaching change.[20]

As Bernardo's and Linda's actions suggest, leadership-mode interventions usually involve speaking, as with asking questions, stating what one sees as real, and testing inferences. (While conceivably one could intervene in the leadership mode in some way other than through speech—for example, by posing a question to a group in writing or drawing a picture on a whiteboard—our concern here is with interventions of the spoken variety.)

Acting in the leadership mode involves in-the-moment choices about what we say, how we say it and, more generally, how we interact with others. An intervention might be no more than a single question or statement within a longer conversation. This implies that the leadership mode is something we can go into and out of, even within the space of a single conversation. Of course, for substantial change to result, many more such interventions would be needed, probably over an extended period and involving numerous contributors.

One example of an action taken relationally was Bernardo's presentation of his ideas to the CSG. His intervention may be seen as relational in that he openly declared assumptions he had made and feelings he had experienced, and he invited feedback from other CSG members. Bernardo's action is very much an intervention in the leadership mode: a specific, relationally-oriented act that contributes to the process of learning.

Linda's question to the group as to whether members were trying to protect a collective self-image of being innovative represents a second example. Here she surfaces an observation ("I couldn't help noticing how strongly some of us reacted to and disagreed with Bernardo's observations."), draws an inference ("It's as if we're trying to protect the self-image of our organization as doing innovation well."), and invites reactions to that inference ("But now I'm wondering how much that image reflects reality."). As it happened, no one took up Linda's question, but perhaps this is not surprising given the likely sensitivity surrounding the topic. (An option for Linda, later in the conversation, would be to point out that no one responded to her question, and to inquire into what was going on such that no one did.)

Another example of a leadership-mode intervention occurred when Bernardo expressed that it may be premature to identify strategies. With his reluctance to speak out in earlier CSG meetings, he might not have voiced such a concern easily. The relational quality of Bernardo's intervention is evident in his acknowledging concerns expressed by others (such as a danger of the meeting becoming a "talkfest on innovation"); his giving reasons for why he thought identifying strategies might be hasty; and his non-dogmatic stance ("It seems to me").

One intervention that would not, in this reckoning, be regarded as being in the leadership mode is CEO Al's statement, "What we need is to get our heads around some strategies for making it (innovation) happen." Nothing in what Al said suggests openness to other views, nor any attempt to discover and disclose what might have been hidden for him. If anything, his statement might be accurately interpreted as an attempt to steer discussion away from deeper exploration of the innovation question, and turn it back to the relative security that discussing strategies implies.

We can summarize this section as follows: There are three essential ingredients for leadership-mode activity: a group of two or more is dealing with a contentious problem; at least one member has an intention towards deep-reaching change; and one or more members actively seeks to build shared meaning through relational processes.

Reflecting on the Differences with Transformational Leadership

Let us review briefly the main differences between learning-centered leadership and transformational leadership as described in Chapter 1. Each of the two orientations toward leadership is concerned with achieving change. Transformational leadership emphasizes leaders as individuals who are thought to possess certain qualities (such as a being able to "see farther" than others, inspire people, and model desired behaviors). While transformational leadership puts the accent on influence processes, with the leader articulating a vision and communicating it to enlist others, learning-centered leadership emphasizes processes of joint sense-making, with the emphasis on relational actions that enable hidden intelligence, wisdom, and experience relevant to the problem to be accessed and applied. Learning-centered leadership puts the question of leaders to one side, with leadership instead being viewed through two lenses, each directed to different aspects of the same learning-based processes. One lens is focused on higher-level processes to be performed over a period (concerning current realities, preferred futures, and energy for change), and the other on the specific interventions made by individuals at points in time, to contribute to these processes.

In Chapter 1 we discussed some difficulties with transformational leadership. We noted that transformational leadership contains no mechanism through which either leaders or followers can test the degree to which they are being given full and open information, as opposed to being told what others want them to hear. In particular, we noted the obstacles "leaders" face in testing for concealed thoughts and feelings that might represent opposition, or at least ambivalence, toward the leader's vision.

We cannot directly compare learning-centered leadership with transformational leadership in terms of the traction they offer to a group for dealing with contentious problems. But, we can consider how successful a transformational approach might be in relation to our innovation case story. Would a transformational leader—whether the CEO or someone else—be able to chart a vision for innovation in the company and impart that vision so as to inspire and align people to bring about a greater focus on innovation? Any such effort would likely be difficult going, in view of what we have heard about the range of attitudes held by the Corporate Strategic Group members, as well as other employees' being concerned about not being listened to. There is little ground for believing that a leader-out-front approach would lead to any quick or substantial changes in either employee perceptions or behavior with respect to innovation.

This is not to say that learning-centered leadership is without challenges of its own. One challenge, for example, is that some practitioners might believe they are enacting learning-centered leadership, when in practice they are demonstrating more conventional approaches. The intention here is not to uncritically assert superiority for learning-centered leadership over other leadership forms, particularly transformational leadership. Rather, it is to establish learning-centered leadership as a different, viable, and useful means of framing leadership. This is vitally important given the overwhelming dominance of transformational perspectives. There is room at the table of leadership for both transformational/influence-based and learning-based conceptions.

This notion of "room at the table" is particularly important when we remind ourselves of the potential benefits of learning-centered leadership. One is that some people, who do not self-identify as leaders, will find the prospect of intervening in the leadership mode more in keeping with their self-image. One workshop participant put it this way: "It's great to know that you don't need a personality transplant to do learning-leadership work." If more people contribute to the work of leadership, there is the prospect of a wider range of talent, intelligence, and experience informing efforts to deal with contentious problems.

It is not just the range, but also the *depth* of intelligence we will potentially be able to apply to a contentious problem. Learning-centered leadership takes as a starting point that each of the parties involved in a contentious problem is likely to be a source of intelligence relevant to the problem, but the application of that intelligence is limited because of pervasive defensive behavior patterns. A core challenge is to draw forth this intelligence through learning-leadership interventions made relationally. This is not a matter of "doing things" to people, but of engaging them at a deep level. To the extent that this occurs, the group gains appreciation of the current problem and what it might mean to overcome it, which generates energy to fuel efforts toward change.

There are no magic bullets, nor any guarantees of success. And there are risks involved (which we will discuss in Chapter 5). Yet, when suitable opportunities present themselves, learning-centered leadership and leadership-mode interventions offer the prospect of groups and individuals being able to confront complex realities and find common ground as a springboard for action, where previously there may have been only division or an unsurfaced issue.

Chapter Summary

The chapter featured a case story in which Bernardo sought to get his executive colleagues to engage with the issue of fostering innovation in his company. Using the case as a launch pad, we considered learning-centered leadership as involving people in jointly constructing meaning in relation to a contentious problem by drawing out, examining, and integrating diverse perspectives.

We saw that a relational orientation is critical to learning-centered leadership processes. This is characterized by intentional efforts to put processes of joint thinking and action ahead of direct task achievement; it also entails a willingness to pay attention at a deep level to the views of others, as well as to reflect on one's own views and assumptions. A relational orientation is critical in view of the pervasiveness of defensive behavior patterns in most organizations. Only through relational processes can we possibly tap into the unspoken wisdom and intelligence that stakeholders to a contentious problem possess.

We looked at learning-centered leadership through two "lenses." One lens emphasizes the "higher-level" leadership processes that need to unfold in a group over a period with a contentious problem. This work involves people jointly establishing current realities, clarifying a preferred future (including sound purpose and shared vision), and harnessing energy for deep-reaching change. The second lens focuses on the same processes, but emphasizes learning-centered leadership interventions—actions taken by individuals at specific points in time. These interventions, which must be made relationally, primarily involve acts of speaking, such as giving voice to previously undiscussed topics, or asking questions to reveal deeper aspects of issues, in order to help the group move toward the changes it desires. When we make these learning-centered leadership interventions, we are functioning "in the leadership mode."

We drew on the case story to illuminate the higher-level processes of establishing current realities, clarifying preferred futures (purpose and vision), and harnessing energy for deep-reaching change. In relation to current realities, an image of an iceberg was used to suggest that the work of establishing what is real to stakeholders involves delving below the waterline to surface hidden, implicit, or subtle aspects so that they may be scrutinized and integrated with other insights. We looked at how the work of engaging with implicit aspects is made difficult because of pervasive defensive practices and patterns. This creates some risk, which we must acknowledge. Relational working helps ameliorate these threats, as we saw with Bernardo.

In relation to clarifying preferred futures, we saw, firstly, the importance of being clear about our purposes. Learning-centered leadership implies a purpose that involves making a worthwhile difference for others, that can be stated explicitly, and which is contestable. The second aspect of clarifying preferred futures was developing a shared vision. Here, we emphasized the importance of vision as a process, distinguishing it from vision as a product. Building momentum for change was presented as an ongoing process of creating and sustaining intrinsic motivation through actively engaging stakeholders in change-related processes.

While the processes of establishing current realities, clarifying preferred futures, and harnessing energy for change may unfold over an extended period, we recognized that making learning-centered leadership interventions is something done in the present moment. Undertaking such action is the essence of acting "in the leadership mode," which we defined as intervening relationally toward building shared meaning in a context of efforts to enable deep-reaching change with a contentious problem.

We also reviewed the differences between learning-centered leadership and transformational leadership. We noted that while learning-centered leadership has its own challenges, it offers particular benefits, including the prospect of involving more minds in the work of leadership, and bringing more of the available intelligence to bear on the contentious problem.

Questions for Reflection

2.1 Consider a contentious problem with which you have had some involvement. How might different stakeholders have construed that problem?

2.2 In what particular ways, if any, does the concept of learning-centered leadership challenge your established ideas about leadership? What is one aspect of learning-centered leadership that you need to think more about?

2.3 Think of a recent situation where, potentially at least, you could have intervened in the leadership mode. What specific actions might your intervention have entailed?

Chapter
THREE

The Roots of Leadership–Mode Action

" I don't know if I could do that. It sounds too risky." Alice, the high school assistant principal referred to in the Introduction, is trying to change the school's culture to develop more of an emphasis on learning by all students. She is replying to a suggestion from her external coach, Juanita, that she (Alice) ask the school's principal to be personally more involved in the change process.

Through the chapter we shall "sit in" on portions of the conversations between Alice and Juanita—a consultant leadership coach—over several weeks as they discuss Alice's efforts towards school change.[1] While this case has a school education setting, executives and managers in business and government organizations often face issues similar to those confronting Alice. The case offers lessons that are relevant to those practicing learning-centered leadership to enable deep-reaching change in potentially any organizational setting.

We draw on Alice's experience to shed light on three critical yet interrelated concepts for learning-centered leadership and the leadership mode[2]:

- Relational working

- Mindful working

- Practice-basis.

Each of these concepts represents an orientation crucial for engaging with leadership-mode work. To inhabit them, it is necessary to go beyond mere intellectual understanding. These concepts relate to the psychological stance necessary for approaching leadership work from a learning orientation. The concepts speak to the proposition that capability in this area has an inner dimension. This is of prior importance to mastering any particular knowledge, techniques, or methods. At the same time, each of the concepts has implications for action. Together the concepts provide much of the underpinning for the ARIES practices and tools described in Part 2.

Alice has been trying to get some of the school's more experienced and long-serving teachers to change their approach to teaching and learning. Her thinking is that the school needs to better cater to the needs of individual students. She believes also that the school must better equip students to learn independently throughout their lives.

Rather than the teachers positioning themselves primarily as experts delivering course content to students, Alice wants them to embrace more of a guidance role with students. She has been encouraging the teachers to work alongside the students, to ask them useful questions, challenge their thinking, and support their more independent learning. At the same time, Alice expects that the curriculum will be covered and that desired learning outcomes will be achieved.

Since being recruited twelve months ago, with a brief to build a more contemporary learning culture in the school, Alice has tried several strategies to bring about change. She has sent staff members to development programs, brought in specialists to help the teachers try out new practices, developed and reviewed improvement and monitoring strategies with them, and recruited teachers from elsewhere to inject new blood. She has talked with the teachers about her vision for the school and invited input from them.

Despite all the effort, Alice is frustrated that several of the long-term staff still seem to be clinging to their established practices and habits. "These people are subscribing to an out-dated teaching and learning model," Alice says to her coach. "They prefer the old ways with the teacher as the content expert in the front of the room. They keep disagreeing with my views about the need to modernize our teaching and learning practices without ever really explaining why. These people don't want to change. There's no doubt about that."

Alice accepts that, at least from a more conventional perspective, the teachers are professionally competent and committed to their roles. She acknowledges also that most are well regarded by the parent community and students. Alice wants most of them to stay—but to modify their teaching styles. Adding to the pressure she feels under, Alice is worried that the school principal is becoming impatient with her lack of apparent success in changing the culture. "She keeps asking me for progress reports, and I'm continually finding excuses to avoid talking to her," Alice admits.

"Can we come back to your point about the teachers not wanting to change?" Juanita asked. "What leads you to be so sure of this?"

"It's hard to put a finger on it. I guess I'd put it down to professional experience and judgment," replied Alice. "But they have taken every opportunity possible to avoid change."

Relational Working

Seeing Oneself as Part of the System

One of the exhibits at Questacon, the National Science and Technology Centre in Australia's capital, Canberra, is Curve Ball: at one level a fun ride and game for children; at another, a powerful reminder that what we see is not necessarily objective reality, as we might presume.

Imagine a seesaw-like structure, with two partners seated in opposing chairs. Instead of going up and down, however, the riders spin round and round. Before the ride starts, the participants are each given plastic balls to throw to the other. No problem here: most can throw and catch the balls without difficulty. The contraption then begins to rotate. The players' task, as they whirl, is to keep throwing and—if they can—catching the balls.

Plenty of balls are thrown, but they usually miss the catcher's outstretched arms by a wide margin. The participants laugh at their apparent inability to accurately toss and catch the balls under the ride's conditions. Occasionally, though, a rider is able to take account of the circular motion and pitch a ball accurately to her partner.

Alice visited Questacon during a school vacation after the last conversation with her coach. Here, following her return, Alice recounts to Juanita her experience of the Curve Ball activity, which she did with her son, Ben.

"As Ben and I whizzed around, I was amazed at what happened when I threw the balls to him. Each ball curved noticeably to the left. I saw it with my own eyes! At least I thought it did. Only after stepping off the ride did my reasoning kick in. What appeared as a curve in the ball's flight was a reflection of my change of position as I spun around.

"This got me thinking back to our last conversation, when I told you the teachers were opposed to change and you asked what made me so sure."

"Yes, you did seem pretty certain about that."

"Having been a science teacher, I understand that what we see depends on where we stand. And I know that all sorts of factors—including our backgrounds, experience, and training—condition how we interpret the world. But that is theory. It's quite another thing to be confronted by your own lack of objectivity in practice."

"I imagine it would be pretty unsettling."

"I've always thought of myself as a fairly impartial observer of the world. But the Curve Ball experience, following our discussion last time, prompted me to question this assumption."

"What insights or implications does this questioning open up for you?" inquired Juanita.

"Well, I've been regarding the teachers as uninformed about contemporary approaches to teaching and learning, and as essentially self-serving in their outlook. But what if there are other aspects of the whole change effort that they can see, but that I haven't seen, or can't see, or at least that look different to them?"

Juanita encourages Alice to take her thinking further. "Where does the possibility that they might see other realities lead you?"

"I suppose I should be less concerned with pursuing my own change agenda and more open to their views."

"And how might you demonstrate that in practice?"

"More attention on my part to listening and asking questions might be a good start," observed Alice.

"Perhaps there's a way of reframing the problem between you and the teachers," suggested Juanita. "What if you step back? Could you mentally construct the problem as involving a larger system of which you and the teachers are all part? You could then ask what an 'invisible observer' might see. What would the situation look like to someone who is outside the system, someone whose actions did not impact on the school or the change effort?[3] This might help you to appreciate the challenge more holistically, to take into account your own actions as well as those of the teachers."

Relational Working as Distinct from Detached Working

Juanita proposes a shift of attitude for Alice in her approach to achieving change in the school: from working in a relatively detached manner toward the achievement of her own objectives, to one of working more *relationally* with the teachers, while still being attentive to her own interests. We work relationally when we enter into the world of others through listening, observing, asking deep-reaching questions, expressing our views without implying certainty, and being prepared to learn. These processes facilitate joint exploration, enabling new understandings to emerge. They are difficult to accomplish in practice, but not impossible.

The differences between working relationally and working in a more detached fashion are illustrated in Figure 3.1 below.

FIGURE 3.1 Detached Working and Relational Working

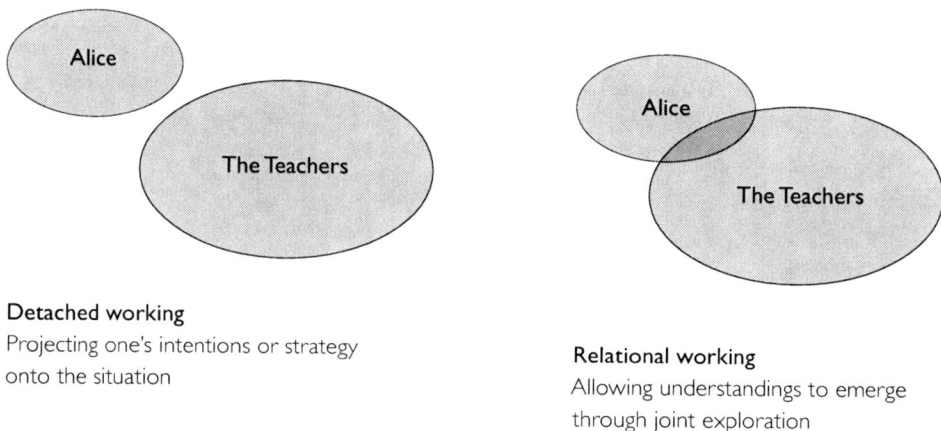

Detached working
Projecting one's intentions or strategy onto the situation

Relational working
Allowing understandings to emerge through joint exploration

The detached-working stance, represented by the first pair of ovals, emphasizes a sense of separateness, of solid boundaries, between self and others. When we work out of this mindset we assume that we are *outside* the system we wish to have an impact on, as shown in the figure with Alice separate from the teachers. In this mode we act as external agents; we analyze problems and seek to bring about change in the behavior or attitudes (or both) of others through the application of various strategies and tactics.

Detached working implies taking action to achieve our objectives, without making those objectives fully explicit to those affected. In the case story, Alice had applied multiple strategies to achieve change in teacher behavior. These included sending the teachers to professional development programs and sharing with them her vision for teaching and learning. The rationale behind these strategies was never discussed with the teachers. Detached working involves keeping the thinking behind our strategies at least partly concealed. In terms of the iceberg metaphor from Chapter 2, that thinking is below the waterline. We might even expect someone deciding on strategies affecting others, as Alice has been, to be somewhat circumspect in revealing the thinking behind his or her actions, in view of the potential for embarrassment for all concerned.

This relatively detached form of working does not necessarily imply an emotionally cold, aloof, or high-handed personal style. Rather, the detachment aspect refers to the general practice of developing and applying tactics and strategies designed to have a desired impact on others while keeping a veil over your deeper thoughts and feelings. It does not refer to your general demeanor, to whether you are friendly, consultative, or interactive. Nor does our description of detached working suggest manipulation. It is not necessarily manipulative to consciously withhold some of your pertinent thinking and emotional content unless, of course, your intention is to deceive others.

The detached stance is common in many organizational change efforts. Such a stance reflects assumptions that we, as change agents, consultants, or interveners, are outside the system on which we wish to have an impact, and that we are better placed than those within the system (by virtue of having greater knowledge, expertise, or understanding, or a more comprehensive view) to determine the nature of the change required and the process for achieving it. In a sense, a detached stance involves doing things to—or that have an impact upon—others, in the hope of achieving some positive result that we have in mind.

When asked, some change agents respond that they do not usually function in a detached stance, as their approach is "consultative." However, consultation-based approaches generally still reflect a detached stance. When we consult with others we are obtaining their inputs and views on changes that we initiate and design. No matter how extensive, a consultative approach still keeps the person (or group) who is initiating change in control. It is they who decide how much, if any, of the input to accept.

Relational working, as reflected in the second pair of ovals above, involves a different mindset. Rather than seeing ourselves as separate, we see ourselves as a part of the system that is experiencing the problem of concern. The others within the system also have an interest in the problem—so we are not detached from them. We acknowledge that by working relationally.

To work relationally is to place, *at that specific time*, the processes of thinking and acting together ahead of direct task achievement. This is not to say that outcomes do not matter, just that in this mode, outcomes are allowed to emerge from joint work rather than being the primary focus.

When we work relationally, we surrender some of our own need for direct control and hold open the possibility that the combined intelligence, wisdom, and experience of the group can yield deeper, more integrated understandings about the problem and about preferred directions. This is the payoff—and why it is desirable to use a relational approach with contentious issues and problems.

Working relationally is not simply a matter of applying straightforward tactics or skills. This work requires a particular kind of stance toward our work on a contentious problem. This stance has three elements:

- The intentions we hold;

- The assumptions we operate by; and

- The behaviors we demonstrate.

Intention refers to our purpose; what we are trying to do. When practicing learning-centered leadership we consciously seek to enter into the worlds of others— and allow them to enter into ours. This is our intention. We are making a deliberate choice, in the particular instance, to try to learn more about others' perceptions of the issue, and to let them find out more about our way of seeing. We are choosing *not* to apply strategies towards others without making those strategies explicit.

Assumptions refer to what we take as given. Working relationally means we bring a specific set of assumptions to a problem situation: that all the parties in this context have a contribution to make; that no individual's analysis (including our own) will be complete; and that the dynamics associated with authority structures will, in all likelihood, encourage at least some people (including, perhaps, ourselves) to suppress some of their relevant thoughts and feelings.

Behaviors necessary to enact a relational approach include listening and observing non-judgmentally, reflecting on different meanings, asking questions to learn more about others' perceptions, giving voice to our own views non-dogmatically, and combining possibly disparate perspectives into common understandings. (Such behaviors are explored more fully in Part 2, in the context of the ARIES practices.)

Relational working is a more elemental form of collective effort than what is implied when we speak of acting in a cooperative or helpful manner, coordinating our actions with those of others, or consulting with others to gain their input. Neither is relational working simply a matter of being an open-minded person; rather, there is a critical emphasis on the choices we make and the actions we take with respect to a specific issue at a point time. Choosing to work from a relational stance in a particular instance—and following through with action—is not easy to do. For one thing, such choices can trigger fears and uncertainties. We need to be able to "hold" these and take action anyway.

If we are unable to embody these intentions, assumptions, and behaviors, we are unlikely to get far in building common understandings with respect to a contentious problem. Instead, we are likely to quickly fall back into the default of detached working—applying our intentions and strategies towards others while keeping hidden some of what we are trying to do. Then, the kinds of mutual suspicions and defensive behaviors that have characterized Alice's efforts at school change are likely to prevail.

Before returning to the case story, I would like to acknowledge here that the distinction I draw between relational working and detached working has its origins in two books that I read nearly twenty years ago as a graduate student: *The Observing Self*, by Arthur Deikman;[4] and *Science, Order, and Creativity* by David Bohm and F. David Peat.[5] (See the endnotes for more information.)

Relational Working in Practice

In their discussion of relational and detached working, Alice asked her coach, Juanita, for a concrete suggestion as to what she might do to demonstrate a more relational style.

"I don't want to be prescriptive," replied Juanita, "but one possibility would be to work towards talking to the teachers more about your observations—what you see as actually going on in the school relevant to the change issue—as well as about your responses to what you observe. You would need to offer these inputs as being from your own standpoint, rather than as some sort of definitive assessment. Then, try asking the teachers about what they see and about the thinking and feeling behind their views. Of course, you would most likely need many such conversations to establish a depth of mutual understanding.

"This kind of working is obviously not easy," Juanita continued. "What kinds of issues do you think adopting a relational stance in working with contentious problems might raise for you?"

"One problem," said Alice, "is that doing this with other stakeholders—

especially in being open to their views—is hard when you already have relationships, perhaps difficult ones, with some of those involved. Through most of my school-change work for the past twelve months I have assumed that the teachers are variously unable or unwilling to really engage with contemporary teaching and learning approaches. My head is full of thoughts and feelings—not all positive—about some of these people."

"I appreciate that working relationally can be tough going," replied Juanita, "but I don't know that the alternatives are ultimately any easier. The main thing is to focus on what is actually happening today, and to put to one side all your history and experience with the teachers, as well as your assumptions, beliefs, and feelings about them as people—except as directly relevant to what is transpiring today. If you were an aspiring international chess champion playing today in a championship competition, hopefully you would not be worrying very much about the last match you lost to your current opponent, or her playing style, or how you played yesterday. You need to address your attention to the present moment. In your situation, that means aiming to deal with each interaction with the teachers as novel and fresh, and being receptive to what they say and do, and to what occurs at that time.

"On this matter of openness to the teachers' views, your experience with the Curve Ball activity tells me that you understand intellectually why this counts. The area for you to work on concerns how you practice, or model, openness in your interactions with others. I suspect this is mainly a question of loosening the hold you have on your own views. Can you regard them as provisional, as open to question, as reflecting your current assessment of the issues, rather than as an expression of your person?[6] This need not mean surrendering what you hold as true, just allowing some permeability.

"One implication is for you to become more adept at taking disagreement with your views as just that, a difference of opinion, rather than as an attack on you as an individual, or on your "leadership." Another challenge is to work at developing a more exploratory attitude with regard to others' views. Seek to find out more about the meanings and experiences behind those views, rather than being dismissive of them. And, of course it is critical not to just *talk* about the importance of openness, but to actively demonstrate how much you value it through the quality of your interactions."

"I think I can make some progress in the directions you describe," said Alice. "But no matter what changes I make personally, there is no guarantee the teachers are going to reciprocate. I can't imagine some of those people seeing themselves as part of the system, let alone regarding my views as worthy of consideration."

"That is true," Juanita acknowledged. "Some—or even all—of the teachers may be unable or unwilling to adopt a more relational stance with you, at least in the short term. You cannot control how they interact with you, but keep in mind that the most important element here is your bearing *towards them*. You can expect to make progress in leadership-mode work only insofar as you are able to hold reasonably positive attributions of those you are working with.

"By this I mean allowing that the teachers probably have reasons for their actions that make sense to them—even if those reasons are not evident to you. Unless you have very good reasons to believe otherwise, start from the assumption that they will be able to act with sufficiently good intent, with acceptable competence, and in a reasonable manner in any given situation. That mental orientation is a starting point for working in the leadership mode. If, on the other hand, you work from predominantly negative assumptions about others, you are actually likely to encourage defensive behavior, which is at odds with the candor you seek.

"And remember that working relationally is an ideal; something to work towards. You cannot realistically expect everything to change at the outset. If you find you cannot work in this way with some people, well, so be it. You could try putting more of your energy—initially at least—into working with those who seem to be more curious about new approaches."

"Here's another problem," said Alice. "The teachers are expecting me to lead. Won't I seem weak or indecisive if I'm open to considering all views? The school appointed me to have a vision, to shake things up, to establish the new direction. I don't want to come across as wishy-washy."

"This comes back to your own concept of leadership," answered Juanita. "Do you view leadership much as the teachers you talk about see their role—as mainly to do with a strong individual standing out front, charting the course for others to follow? Or is your model of leadership more a matter of gently prompting and encouraging people towards a future that you aspire to and that you would like them to share? Or is your concept more in line with the kind of learning-centered leadership we have been discussing, with its emphasis on joint exploration?

"If it really is the latter, you need to clarify your own beliefs and expectations about leadership as well as dealing with the teachers'. Do you provide "strong and decisive" leadership because that is what they expect? Or do you strive to act in ways that are truer to your own beliefs?

"Let me pick up that point about what the school principal wants," added Juanita. "My understanding is she expects you to change the school's culture. 'Shaking things up' implies a theory about how to get there; about a means towards an end. Having an in-depth conversation with her would probably be a good idea, if only to learn more about her concept of change. I take it you haven't had such a talk yet?"

"That's right," said Alice, "but it's on my to-do list."

Both relational and detached approaches are necessary; it is not a matter of one being better than the other. Neither is there any sharp line dividing them. Most of Alice's day-to-day activities in managing the school might actually call for a more detached orientation, for focusing on what needs to get done rather than seeking to build shared understandings about underlying issues. The deep-process orientation of working relationally is just not necessary for many activities, particularly those with an operational focus. Alice would probably not achieve much if she adopted a relational stance in situations where it was not needed. Yet, with troublesome problems, the concept of working relationally offers the prospect that thinking together can enable a deeper, more compelling truth to emerge.

As Alice's experience suggests, a relational approach is easy to assert, but difficult to enact, particularly if—like Alice—you tend to define yourself as a "leader." It takes courage and strength to treat your own views as contestable, to be open to the possibility that others might offer insights that make more sense to the group than yours, and to deal with the uncertainty and vulnerability that comes with this territory. Alice is perhaps beginning to shift her stance in relation to the teachers, but her apparent reluctance to speak with the school principal suggests she has some way to go.

Mindful Working

In their next conversation, two weeks after the last, Alice described to Juanita a meeting that did not work out the way she intended.

"I met with some of the senior teachers to discuss a new performance management system that I want to implement. It's a system that's been used successfully in other schools. The aim is to help reinforce the kinds of teaching and learning practices that I'm trying to encourage and to keep the school moving forward, not to catch people out. I'd gone to a lot of effort to consult with the staff about it, and I was confident that people were coming to accept the system.

"But then there was a blow-up, almost a rebellion. Two of the more experienced staff publicly accused me of setting up a system that would make it easier to get rid of teachers that I don't want. One of them yelled something about me 'just trying to control them,' then they both walked out. I know I need to put myself within the system and work jointly with the teachers towards change, but some of these people are simply resisters."

What I am terming "working mindfully" refers to our maintaining an open, receptive, inquiring, and diligent stance with regard to both external stimuli and our internal states. We have seen that acting in the leadership mode involves making real-time choices about how we speak and act. The choices we make are likely to be more productive to the extent that we have our "antennas up" and can tune in and engage with signals, even faint ones, coming in from our environment. Working mindfully implies paying attention, as well, to what is happening within us, including our thoughts, feelings, assumptions, and impulses. Discerning a wide range of signals, interpreting them with care without rushing to judgment, and then acting according to what makes sense in that moment is to act mindfully in the practice of leadership.[7]

Sometimes the nature of mindful working is revealed by its absence. Consider this example.

The executive team of a business banking division was considering quarterly performance data at their regular meeting. The divisional head was in the process of congratulating his colleagues on a successful quarter. In the midst of that, one member of the group spoke up. He told the group that he had recently seen some new research that showed that their bank had slipped two rungs on an industry customer perceptions ladder. The chief executive glared at the executive who put forward the information, and then continued with his talk as though nothing had happened. There was no further discussion of the industry ladder.

What might mindful working have looked like in this instance? There are no objective standards or hard and fast rules. It is more a matter of considering what actions might have reflected an attentive, open, thoughtful, and suitably responsive stance in the particular circumstances.

Perhaps the chief executive was already aware of the data. If so, he had a choice to make about disclosure. Perhaps he could have acknowledged the— presumably significant— data at an appropriate point in the meeting, putting it in a larger context that meant congratulations were still in order. If he was previously unaware of it, he might have invited the executive who mentioned the research finding to share more information at the meeting or at a later time. Conceivably, he might have spoken with this executive after the meeting, taking that opportunity to disclose his reaction (surprise, embarrassment, or whatever it was) to hearing this information raised at that particular point and, if he was not previously aware, to inquire into the nature of the findings.

The executive who raised the information might have given more consideration to the reaction likely to greet his mentioning the research findings at the same time the chief executive was reviewing the quarter's performance, and prepared accordingly. Was he clear about his intentions? If so, then the executive might have paid more attention to timing. He might also have prefaced his remarks by stating that he had some information that could alter the group's perceptions of current performance, suggesting that the group might want to discuss these findings. Was the group interested? Alternatively (or additionally), this same executive might have approached the divisional head following the meeting. He might have revealed his concern about the head's reaction—without judgment—and sought an opportunity to discuss the findings.

Working mindfully implies that we take care not to react unthinkingly (as perhaps the chief executive did with his glare), and that we pause to ask ourselves about the whole context in which we are functioning, including subtle dynamics that could easily be overlooked. Working mindfully also means that we refrain from pushing to achieve our objectives without being open to new information, which might suggest we need to reconsider those objectives. This is particularly relevant to contentious problems. The more mindful we are, the more alert we will be to the signals—both overt and subtle—that point to the critical factors bearing on a problem.

In the next sections we shall focus on two aspects of working mindfully, drawing upon the work of Harvard psychology professor Ellen Langer in her book, *Mindfulness*.[8] Those aspects are being mindful of perceptions and language, and being mindful of process.[9]

Being Mindful of Perceptions and Language

Imagine two people, previously unknown to each other, sharing a compartment in a train traveling across a large expanse of relatively flat and dry plain. One spends much of her time reading while the other absorbs the scenery, noticing subtle changes in vegetation and topography as the miles pass. After a time, the person observing asks, "Have you done this trip before?" thinking this may explain her fellow traveler's apparent disinterest in the view. "No, but it's basically just all desert," is the reply. "If you've seen one mile, you've pretty much seen it all."

Ellen Langer emphasizes the importance of the categories we use—like mental sorting shelves—to organize our thoughts and beliefs. The traveler who regards the view as "just all desert" appears to be using a very broad category to encompass a potentially huge variety of experience and learning, as compared with the other passenger who is observing more actively and acutely. The language we use, as with the reference to "desert," reflects our way of experiencing the world. Language choices also *reinforce* how we perceive: if we conceive of the view outside the window as just a desert, then just a desert is all we are likely to see.

A more mindful stance, Langer suggests, is characterized by the continuous creation of flexible new categories that take into account specific circumstances and contexts. To think and act more mindfully is to apply greater differentiation in the categories we use; to be less prone to projecting pre-determined filters onto novel situations. It is about refraining from making sweeping, uncritical generalizations and snap judgments.

Consider Alice's use of the term "resisters" to describe some of the teachers. The danger in using such a broad category is that it lumps together certain people as "the problem," and implies that they are necessarily wrong in resisting what is a reasonable change. It might help Alice to apply a more fine-grained categorization in her thinking. This would involve thinking and learning more about *which specific staff* appear unconvinced about the proposed changes and for *what reasons*.

Conceivably, a number of factors could account for the apparent resistance, and different factors (or combinations of factors) might be important to different individuals. For instance, there could be disagreement on pedagogical grounds about the extent to which—if at all—the changes represent improvements to teaching and learning practice. There could be objections to the way the changes are to be implemented; perhaps some people believe they have not had enough say or that their concerns have not been taken sufficiently into account. One factor—already alluded to by Alice—might be teachers' fears about their experience being lost or compromised. Some teachers may have qualms about their ability, or about the effort required, to become proficient in new approaches.[10] Some may fear their jobs are at risk if they cannot make the transition.

An important facet of developing leadership-mode capability involves our thinking in more differentiated and fine-grained terms about the information and experience we rely upon, and reflecting these more nuanced appreciations in the words we choose. As one of my workshop participants put it, "The language is out there; the challenge is to find it."

Being Mindful of Process

It could be a football team winning their game by kicking a goal in the closing moments, a potter removing a beautifully crafted vase from the kiln, or a group of executives reaching an agreement to settle a dispute between two companies. Behind every outcome or result, as Ellen Langer points out, is process.[11] Process refers to the "how" in attaining the outcome; not just the "formal how" in the sense of explicit strategies, steps, and procedures but also the "informal how": the often subtle dynamics unfolding in the actions, relations, and perceptions of those involved as well as from changes in relevant systems.[12]

One aspect of mindful attention to process involves thinking and conversing about the *premises* we hold as to how change occurs in a particular setting. What is our understanding—our concept or theory—of the strategies and dynamics needed to bring about the results we seek? Conversely, what concept or theory of change might be inferred from the actions we are actually taking? What dynamics do we see currently unfolding in our efforts to achieve change? In our school change story, a full range of stakeholders—including parents, students, and other members of the school community, as well as teachers and the school principal—could potentially be involved in such a conversation, to great effect.

There are few signs that Alice has talked much about such matters with stakeholders. However, in their coaching session, Juanita invited Alice to share her thinking as to how the performance management system she was trying to introduce would help advance the changes she wanted in teaching and learning: "How will the system help teachers to focus less on expert delivery and more on enabling student learning?"

"That's difficult," Alice admitted, momentarily averting Juanita's gaze. "Based on what she has seen in some other schools, the school principal has been pressuring me to introduce a performance management system. I think her assumption is that the system will support and strengthen the kinds of behaviors we need to foster. But I'm not sure that it will encourage real commitment to change. In a way I've gone against my own better judgment here. As a way of staying on top of the load I'm carrying, I've tended to blur the cultural change effort and the performance management system together. Perhaps this has been a mistake."

"Maybe so," observed Juanita, "if it prevents you from achieving what really matters."

Without well-formulated and tested ideas about the processes needed for change and how they relate to what is actually occurring, we lack a sound basis for making choices about interventions and strategies. Under such circumstances, as in Alice's case, choices are more likely to be a reaction to political and other factors, such as the preferences of decision-makers for particular methodologies, rather than a considered response to the problems faced. When this is the case, it should not be surprising if results fall short of aspirations.

Of course, conversations about the change process are often avoided, given the implicit threat associated with them. Alice could continue to ignore process, and persist in devising and seeking to implement strategies for "moving forward." Such action would effectively sweep aside questions about the actual and desired processes of change—hardly consistent with our concept of mindful working as thinking and action that is attentive, context-sensitive, and diligent.

A more mindful approach would be for Alice to initiate conversation with other stakeholders, to acknowledge what she sees has been happening (perhaps adopting the "invisible observer" perspective suggested by Juanita), and to inquire as to how they are experiencing the change effort. Part of the challenge here is that Alice might be tempted to mask or step around some of the more contentious aspects of what she sees, and others may do the same. Alice would need to handle her part of the conversation skillfully to prevent it being derailed by defensive behaviors, whether her own or others'.[13] The ARIES practices, in Part 2, could turn out to be handy here.

The discussion of mindful attention to process has so far focused mainly on processes over a period of time, both as they actually unfold and as we would like them to. But we also need to focus on the specific interactions between people. Process also occurs "in-the-moment," and we need to be concerned with the dynamics at play at the time when people talk about difficult issues.

Consider the "blow-up" over the proposed performance management system that occurred in Alice's meeting with the teachers. At one level, this incident may reflect process issues that were building up for some time. At a second level, the process issue that triggered the blow-up may have developed over a few minutes, or even seconds, perhaps as a reaction by one or more teachers to something

Alice said. Mindful working, in this context, requires that we be able to step out of the content of the conversation, and deal with the process side.

In their book *Crucial Conversations*, Kerry Patterson and his colleagues describe the process work that can be done in the midst of a conversation as having three strands.[14] The first strand involves recognizing when a conversation turns from routine to dangerous. They point to signs such as noticing that you feel uncomfortable. Perhaps your stomach tightens or you experience a tinge of fear; maybe voices are getting louder. The second strand is being alert to "safety" issues; recognizing circumstances in which you and others may feel unsafe to speak up. Common reactions in such instances, suggest the authors, are "violence" (verbally attacking others) and "silence" (withdrawing or shutting down). When these circumstances emerge, the need is to slow down, step back from the conversation, regain perspective, and restore safety. The third strand involves paying attention to your own style. It is important to be aware of your tendencies when under pressure such as, for example, seeking to dominate or control the conversation, or going quiet. A key element for ensuring a productive process is being able to self-monitor and self-regulate your own contribution.

We have considered two sides of mindful attention to process: process as change unfolding over time, and process as it relates to the dynamics within a particular conversation. Both are critical for achieving positive outcomes. Yet, in our outcome-driven, get-it-done-today world, the importance of both types of process is easily lost. Process is often associated with red tape and a mechanical following of rules and procedures. "Less emphasis on process and more on outcomes" has become a management mantra. Outcomes do matter. But to focus slavishly on the pursuit of results by the shortest possible route is to risk ending up like the fabled hare, beaten by the slower but methodical tortoise.[15] While process-oriented work can sometimes seem slow and not directly related to tangible, immediate results, the paradox is that paying attention to process today can help build a solid base for making faster and more substantial progress from then on.

As well as a process orientation, we have discussed how mindful working fosters differentiation in thinking and language use. Mindful working is also closely interwoven with relational working, our first concept. This is so because working relationally requires us to be mindful in our interactions with others, and actively attentive to own thoughts and feelings. Echoes of mindful working will be evident in the third concept, too—leadership as practice-based.

Practice-Basis

A small boy, walking in a park with his family, noticed a solitary teenager performing tricks on his bicycle. The older boy was riding the bike as if it were a unicycle, learning forward over the front wheel to lift the rear wheel high in the air. "How do you do that?" asked the small boy. "Practice," said the older boy. "I practice every day."

The importance of practice—in the sense of working repeatedly to hone a capability—may seem obvious for performing tricks on a bike, or for touch-typing, tennis, chess, or any number of other accomplishments. But this is not necessarily so for leadership. Here the emphasis is more likely to be on an individual's qualities (or shortcomings) as a "leader," not on how well or how often she practices leadership day-to-day.

The question of practice came up in Alice and Juanita's next coaching session. Alice talked about her experience over the past two weeks, saying she felt she had moved two steps forward and one-and-a-half back.

"The senior staff have agreed to participate in a conference to explore different approaches to teaching and learning, and that's a good thing. But I must confess that I haven't yet had that discussion with the school principal.

"I've been even busier than usual but it's more than a time issue. I'm finding this whole change leadership business incredibly draining. In my past roles I've been a strong and successful leader. I've thrived on change, enjoyed stirring the pot. But here I haven't achieved the turnaround needed, and I've been having real doubts about my effectiveness as a leader. And this is on top of the load that comes with a job like mine in a large school."

The two women talked about how Alice might better reconcile the various strands of her role and deal with her misgivings. Juanita observed, "Perhaps focusing on your success as a leader is not the best use of your time right now. It might be more valuable to focus on the particular interventions that you're making, or not making."

Like the teenager's advice to the small boy, Juanita's message is about the importance of continually working at building one's proficiency. The leadership-mode concept locates leadership not in a person's capabilities or qualities as a leader, but in the interventions made relationally towards achieving deep change. For Alice, the question then becomes, How well am I enacting leadership processes at this time? This is largely a matter of the choices she makes about when and how to intervene, and of the quality of those interventions.

As with any discipline, building your capacity to intervene productively requires practice, reflection upon your efforts, and more practice still, incorporating what you have learned. In some cases, practice might entail using tools, such as those presented in Part 2, to "rehearse" potentially difficult situations before you step into them. But, primarily, practice implies undertaking leadership-mode work in real situations—if possible, in relatively low risk settings at first. Practice and performance are inextricably linked in leadership-mode work. In effect, each intervention you make is a rehearsal of sorts for the next intervention, as well as being action in its own right.

The cycle of practice and reflection needs to be continued over a period, definitely past the first few efforts. At first, you may find that your initial leadership-mode actions do not bring about the results you want. Rather than concluding "I can't do this," or "This approach doesn't work," the challenge is to persevere at least until your actions become more assured.

Some people confuse practice with intellectual understanding, believing that once they have absorbed the concepts they will—or should—be able to act on them capably. This is akin to a novice skier watching a professional zoom downhill and thinking, "I get the idea here and I can do that." While the capabilities required for leadership-mode work are not difficult to comprehend, the learning required to develop adroitness is not primarily of an intellectual nature. The idea of seeing ourselves as part of the system of concern, for example, is not hard to grasp, at least superficially. But to be able to look at an issue holistically and be aware, in real time, of our own participation and its impact is difficult to do in practice. It certainly involves more than learning a bundle of techniques. The most important capabilities come from within.

As to the nature of these inner capabilities, W. Timothy Gallwey offers an interesting perspective from the world of tennis. Gallwey, a former tennis pro, is the author of *The Inner Game of Tennis* (as well as several other "inner game" books).[16] For him, the quality of one's performance, whether on the court or off, has a lot to do with the kinds of messages we give ourselves, the self-talk that most humans engage in continuously.

Gallwey distinguishes between the "telling" self and the "doing" self. The telling self is the inner voice that you might hear when you are trying to perform a skill or task that you find difficult. Imagine a social tennis player continually failing to get her serves in. She admonishes herself: "You're trying too hard. Relax." This is the telling self at work. It is that part of us that judges, criticizes, corrects, and advises us on our own behavior.

The doing self, on the other hand, is the side that gets on with the action. Gallwey describes it as comprising the know-how, wisdom, and skill embedded in the brain, body, and memory. It is built up with experience and learning, but much of it is beyond the reach of conscious awareness. To gain a sense of the doing self, think of a skill that you perform well. It does not matter what the skill is. Now, imagine yourself actually performing this skill to the limits of your ability. Chances are your doing self is largely in charge of the action and your telling self is relatively quiet.

The key to successful performance, argues Gallwey, is to quiet the telling self and allow the doing self more space to perform the action. This is not a matter of suppressing the telling self. It is, he suggests, more a case of quietly and non-judgmentally observing your performance of the action, creating a mental picture of a good outcome, and then trusting your doing self to perform the action. If you fail to get the result you want—say you serve several balls in a row that are too long—calmly observe what is happening, re-imagine the desired result, and again allow yourself to make it happen.

Of course, this is much easier said than done. The telling self has a pesky habit of reasserting itself, even when we believe it settled. The effect can be to "trip-up" the doing self, to throw it off balance. Imagine our tennis player again. She tells herself: "Your serve is too stiff, too mechanical; you need to be more spontaneous." Then she realizes that her telling self has taken control. "Stop giving yourself advice; just let the serve happen." Here the telling self is still very much in the ascendancy; it bobs up unexpectedly, insidiously. Allowing the doing self to act is obviously challenging. This can be especially so in the early stages of practice, when the emphasis is on basic technique. We shall look in Chapter 6 at some ideas for quieting—rather than suppressing—the telling self so that we are better able to do what needs to be done. For now, let us consider how Gallwey's construct might be applied to leadership-mode practice. We return to Alice's conversation with her coach.

"Let's think about the need for a chat with the school principal," said Juanita. "I sense your telling self has been very active here."

"Yes, I suppose it has. I've been doing a lot of negative self-talk, about how I'm not succeeding and so on—to the point where I have felt pretty much paralyzed about how to actually approach the principal on this issue."

"That makes sense to me," replied Juanita. "I would like you, right now, to see if you can create an image in your mind of a successful conversation with the school principal. Then please describe the challenge of undertaking that intervention in light of Timothy Gallwey's ideas and the other concepts we've discussed."

After a few moments, Alice responded: "I did manage to see myself in conversation with the principal. And I need to make this meeting happen in reality, not just in my mind. I can't keep running away from this. I need to talk candidly with her about what's working well and what's not.

"With regard to the relational working concept, I need to be less concerned about managing my relationship with the principal (so far, I've done that mainly by avoiding her), and instead see myself as working alongside her. I need to own up to my contribution as a part of the system needing change, and also encourage the principal to see that she's part of the system, too. I need to ask for her active support while making clear that this is not a matter of me failing. Visible support from her will demonstrate to the teachers that the school is serious about this change effort, and that it's not just my personal priority.

"I think the principal and I share similar visions," Alice continued. "The questions are more about how to get there. From a mindful working perspective and, especially, a process perspective, I need to see this is as the first of several conversations about our theories of change. I also need to talk with her about the performance management system and how that fits in."

"There's also the process-in-the-moment aspect," said Juanita. "What would you do if she became defensive or angry?"

"Well, keeping my mind clear would help. If I can do that, I will have some chance of stepping out if things start to unravel, and getting the process back on track. I must be careful not to do all the talking or to let myself be captured by the ideas I want to get across. I need to inquire about how she sees the issues, and be prepared to receive some criticism. If she is critical, I'll ask for an opportunity for us to work together more collaboratively in order to get on top of the change process.

"But perhaps the main thing is that, having given the meeting some prior thought, I need to trust myself to handle it well. I need to avoid getting caught up in thinking about all manner of scenarios and trying to tell myself what I need to do in each. I have to give my 'doing self' some room to act."

"That all sounds good to me," Juanita said. "Just one thought. If the conversation does go in unexpected or uncomfortable directions, be very clear about your primary purpose in seeking the meeting, and make sure you get that across—even if it takes a follow-up communication after your face-to-face meeting. I'm looking forward to hearing how it goes."

The concepts of relational working, mindful working, and practice-basis are all connected. Each offers a different angle on learning-centered leadership. Yet, the concepts flow into, and through, one another; the distinctions between them are soft, more a matter of emphasis than of sharp delineation.

Relational working is at the core of a learning-oriented perspective on leadership. It is not possible to intervene in the leadership mode (as defined here) without at least an element of relational working. The fundamental challenge of working relationally is learning to step back from attachment to your own views, to see yourself as sitting at least partly within the system you are seeking to change, and to deal with the issues that arise. As Alice's experience suggests, this is difficult to do in practice, though it need not be overwhelmingly so.

Mindful working accentuates thoughtful, attentive action; it is a stance characterized by receptiveness to new inputs and a disinclination to rush towards judgment. This chapter has highlighted two aspects of mindful working: using language in order to see the world in more differentiated terms, and attending to process as well as outcomes. Common to both is an attuning to subtle phenomena and a willingness to suspend judgment and look beyond what may seem obvious, allowing that this may require reappraising previously taken-for-granted truths. Alice's success in changing the school's culture is likely to hinge, at least in part, on the extent to which she can mindfully engage with what is going on around her, including with the teachers and school principal. She must be prepared to experiment with intervening in different ways. This brings us back to the matter of practice.

The focus on practice reminds us that what counts is not how good a leader we are, but how well we identify and undertake leadership-mode interventions. Those of us wanting to work—at least some of the time—in the leadership mode are all practitioners (whether we think of ourselves as leaders or not). As with tennis or any other discipline, practice is required as long as we are keen to improve; we should not expect to reach a point where practice no longer benefits us. For someone like Alice, who has tended to regard herself as a leader, this may involve some difficult re-learning. Yet, perhaps it is the very notion of a continual quest to develop our proficiency that makes working in the leadership mode such an interesting and challenging game.

Post-script: Alice Meets with the School Principal

After leaving Juanita, Alice arranged to meet with the school principal. That discussion occurred a few days later.

After listening to what Alice had to say, the principal replied: "I'm relieved that we are finally talking. I've been aware for some time that trying to change the culture is a tough job. Some of these people can be very difficult. That's why I've been asking about progress. But I didn't want you to feel like I was trying to take over, so I chose not to initiate a more formal discussion with you.

"This is a whole-school change issue, so it makes sense that we both be involved. I think you have made some mistakes, but basically I have a lot of confidence in your abilities. By working together—assuming we can establish goodwill with the teachers—we should be able to achieve the shift we need, though it will no doubt take a while."

Chapter Summary

This chapter delved into three concepts underpinning learning centered-leadership and leadership-mode action: working relationally, working mindfully, and practice-basis. The story of Alice's efforts—with the assistance of her external coach, Juanita—to bring about change in teaching and learning practices in her school illustrated these concepts.

Relational working implies seeing yourself as at least partly within the system that concerns you, and acting accordingly. As well, it asks you to inquire into others' views while also holding your own views open to review. Relational working asks you to adopt a receptive stance even in situations where you have already established, and perhaps difficult, relationships with other stakeholders, and to accept the reality that others may not reciprocate by displaying receptiveness to your views. Detached working, in contrast, sees the intervener as an external agent operating upon the system, applying strategies and tactics to bring about change involving others.

The discussion of mindful working drew on the work of Ellen Langer to look into two aspects: the need to work towards differentiation in perceiving—rather than applying sweeping generalizations and unchanging categories—and the necessity for attention to process. Process was considered both in relation to the subtle change-related dynamics occurring over a period, and—at a more micro level—the dynamics occurring within a particular conversation. Critical to process work is the ability to step outside of the conversation's content to deal with shifts in mood or atmosphere, such as when someone (ourselves included) displays anger, or the conversation seems stuck or stalled.

A practice-based perspective goes to the idea that the leadership-mode concept is about taking actions of a particular type (relational, deep-reaching, and change-oriented). The question is not how good a leader any particular person is. The more relevant question is, What kinds of interventions are they making? And, How well are they making those interventions? As with any discipline, practice is a critical element. But this is not just a matter of trying harder. The challenge is to engage with the inner dimension: to become more adept at observing one's internal processes, at intentionally trying out different approaches, and at reflecting on the results—without adopting an overly self-critical stance.

Questions for Reflection

3.1 Recall an instance in which you had a positive experience in working relationally. What aspects of this experience lead you to think of it as involving relational work?

3.2 Think of a time in which you observed someone behaving mindfully. What was it about their behavior that prompts you to regard it as mindful?

3.3 What is one challenge for you, personally, in adopting a practice-based approach to your exercise of leadership? How might you go about dealing with this challenge?

Chapter
FOUR

. . . .

Re-interpreting the Leadership-Management Relationship

" The expectation is that we deal with the here and now, the urgent. Leadership is important, too, but it's hard to get to."

"Usually, I take the expert role in solving problems in my area. I can now see that's the management mode. The leadership mode is another option for when I want to help the other person take charge of their own problems."

"I find the leadership and management distinction helps me be more conscious of how I'm allocating my time. I'm going to work at freeing up some time for leadership."

"My preference is for the more concrete side of things, so I probably lean towards management. I like the idea that I might start off a meeting with my managers with a clear agenda but maybe go into leadership to drill down into a particular issue. And then we can come back to management to decide on what to do next."

"I recognize that I need to do more leadership. It's handy to know that when I do move into the leadership mode I can move back to management again—such as when I need to sort out a problem with one of our suppliers."

These comments, typical of those made by participants in my workshops after discussing the leadership–management relationship, suggest that we can potentially make sense of the relationship, and that there is practical benefit in doing so.[1] Yet, such views are at odds with a common assumption: that little is to be gained from seeking to differentiate the two. This assumption is another one of the "vines" obscuring our view of leadership, referred to in Chapter 1.

The terms leadership and management are often bandied about and sometimes used together, as in the names of professional institutes and academic journals. But serious consideration of the relationship tends to be lacking. For all the many hundreds of books on leadership, relatively few appear to deal in a thoughtful way with the question of how leadership relates to management. It is as if the relationship between them is seen as just too difficult to fathom, too complex and multifaceted to be deconstructed.

Here, I propose that the relative lack of careful attention to the relationship reflects in large measure the confusion generated by the other three vines of leadership discussed in Chapter 1.[2] Those vines represent the out-dated assumptions that:

- Leadership is equivalent to leaders;

- Leadership is the province of people in positions of authority; and

- Leadership essentially involves influence processes.

The assumption that there is little value in seeking to distinguish leadership and management seems to be an "offshoot" of these out-of-date assumptions. In turn, these vines also get in the way of our seeing how management and leadership are distinct, as well as how they relate to and complement each other.

To appreciate the distinction between the two, we need to continue our work of pulling back these vines and holding them clear. In doing so, we might discover that distinguishing leadership-mode action from management-mode action gives us significant additional traction in dealing with contentious problems. This is a potential benefit that awaits discovery.

Our purpose in this chapter is to clarify a vision of leadership-mode action in relation to action in the management mode such that each complements the other, while recognizing that such complementarity also brings challenges. In the following section, we look into how the conventional assumptions concerning leaders, authority, and influence make it difficult to see leadership and management in relationship.[3]

First, though, let me recognize some other writers whose ideas—not necessarily on leadership and management as such—have informed my thinking and the development of the ideas in this chapter: Chris Argyris and Donald Schön,[4] Arthur Deikman,[5] John Kotter,[6] Robert Quinn,[7] and Joseph Rost.[8]

How Conventional Assumptions Obscure our View of the Relationship

Leadership and Leaders If leadership is equated with leaders, discussions on leadership and management can quickly turn into comparisons between leaders and managers. In such comparisons, managers tend to come off second best, sometimes portrayed as fulfilling a foot-soldier role in keeping the existing order of things moving along. Leaders, on the other hand, are often portrayed as undertaking the more elevating, enriching, and high-status work of building visions and mobilizing people.

Consider these three statements comparing leaders and managers by the noted leadership scholar Warren Bennis: "The manager imitates; the leader originates," "The manager relies on control; the leader inspires trust," and "The manager is a copy;

the leader is an original."[9] Who would want to think of themselves as a manager rather than a leader after reading a comparison like that? As another prominent leadership scholar, Gary Yukl, notes, any attempt to sort people into two categories, where one of the categories is of clearly lower status, is problematic.[10] For this reason, the common equation of leadership and leaders tends to put a damper on serious consideration of the leadership-management relationship.

Here, the focus is on *processes:* the processes of leadership as distinct from those of management. The accent is on the kinds of work performed at different times—recognizing the importance of both types of processes—rather than on categorizing people. This enables us to effectively bypass the prevailing tendency to compare leaders and managers.

Leadership and Authority The assumption that leadership is the domain of people in authority gives rise to problems, as I pointed out in Chapter 1. One example is the difficulty those in positions of relatively little authority experience when they try to exercise leadership. But, management is also widely assumed to derive its basis from authority. The belief that *both* leadership and management are grounded in authority has added to the confusion of the two.

In this book, as discussed in Chapter 1, authority is positioned as a background factor, not a requirement, for leadership-mode work. In contrast, authority is one of the defining features of management-mode work, as we shall explore in this chapter. So we are, in effect, loosening the connection between leadership and authority, and reaffirming the view that management is based in authority. In this view, authority is fundamentally a matter of management, not leadership.

Leadership and Influence While notions of influence are integral to most contemporary constructions of leadership, influence is important in management, too. As so many popular management books advise, influence is critical in "getting things done," whether in convincing your manager to support a project or to persuade a business partner that your proposed strategy will meet his needs.

As with authority, pervasiveness of talk about influence adds to the cloudiness surrounding the leadership–management relationship.

With respect to leadership, we have highlighted the importance of learning rather than influence, as discussed in Chapter 2. This shift in emphasis should help to reduce—if not remove—influence as a source of confusion in our attempts to make sense of the leadership–management relationship.

The identification of leadership with leaders, authority, and influence obstructs our view of management as well as its relationship to leadership. It is true that the view will probably never be entirely clear. A degree of ambiguity is almost certainly inevitable, but we can sharpen our understanding of the relationship if we:

- Think of leadership and management as both being grounded in processes rather than in individuals;

- Regard authority as a defining feature for management and as a contextual feature for leadership; and

- Consider leadership as based in learning—while recognizing that influence is an important, if not defining, feature of management.[11]

We move now to considering the concept of the management mode, delving into the nature of management only as far as necessary to clarify the relationship with leadership.

Understanding the Management Mode

"During my meetings I bring up agenda items pertaining to the group's area of responsibility. We may have a customer with a dramatic increase in unexpected volume that requires immediate attention. I will start by asking them to clearly define the problem; then we start listing alternatives to fix our problem. I keep prodding them to give more alternatives and will only volunteer some of my alternatives after I have exhausted all of their alternatives. All of them understand that no alternative is wrong or inappropriate, that we want to get everything out on the table. After the options are out, we then look at the up and down side of each and continue to proceed to narrow them down until we have a basic course of action. This is the way we solve the problems of the day, week, or month."

This extract, from *Leading with Questions*, by Michael Marquardt, quotes an executive describing how he works with his group to solve operational problems.[12] As it happens, the action recounted by the executive is typical of the management mode. The management mode has three characteristic features:

- The focus is primarily on the explicit, rather than implicit, aspects of a problem (whether operational or more strategic in nature);

- Considerations of task are given priority over working in relationship; and

- The basis, or legitimacy, for action comes from authority.

Focus is on Explicit Aspects of a Problem

When a person functions in the management mode, the accent is on "things," such as plans, business systems, strategies, governance arrangements, databases, reports, structures and measures. These things are perceived to have an existence in the external world separate from the person perceiving them. In terms of the iceberg model (from Chapter 2), the focus is primarily above the waterline; it is on explicit, overt, or tangible matters that we are capable of observing and/or documenting. In the example about handling operational problems, a tangible matter of concern to the executive is the customer's "dramatic increase in unexpected volume."

Task has Priority Over Relationship

The second feature of the management mode is an emphasis on undertaking tasks. The management mode emphasizes doing or acting. Examples include assessing customer needs, allocating resources, delivering product, improving business processes, monitoring performance, measuring results, and so on.

To act in the management mode implies operating on the surrounding environment to achieve individual or group objectives, perhaps doing so jointly with others, but with the emphasis more on task accomplishment than on working in relationship. In the extract about the executive's meeting, we see the task orientation in the focus being put on the staff to identify a course of action to deal with the customer's volume increase.

It is important to note that giving priority to task accomplishment in a particular situation does not imply a rejection of contemporary human resources concepts to do with including, respecting, and valuing people. In the example, the executive apparently values the input of his team members in that he relies on their cooperation to identify and assess possible solutions. But, the interaction is not of the relational variety considered in chapters 2 and 3, with its emphasis on joint inquiry. The executive here maintains control of the interaction; for instance, he does not reveal his alternatives until the team members have exhausted theirs.

Basis is in Authority

We have said that to act in the management mode is to focus on the explicit side of problems, and to put task above relationship in the particular instance. What enables us to take such action? It is the authority we hold, even if that authority is expressed in subtle ways, or only alluded to obliquely, as in the executive referring to "my meeting." Authority is what gives legitimacy to actions in the management mode.

Authority takes different forms—and we shall briefly outline three types insofar as they are relevant to the leadership-management relationship:

- Supervisory authority
- Technical/professional authority
- Implied authority.

Supervisory Authority This is the authority that characterizes manager-subordinate relationships, and is the form most customarily associated with management.[13]

We tend to link the use of such authority with the giving of direction and the application of sanctions. Often, supervisory authority is not overtly referred to, but it is there, in the background, shaping the interaction.

In today's workplace, relying directly on supervisory authority is generally not the best approach for getting things done. Good management practice involves working with others in ways likely to elicit cooperation and goodwill. Nevertheless, employees tend to be aware of the presence of authority, as we saw in Chapter 1; they may elect to suppress thoughts and feelings if they sense that to speak up might displease those holding authority over them.

Technical/Professional Authority This is authority conferred upon people to allow them to perform particular services or functions. (The definition is a variation of one Ronald Heifetz proposes in *Leadership Without Easy Answers*.[14]) Examples include the authority that a parking enforcement officer uses to issue an infringement notice, the authority an auditor uses to review a set of financial accounts, or the authority a doctor in a hospital uses when ordering diagnostic tests. Often, people acting with technical/professional authority are in an advisory, rather than decision-making, role. In such instances, the exercise of authority is more about having a "seat at the table," about being in a position to put forward one's views and to advise, rather than about making decisions. An example is a human resources manager proposing a recruitment strategy to a line manager.

When the human resources manager proposes a recruitment strategy, we could say she is operating in the management mode. The explicit aspect of the problem being dealt with is the recruitment strategy; the task aspect is *proposing* the strategy; her authority comes from her specialist role. The point of making that distinction is not to label every action by a professional or technical person in which they rely on their authority as being in the management-mode, but to encourage us to consider whether alternative interventions, reflecting a learning-leadership stance, might be available. As an example, let us imagine a leadership-mode alternative to this intervention. For instance, the HR manager might work with the line manager to explore the underlying problem for which a "recruitment strategy" has been seen as a solution. They jointly identify deeper issues which are resulting in increased rates of staff turnover. Together, they work towards developing a vision of the future in which these issues have been overcome.[15]

Implied Authority This category describes the authority that people claim to hold as their "right," even when they cannot specify the basis for that authority. (It may, in fact, have an explicit, statutory, or other basis). Examples include a person asserting the moral authority to speak up and complain that a colleague has no right to bully her, or a father asserting parental authority in order to negotiate a homework agreement with his daughter.

With this category, we are including authority that people *expect* to be able to exercise, whether in the workplace or in their lives outside of work. The inclusion of this category underscores that management-mode action can occur in circumstances that we might not ordinarily associate with "managing." Consider the father negotiating with his daughter as an example. An implication here is that if a person is acting in relation to the explicit dimension of a problem (such as a homework agreement), is favoring task action (negotiating the agreement), and is relying on the authority they believe they have ("my authority as a parent"), then we can describe them as acting, in that instance, in the management mode.[16]

Again, identifying this form of authority with management-oriented action encourages us to think about the possibility of leadership-mode intervention alternatives. Perhaps what to the father is a homework problem, to the daughter is more a problem of her father being too controlling. We might imagine the father (or the daughter) seeking to establish shared meaning in order to create a fundamental change in the way they relate to each other, incorporating homework-related considerations. Such action is suggestive of the leadership mode.[16]

The key point from this section is that we act in the management mode when we rely on authority to focus attention on the explicit aspects of a problem and on task attainment, as a priority over relational interactions. Identifying specific actions as being in the management mode sensitizes us to consider the possibility of learning-leadership alternatives.

Deepening our Understanding of the Management Mode

While attention to task accomplishment is integral, the management mode is not only concerned with implementing plans, executing decisions, and attending to day-to-day matters. Management mode work can also encompass activities that might be thought of as more strategic: where complex questions as to possible courses of action need to be considered, and where higher-order cognitive processes are critical. Activities such as determining a corporate strategy, reviewing a merger proposal, or deciding on whether to launch a new product line or to close down a business can all be considered as being in (or mainly in) the management mode, insofar as they involve a focus on the explicit part of a problem, have a task orientation, and are legitimized by authority.

When we choose to address a problem in the management mode, we are assuming, though perhaps not consciously, that the problem requires action other than the kind of relationally-oriented, joint exploration discussed in chapters 2 and 3. We may make that assumption because we see the problem as largely technical (with a single solution to be found). Alternatively, we recognize the problem is contentious—with multiple possible interpretations—but we see the contention as something to be controlled or "dealt with," rather than as a potential source of intelligence, insight, and energy.

Many kinds of action are possible in the management mode, with the core element being that we are "operating on" the problem; we are taking some kind of action in relation to it. We might be trying to push our own views through in the face of perceived opposition; we might be trying to broker an agreement or compromise; or, we might be seeking to find a solution through "arguing" the matter out with others. We might set about obtaining additional information (e.g., more data and/or specialist advice or assistance). Possibly, we could be using our authority to defer, re-allocate, or shut-down activity. Whatever the form of action, we are utilizing the more detached style of working (as described in Chapter 3 in relation to Alice), rather than a relational style, in which we consciously view ourselves as having a connection to the problem, and we hold our own views as open to question.

We are now in a position to summarize the key differences between the management and leadership modes.

In general, we are operating in a **Management Mode** when we:

- Assume that a detached, rather than relational, style of working is needed to bring a problem, whether technical or contentious, under control;

- Focus on the explicit aspects of the problem/issue;

- Focus on tasks and actions; and

- Rely on whatever authority we hold.

By contrast, we are in a **Leadership Mode** when we:

- Assume that the problem we are facing is not technical, but contentious—reflecting different perceptions—and that dealing with it effectively will require shifts in thinking, and perhaps behavior, by some or all stakeholders;

- Focus on both the implicit and explicit aspects of the problem, recognizing that engaging with defensiveness (including our own) is likely to be a key factor in making progress; and

- Focus on working relationally to "mine" collective intelligence and build shared meaning so that integrated understandings, directions, and solutions can emerge.

Leadership and Management as Complementary Processes

Now that we have effectively distinguished leadership from management, it is important to point out that the management mode is not the opposite of the leadership mode; it is different. Regarding the two as opposites only leads into unhelpful debates about whether one is superior to, or more important than, the other. Rather than thinking leadership *versus* management, it is more productive to think in terms of leadership *and* management; they are complementary.

The complementarity can be seen in the story of Alice's efforts toward school change in Chapter 3. Her earlier actions, such as sending staff to development programs and developing improvement strategies, indicate that she was working in the management mode (though the management-mode side of her work was not named as such at that point).[17] Later in the story, there were signs that Alice was moving in the direction of working jointly with the teachers to think about teaching and learning practices. This suggests she was taking more of a leadership-mode stance. To achieve substantial change, Alice would very probably need to make many interventions—in each of the modes—over a lengthy period.

Just as the two modes are not opposites, there is also no sharp separation between them.[18] At one level, each mode does have clearly distinguishing features, but there is also a degree of ambiguity in the relationship. Some activities are hard to label as either leadership or management.[19] As with the relationship between the three leadership-mode concepts in the last chapter (relational working, mindful working, practice-basis), it is more productive to think of the leadership-management distinction as a soft or permeable one, acknowledging that in some situations the differences can be difficult to discern.[20] (In Figure 4.1, below, the ambiguity is represented by the overlapping area of the circles.)

FIGURE 4.1 Relationship of Leadership and Management

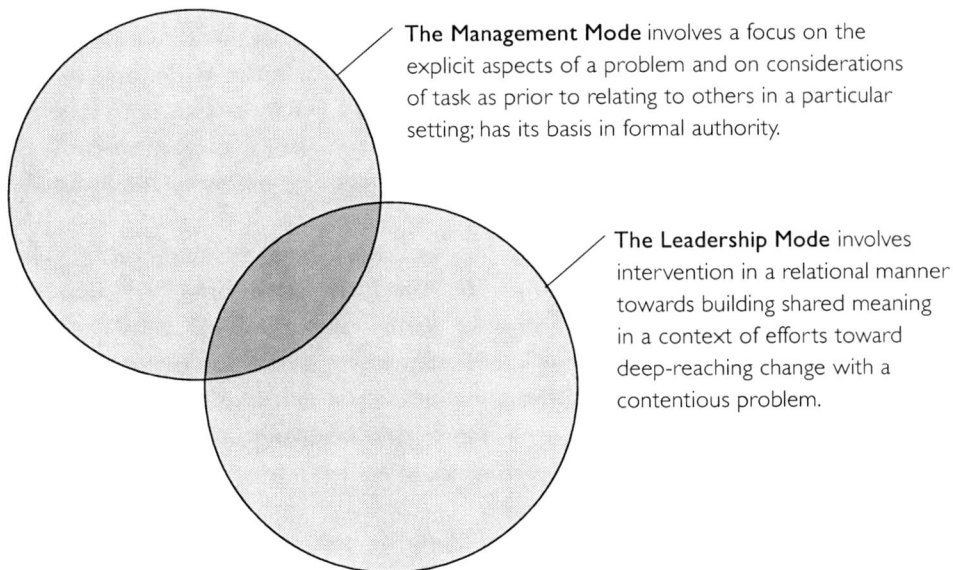

The **Management Mode** involves a focus on the explicit aspects of a problem and on considerations of task as prior to relating to others in a particular setting; has its basis in formal authority.

The **Leadership Mode** involves intervention in a relational manner towards building shared meaning in a context of efforts toward deep-reaching change with a contentious problem.

The point, therefore, is not to try to assign each and every action you take (or observe) to one or other category.[21] Nor is there likely to be much value in "typing" people as being oriented more toward one mode or the other. While it might be presumed that most will have a preference for one or the other form, conceivably just about everyone in an organization needs to do some of each, even if a very small amount. (Of course, the preferences of work colleagues come into the equation; if your co-workers are mainly inclined toward leadership, there may be little need for you to demonstrate capability in this mode.) Likewise, the relative importance of the two modes can be expected to vary over time for any individual—though not in any predictable fashion, being more dependent on circumstances at a particular time. It might also be expected that those further up the organizational hierarchy would perform—or at least be expected to perform—more leadership work than their less elevated colleagues. Ideally, virtually anyone in an organizational role could develop the capacity to function to at least some degree in each mode, and to be able to move into the appropriate mode as required. In practice, this is difficult, particularly because many forces come together to encourage a predominance of the management mode.

Leadership in the Shadow of Management

Although we tend to attach greater importance and status to leadership than to management when we think of the two in conceptual terms (as suggested at the beginning of this chapter),[22] when it comes to *practice*, management generally takes precedence over leadership.

The idea that management, rather than leadership, tends to constitute the bulk of effort in organizations is not new. Prominent authors including Warren Bennis, John Kotter, and Stephen Covey have variously made this point.[23] Perhaps not so well understood are the patterns and dynamics that tend to keep leadership playing second fiddle to management. Gaining an appreciation of these factors is essential if we are to better capture the potential for mutually supportive actions in the two modes.

Managers and professionals attending my workshops routinely state they would like to do more leadership work, but that there is "no time." The sense of not having enough time to do the things we want—or need—is obviously a struggle with which many of us in today's pressure-cooker world can relate. There is relentless pressure to produce short-term results; to satisfy customers, boards, and regulatory agencies; to keep day-to-day business moving along. These all tend to reinforce a "deliver now" task-orientation, as well as a preoccupation with the explicit aspect of problems.

Under such pressures, people are likely to put their energy into what Stephen Covey, in *The Seven Habits of Highly Effective People*, termed "urgent" rather than "important" matters.[24] As the old expression goes, it's the squeaky wheel that gets the grease. Important—but less pressing—matters, such as building a shared agenda for the future, or integrating knowledge from diverse perspectives, can be effectively crowded out by forces to perform management-oriented functions.

In addition, the payoffs from leadership work can take some time to become evident—assuming they eventually do. This further buttresses the bias towards management-mode work. As one general manager put it, when discussing a proposal to develop learning-centered leadership among his managers, "What is this going to do for my next quarter sales results?" The answer is probably very little. Learning-centered leadership involves acting in the present for benefits that are often deferred, as with developing the capability of the general manager's business to achieve future results. Such delayed benefits are difficult to quantify, at least initially. Something of a leap of faith is required to justify investing in leadership in the short term, believing it will pay dividends at a later time. A degree of both courage and conviction is necessary as well, for we must deal with the combination of uncertain future outcomes and short-run pressures to perform.

These same pressures also ensure that the effectiveness of one's performance is most likely to be judged on the basis of management, rather than leadership. Consider the case of Gary, a middle manager and former union organizer. Gary enjoyed getting involved in all sorts of innovative activities in his organization. A lover of ideas and of change, Gary was credited by his colleagues with kick-starting several important initiatives. Yet, his boss regarded him as lacking in the management of ongoing tasks, noting timeliness and tuning in to stakeholder expectations as "areas needing improvement." If, like Gary, you are not seen, first-and-foremost, as able to deliver the results or outputs that stakeholders require on a day-to-day basis, you are unlikely to command a great deal of credibility for your ability to enact leadership, learning-centered or otherwise.

Learning-centered leadership, with its emphasis on working relationally on deep-seated problems, necessarily brings us up against sensitive and emotionally-loaded issues and the fears and anxieties that accompany these. Will I be seen as rocking the boat? What if people do not like my ideas, or do not share the vision? How will I deal with those who oppose me? Will my leadership be seen as effective? It can be easier to avoid engaging in leadership action than to face such fears directly. Because of the strong management focus in most organizations, such avoidance can usually be rationalized without difficulty; you can easily tell yourself, or instance, that short-term task priorities necessitate your focusing on management-oriented work.

A preoccupation with the management mode relative to leadership can act as a shield, a false protection that prevents us from deeply engaging with reality. It can enable us to skirt around the more troublesome, covert side of issues that leadership implies. The task emphasis associated with the management orientation sees problems as "out there," apart from us. This distancing protects us from having to face up to how we may be contributing to the creation and framing of those problems. In contrast, the relational emphasis in the leadership mode requires that we place ourselves at least partly within the system of concern. We saw this in the Chapter 3 story concerning Alice and her efforts to achieve school change, where Alice discovered she needed to focus less on "operating on" the teachers, and more on working in relationship with them. A central question for practitioners in the leadership mode is, "In what ways might my own behavior or approach be contributing to the problems with which I am engaging?"

Another reason for its dominance is that working in the management mode brings its own satisfactions; for many, it provides a great sense of fulfillment. "Fixing" problems can seem to be more personally satisfying than the process-oriented work of delving into underlying (non-technical) causes and building shared vision. To the extent that we do it successfully, our focusing on tasks and the explicit aspects of problems yields immediate, positive feedback and affirmation; the more nebulous nature of leadership-mode work means these benefits are often harder to come by.

Although the theme being explored here concerns how and why the management mode overshadows leadership in practice, it is, quite ironically, the case that management skills are not well developed in many organizations. In addition, those who need to apply them, often do not. Technically oriented people, in particular, frequently prefer to focus on their area of passion—be it software development, teaching, accounting, neurosurgery, or whatever—rather than attend to management-oriented work. In these instances, developing management proficiency should be an important priority.

The concern here is not with the management mode as such, but with the pervasiveness with which a management perspective on problems tends to eclipse a leadership view. Often, leadership seems to exist in the shadow of management; in more extreme cases, the eclipse is virtually total. When that is so, leadership is a largely untapped potential, as suggested in Figure 4.2.

FIGURE 4.2   The Management Mode Commonly Eclipsing Leadership

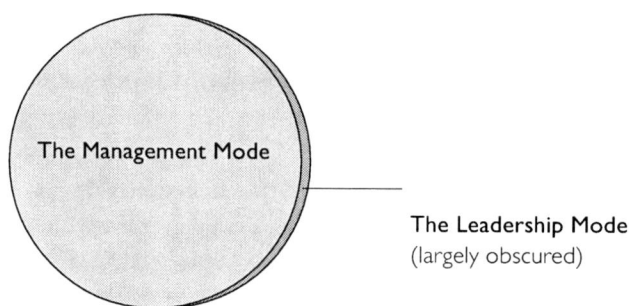

The Management Mode

The Leadership Mode
(largely obscured)

The dominance of the management mode tends to be self-perpetuating. If few people are actually practicing leadership, there will be hardly any role models to inspire and support others. In these circumstances, those who are potentially interested in practicing in the leadership mode receive few signals indicating that such actions are encouraged and valued.

The core problem is that the management way of seeing and acting does not recognize or provide any mechanism for engaging relationally with the implicit domain. It does not concern itself with the realm of hidden, but vital, perceptions, assumptions, feelings, and experience that we saw in chapters 2 and 3 as being so critical to dealing effectively with contentious problems (and thus, critical to learning-centered leadership). In environments that value the explicit over the implicit, task-oriented working over relational working, and authority over collaborative processes, it is difficult to create conditions to support the kind of deep-reaching conversation needed to explore what is really going on, develop shared vision, and generate energy for change. An organizational obsession with "things," tasks, and authority can snuff out virtually all efforts towards leadership. Leadership becomes almost encased within a management-oriented view of the world.

The pre-eminence of the management mode does not come without cost. Continually playing catch-up can become the order of the day; deeper issues remain unattended, perhaps undiscussed, while patch-up solutions are applied, possibly to the organization's eventual detriment. Frequently, the lack of meaningful engagement with deep-seated issues becomes a major source of dissatisfaction for both employees and other stakeholders. Reality can come to be defined in pessimistic terms—"This is the way it is, get on with it"—reflecting a sense of powerlessness that people at all levels feel about their capacity to effect or change anything important.

Differentiating between leadership and management does not, of itself, eliminate such problems, but it does provide a structure for thinking and acting differently in relation to them. Our first step in realizing this potential is to strive to recognize what is unambiguously leadership and management, and to carefully consider our use of each, while also being alert to the ambiguity at the interface of the two modes.

"Seeing" Leadership in Relation to Management

The vision inspiring this chapter is that our understanding of the two modes will lead to more informed action. That means being able to interweave the two productively as circumstances suggest, possibly on a moment-by-moment basis. To do so, we must be able to consciously *choose* between the two modes at a point in time (a theme to be developed in the next chapter). That is why we must be able to distinguish leadership from management action.

Unless we can absorb this distinction ourselves, and help others to see it, it is likely that management-mode thinking and action will continue to overwhelm leadership in most organizations. The prospect is that leadership will exist as little more than lofty words and perhaps good intentions, as an espoused value rather than an enacted value. If the status quo continues, people will believe they are enacting leadership when their activities could be described more accurately as management-related. The kind of leadership we are discussing here would remain just an untapped potential.

This should be a concern, but not an obsession. Echoing the concept of mindful working from Chapter 3, we need to become aware of the differentiation between leadership and management, without becoming preoccupied or unduly distracted by it. An illustration of this attitude comes from an interview on Australia's *Radio National* with a former prisoner.[25] Asked how he looked back on his life in jail, the ex-inmate talked about the need to "see it, but not stare at it." The need he expressed is to notice, to be aware, but not to become consumed by such thoughts.

Distinguishing leadership and management processes is a step in empowering ourselves to make conscious choices about how to act, to move between the two modes as circumstances require. As the comments at the chapter's beginning suggest, making the distinction can help build awareness of different action possibilities. Having an appreciation of the two modes and how they fit together enables us to assess how much of each we are actually doing, and how much we need to do. If we understand, and seek to develop our capability in leadership-mode interventions as well as those of the management mode, we can potentially develop a much stronger and better-rounded repertoire of responses to the challenges we face.

Holding the two modes apart is not a matter of agonizing over whether particular actions represent leadership- or management-mode work, or striving to attain some preconceived notion of balance. It is more a matter of reflecting from time to time on the choices one makes and on the relative amount of attention we give to each mode. Obviously, if you find yourself practicing very little leadership—or none at all—it might be opportune to consider what factors are driving this outcome, and what options are open to you. To the extent you are able to catch yourself making decisions about intervention strategies, you may open up more opportunities for trying a leadership-mode approach. (The following chapters provide more guidance on how to take advantage of such opportunities.)

Obsessive concern is not the answer, nor is under-playing the significance of the leadership-management relationship. Such under-emphasis is sometimes indicated when people acknowledge that the two forms of action are different, but then act as if the difference is of no consequence. One workshop participant put it like this: "Yes the differences are interesting, but can't we just note them then move on?" To do so is, in effect, to allow the dominance of the management mode to continue unrecognized, unquestioned, and unabated. Yet, it is easy to turn away from serious consideration of the relationship.

Imagine you are in a city you have not previously visited. You are walking through a shopping area when you come across two young street performers. One a baritone, the other a tenor, the two men are performing a jazz classic. You listen for a few moments. You notice that while each of the voices is pleasing in its own right, one of the voices basically overpowers the other. Somehow the idea of the two singers as a duo is not effectively realized. You move on.

So it is with leadership and management. The common confusion between leaders and leadership, the multiplicity of leadership models (most of them influence-based), and the dominance of management processes in most work settings all make it harder to imagine and seriously envision the prospect of leadership and management enhancing one another. As with the two discordant singers, the prospect can seem more pipedream than reality.

Yet, setting aside ideas about "the leader," and about leadership as grounded in authority and influence, as we did in Chapter 1, opens up scope for conceiving of the leadership and management relationship afresh. To the extent that we are able to recognize, and set aside, our well-worn assumptions about leadership, we will have a clear vantage point for developing our practice in the leadership mode in light of the relationship between the two.

Interweaving the Leadership and Management Modes

The essential message is that each of the two modes provides something not found in the other. Once we see the distinction, the potential arises to create a more complete set of pathways for intervention. There are no hard and fast rules as to how best to combine the leadership and management modes to good effect. While sometimes you might intervene primarily in one mode, on other occasions you may find that utilizing the two modes in close conjunction gives added traction. Below are some illustrations that demonstrate how actions taken in each mode can beneficially round out efforts in the other.[26]

Re-orienting the Executive Group This group spends most of the time in its extended monthly meetings discussing pressing business issues, sharing information, and coordinating activities (management mode). The chief executive is frustrated that the group does not give more attention to some of the "bigger" issues involving complex change, and that members seem to place low importance on their membership of the group in comparison to running their own parts of the business. He initiates conversation with group members about their perceptions of the group and of him; he declares his own dissatisfaction and inquires into how others feel about the group (leadership mode). As an outcome of these conversations, the group decides to restructure their meetings (management mode)[27] to enable more time for conversing and coming to new understandings of the previously neglected issues (leadership mode).

The Customer Survey A divisional head arranges for a customer survey to be undertaken in order to assess satisfaction with her division's products and services. On receipt of the results, which identify some significant issues, the head and her executive colleagues compare the results with those of a previous survey and with industry benchmarks, and identify some potential action strategies (management mode). The head also works with mixed groups of stakeholders from different parts of the business, as well as external partners, to make sense of the underlying messages and implications for change (leadership mode).

Executive Performance Problem A general manager is unhappy about the performance of one of his managers. The general manager arranges for an external review of the manager's area (management mode), which confirms several problems. The general manager and the manager agree on an improvement strategy and monitoring process (management mode). After a while, and noticing the manager still seems dissatisfied, the general manager initiates a conversation with him with a view to uncovering and working on any deeper issues, including those affecting their relationship (leadership mode). One issue that emerges is a lack of support by the general manager; this is factored in to a revised improvement plan (management mode).

Organizational Restructuring Due to concerns about the quality of customer service, an executive team initiates a restructure to create incentives for staff to improve their skill levels, and to better reward those with advanced skills (management mode). A discussion paper is prepared and circulated among the staff, to gain input on the proposals (management mode). As the discussion paper attracts little response, the executive team rethinks its approach and initiates conversations with groups of managers and staff to better understand the reasons for the customer service problems (leadership mode). As a result, the restructure plans are modified (management mode).

Leadership and Management in the Classroom A schoolteacher engages her class in a small group dialogue process to explore the implications of climate change, and to consider how everyone's behaviors, including her own and those of the students, can contribute to making a difference (leadership mode). During the dialogue she monitors the participation of individual students and seeks to draw out those who are holding back (management mode).

Dealing with Risk Keen to reduce its exposure to workplace accidents, a business unit institutes a program to categorize and evaluate major risks, improve its risk assessment and treatment processes, and ensure that employees are appropriately trained (management mode). In addition, employees are involved in ongoing conversations and action learning projects, designed to strengthen the organization's capacity to recognize and respond to risks before they have an adverse impact (leadership mode).

These examples have illustrated how leadership- and management-mode interventions can potentially support and reinforce each other. The leadership mode contribution is in the joint thinking; it is in the relational processes of achieving well-grounded understandings of the issues, contemplating preferred futures, and drawing forth energy to make change happen. The management mode shows its usefulness when the need is to focus on the harder, more concrete aspects of the problem, and to take action to improve or remedy the situation, with the legitimacy of the action stemming from authority.

Activating the leadership mode and interweaving it with management requires bringing it out of the shadow of management. This is not a matter of seeking to put leadership on a pedestal, or to mark it as more important than management. It is more a case of striving to ensure that leadership is valued and enacted in practice when it is needed, not just declared as important. Bringing about a greater emphasis on leadership-mode practice for ourselves and others requires facing up to the kinds of obstacles described in this chapter. For many of us, the greatest challenge may be to deal with our own fears and anxieties about undertaking this work. Leadership-mode work involves an element of personal choice. Admittedly, such choices are constrained by the realities of the modern workplace, but a degree of choice exists nonetheless. The challenge is to find openings, and then to act on them.

Chapter Summary

In this chapter, we set about untangling the fourth "vine in the forest of leadership," the assumption that leadership and management cannot be gainfully separated. We recognized a need to set aside questions of leaders and managers in order to distinguish leadership processes from those of management. Without a process emphasis, we would bump up against the problem of leader-manager comparisons relegating managers to a second tier. We saw also how the other vines—those identifying leadership with authority and influence—contribute to confusion regarding the leadership-management relationship.

The management mode was defined in terms of a focus on the explicit aspects of problems and a concern with task accomplishment, with its legitimacy deriving from authority. The leadership mode was defined earlier as involving relational thinking and action in order to build shared meaning on contentious problems in the pursuit of deep-reaching change.

While both modes are necessary, it is the management mode that predominates in most organizations and settings, often overwhelmingly so. Some reasons for this dominance were canvassed. One consequence of the pre-eminence of management processes is that leadership can become little more than an espoused value, while most action reflects a management-oriented way of seeing.

The leadership mode is different to, but not the opposite of, management; they are complementary. Maintaining an awareness of the differences between the modes—while recognizing a degree of overlap between them—opens up the prospect of making much more informed and intentional choices in our use of the two modes. We can utilize one or the other mode, or interweave both, in particular circumstances, as well as become more aware over time as to the relative attention we are giving each mode. Some examples were provided to illustrate how interventions can draw upon the complementary nature of the two modes, and to show the power of doing so.

Questions for Reflection

4.1   Thinking about your own organization, in what specific ways, if any, do you find the distinction between leadership and management helpful?

4.2   What proportion of your own work would you consider to be management-mode oriented? What proportion would be leadership? Based upon our discussion here, how satisfactory does this split now seem to you?

4.3   What implications, if any, do your responses in Questions 2 have for your approach to your work?

Chapter
FIVE

Active Choice and the Leadership Mode

" I accept that leadership and management are different. And I can see that I need to recognize the leadership mode and pay attention to it. Otherwise, I could continue doing nearly all management, without even being aware that I'm ignoring leadership. The problem I have is that actually doing leadership is difficult. I'm going against the dominant culture. Then I'm dealing with all these emotionally-charged issues. I have to put myself on the line—and that's daunting, as I've discovered."

Maria – business unit manager

As Maria observes, enacting the leadership mode requires first becoming aware of it as a way of thinking and acting that is distinct from management. Also critical is one's frame of mind. (We must abide by the concepts from Chapter 3: working relationally, a mindful stance, and an orientation towards practice). On top of this, we must move from a leadership standpoint into the management mode and back again as appropriate. There is no denying that this is challenging.

If we are to function effectively in the leadership mode—even if only on occasion—we need to intentionally choose to do so, and to follow through with action. Without the deliberate exercise of choice, implicit choices will be made anyway. And given the pressures that operate in most organizations—some of which we reviewed in Chapter 4—those implicit choices are likely to favor management-oriented action over leadership.

Whenever we come up against a contentious problem—which most assuredly signals a need for deep-reaching change—we have a number of options (which are not necessarily mutually exclusive). We can:

- Sidestep responsibility by saying that it is too hard and there is not much we can do;

- Set about "managing" the change by focusing on the concrete aspects of the problem, getting task work completed, and relying on whatever authority we hold (that is, by opting for the management mode);

- Try to lead others by communicating a vision of the future and seeking to inspire, nudge, and encourage others towards it (that is, by practicing a more conventional form of leadership).

Or, we can seek to intervene from a learning-centered leadership standpoint.

To make an informed choice about how to act, we need to be able to see these problems as also presenting opportunities for deep and positive change. We must be able to assess the potential benefits to both individuals and the organization as a whole, and be able to weigh these against the potential risks to self and others.

If our evaluation tells us that learning-leadership is a choice we want to make, we must be alert to the challenges without allowing our behavior to be defined by them. We must have a vision of we want to achieve, yet also make that vision explicit and contestable. We must engage relationally with others, honoring their contributions, and avoid trying to control them. We must allow a preferred future to emerge and come into being through joint effort, rather than trying to plan the whole process from the outset.

We must also be continuously concerned with risk, threat, and defensiveness. We must act in ways that both disarm threat to ourselves and reduce the likelihood that our own behavior will threaten others, if we are to assist in the emergence of shared meaning.

Making the choice to enact learning-leadership under challenging circumstances is the theme of this chapter. The hidden aspects of an organization's culture, particularly the "underground rules," present a major challenge. These are the unwritten organizational codes that people intuit about "how things get done around here." By following these rules they minimize the prospect of harm for themselves and others.[1] Understanding how these informal systems operate is an important step towards making learning-centered leadership interventions that advance change. To illustrate this, we consider the story of Lee, a spatial imaging specialist seeking to achieve changes in his organization's use of technology. We draw on the story to discuss how learning-centered leadership work can foster more open discussion of underground rules.

As Maria's opening comment about emotionally-charged issues points out, action in the leadership mode inevitably involves engaging with threat and defensiveness, including our own. Learning-leadership work requires we look beneath the surface. By definition, this means talking about matters that are usually not discussed—often because people find the prospect scary. If we are to help open up these matters, we need to interact with others in ways that support everyone's safety. We achieve that mainly by not acting ourselves in ways likely to spark threat. By the same token, we must avoid seeing it as our responsibility to protect others from difficult interactions. While this may be warranted on occasions, if we do so uncritically we may be moving out of a relational style and into a more detached form of interaction.

A detached style can be called for in some instances, including when we find ourselves under attack. Moving into the management mode can help contain threat and restore our own safety. On other occasions—even when the environment is tense—we may be able to intervene in the leadership mode to deepen learning. Again, this is a matter of exercising choice. To illuminate this we consider a story in which Maria utilizes both management- and leadership-mode interventions to engage with a more senior executive who appears to be behaving in a strongly self-protective manner.

To help make our learning-leadership interventions less risky for both others and ourselves, I offer three guidelines: work from observation, attribute reasonableness, and seek to act authentically.

Even when we follow these guidelines, stepping into learning-leadership raises our level of risk by several degrees. Yet, contentious problems present opportunities for deep-reaching change, and the potential benefits—to both people and organization—can be substantial. In deciding how to act, we also need to be alert to the opportunities, which may not be as apparent as the risks. The chapter's concluding section discusses the need for mindful appraisal of the risks and opportunities, so we can make informed choices.

Dealing with "Underground Rules"

Lee, an expert in spatial imaging with extensive international experience, has been recruited by a government organization as a specialist advisor. He is on a one-year contract, replacing a staff member who is on extended leave. Lee aspires to work at the cutting-edge of his field and wishes to achieve significant results in his twelve months with the organization. He is excited by the possibilities, including the idea of developing a group of practitioners working collaboratively across the organization on a range of spatial-imaging-related problems. Within weeks of arriving, Lee recognized that the organization could use its available technologies for a variety of value-adding applications without exceeding its current resource commitment. It appeared that these ideas had not been considered before.

An external colleague suggested that Lee first become more established in his role. Then, he might get things moving by reaching out to individual internal constituents with a view to getting them together to explore the possibilities.

"I doubt that calling a meeting right now would be a smart move," said Lee. "From what I understand, that's not the way things get done around here. You don't show your hand. I have some specific technologies and uses in mind. I will need to talk individually with the various players first and sound them out about their level of support for those applications. If I get enough of them on board, then I might call a meeting."

Lee's proposition that you "don't show your hand" is an example of an underground rule: an unwritten standard for action that an organization's members come to regard as the accepted way to operate, to get things done. The "underground" aspect comes from the fact that these rules reflect people's tacit understandings about how the organization actually operates, which is often quite different from its declared values.[2]

Signs of another underground rule were evident in the Chapter 3 story of Alice's efforts to bring about change in the teaching and learning practices at her school. Alice was finding it difficult to encourage some of the teachers to move away from their "expert-out-front" approach to teaching. Initially, Alice seemed to be avoiding discussion with the school principal about the difficulties she (Alice) was experiencing, perhaps fearful that the principal would conclude that she was not succeeding in the change effort, and—possibly—that she was not competent to do so. Perhaps Alice was operating according to an underground rule along the lines of "avoid disclosing uncertainty, doubt, or lack of confidence." As it turned out, the school principal also felt unable to directly discuss progress with Alice, worrying that Alice would then think the principal lacked confidence in her. It could be that the principal was following a similar underground rule.

If you look and listen closely enough, it is likely that you will see signs of underground rules operating in your own organization. While the specific rules vary, there seem to be some common themes such as, "Do not challenge authority," "Protect others from bad news," and "Avoid being associated with failure." Such rules reflect and reinforce deeply embedded patterns of defensiveness, what organizational theorist Chris Argyris calls "organizational defensive routines."[3] For our purposes, the significance of underground rules is that they can pose significant hurdles for anyone wanting to practice learning-centered leadership.

By definition, underground rules sit below the surface; they are not readily apparent. Identifying them—or at least hypothesizing about them—involves observing behavior and asking, What shared belief might lead otherwise reasonable people to behave in this manner?

While underground rules tend to become embedded over time as informal controls over what gets done and how, it is also the case that, like stones in a flowing river, they are continually being shaped. Underground rules are not determined for all time: they are potentially open to review and change. Individuals can make choices to act differently. The potential benefit in being able to surface and appraise underground rules is that it frees energy. Energy that was being channeled into defensive practices can now be used for productive purposes. Surfacing an underground rule for open review does not necessarily imply mounting a direct challenge, however.

Consider a parallel with sailing. Pressure represented by an underground rule is analogous to a wind blowing towards a boat from the direction of the intended destination. Sailing directly into the wind would end any progress. Instead, the sailor applies the combined energy of the wind and the boat with its sails and keel to tack at an angle to the wind, changing directions as needed. So it is with the leadership mode. To intervene productively we must use the forces available to us, including our own thinking and language skills—and any other available support—to sail close to the winds of organizational resistance, without being either becalmed or sunk.

Returning to Lee's case, when asked about the problem with calling a meeting, he replied that there were big risks in revealing his thinking too early. "Someone might not like the idea of using the technologies more extensively, or of people collaborating across the organization. If they react against these ideas, they could blow the whole thing out of the water before I get to first base."

Lee has made his first intervention-related decision. By opting to first talk with individuals about specific applications, Lee has effectively elected to act, initially at least, in the management mode.[4] The evidence is that he is focusing on concrete things (such as particular spatial imaging tools and specific possible uses); he is concerned with the task of establishing the level of support for employing these applications; and he is doing so with the authority that comes with his role as a specialist advisor in this area. This could turn out to be the best way to proceed, but there is another choice.

What could it look like if Lee chose to step into the leadership mode? (Recall from Chapter 2 that leadership-mode interventions involve acting relationally to build shared meaning in the context of efforts to achieve deep-reaching change with a contentious problem.) Lee might still approach his individual contacts to survey the prospects of calling a meeting to discuss using the technologies more extensively and collaboratively. In each conversation he might acknowledge his understanding that conventional practice would be to discuss the technical aspects and build support with individuals first. He might go further and mention any misgivings he has about stepping outside conventional practice. Then, he might propose a meeting as an opportunity for the group to jointly explore the opportunities and implications of a more ambitious use of the technologies. If the proposed meeting gets off the ground, Lee could make a short presentation about his ideas, but otherwise allow the direction to emerge from the group.

Lee's proposal of a meeting is a leadership-mode intervention insofar as he:

- Frames the conventional assumption about how to proceed as one that impacts everyone and the organization as a whole, potentially adversely;

- Indicates an openness to others' viewpoints; and

- Recognizes that suggesting changes in the organization's use of these technologies may trigger contention, and strives to build shared understandings with his colleagues about how to proceed.

It may be that calling a meeting would be premature. On the other hand, some of Lee's colleagues might be excited by the prospect. They may be ready to contribute insights and suggestions and to actively work towards change. If Lee had made the choice to act in the leadership mode, he might have helped the organization move—if only incrementally—towards a common vision on its approach to spatial imaging, and generated some energy for change.

Decisions about whether to act in the leadership mode or its management counterpart are appropriately made on a case-by-case, even moment-by-moment, basis. Lee's choice may have been a sound one on this occasion. There is no imperative to act in the leadership mode with every potential opportunity identified. The challenge is to become more adept at identifying and evaluating the choices, and to be willing to choose action in the leadership mode at least some of the time.

Dealing with Threat and Defensiveness

The senior executive group of an engineering services organization had been progressively reviewing the organization's business units. Through an informal discussion process, group members questioned their peers, in turn, on how well each of their areas was performing. The group had a stated goal of building a more open and collegial group climate. The group's chief executive believed this would help them successfully tackle some longstanding issues, such as continuing poor relations with one of the organization's major customers.

The final review date had arrived. One of the senior executive group members, Maria, had noticed that the operational area headed by Ivan, the deputy chief executive, had never been reviewed. There had been three prior attempts, but each time, Ivan had managed to sidestep a review. He had excused himself from the meeting, changed the topic, or avoided answering questions directly.

Maria decided to bring up what she had observed. She first considered the risks of doing so, but felt that she was on relatively safe ground as she did not report to Ivan. She also enjoyed a good relationship with the chief executive, whose vision of more openness she wholeheartedly endorsed. Maria saw the review process as an important catalyst for that change effort. She had also recently undertaken a training program in learning-centered leadership intervention skills and was keen to practice for real. Maria decided to intervene by confronting Ivan, yet she would be careful to do so without suggesting that he was deliberately evading the topic.

"Ivan," she said, "this is the last of our planned review sessions, and each unit has been discussed except yours. I have observed colleagues invite you to open up your area for discussion on three previous occasions, but this has not happened as yet. I believe it's important to our future that we all participate.

Could we talk about your area now? Or could you suggest when and how we might best have that conversation?"

The chief executive watched with interest. He often found it difficult to decipher what Ivan really thought. While generally polite, Ivan tended to withdraw in group conversations, except when they centered on matters directly concerning his area. This time, though, Ivan reacted uncharacteristically.

"What kind of game is this?" he demanded, glaring at Maria, his words dripping with anger. "You're practicing this fancy talk from that course you went to, but it's really just word play. It's sanitized language; 'have a nice day' talk. Your problem is you lack the guts to say directly what's on your mind."

Such an outburst would be challenging to most people. Even a more muted reaction—a person walking out of a meeting or shutting down communication—can be difficult to deal with. Yet having to engage with difficult behavior on occasions is an occupational risk if you wish to delve into the underlying aspects of problems and not just operate at a surface level. The temptation, of course, is to hit back. Maria might have been tempted to retort with something like, "You're just afraid of having your area scrutinized. What are you trying to hide?" It is not hard to imagine the blow-up likely to occur if Maria were to retaliate in this way.

The first key in dealing with difficult behavior is, borrowing from the renowned negotiation expert William Ury: "Don't react. Go to the balcony."[5] As Ury puts it, in his book, *Getting Past No*, "Going to the balcony is distancing yourself from your natural impulses and reactions."[6] "Stepping outside," metaphorically speaking, helps you to gain perspective. Even consciously pausing to take a few deep breaths can help you to look more holistically at the interaction, including at your own contribution. Going to the balcony, rather than reacting, is an act of choice.

Stepping out of the conversation also enables us to choose what type of intervention to make. We have the choice of leadership-mode or management-mode interventions, or an interweaving of the two. Let us consider first how Maria might respond in the management mode.

Maria might say something like: "Ivan, you said that 'I lack the guts to say what's on my mind.' I find the tone and content of that remark insulting, and I ask you not to speak to me like that again."

This is a management-mode intervention because it deals with the explicit aspects of the problem (e.g., Ivan's words and his tone of voice, which are observable), and it has a task component (e.g., Maria expresses her displeasure and firmly requests that Ivan not repeat such behavior). In addition, Maria grounds her request in authority. Maria's authority to intervene comes from her membership in the executive group. She would also be exercising implied authority. (As discussed in Chapter 4, implied authority includes the entitlement to be treated with respect, and to protest when spoken to in an objectionable manner.)

Maria's response reflects an accepted model for managing difficult behavior (as adapted from *Asserting Yourself*, by SA Bower and GH Bower):

- Describe the behavior without judgment or labeling.

- Explain its impact without blaming or fault-finding.

- Make a request such as, for example, not to repeat the behavior, or to handle a similar problem in the future in a particular way.[7]

Responding in this way to aggressive, hostile, disrespectful, or otherwise inappropriate behavior is quite reasonable, perhaps even necessary, in order to bring those objectionable behaviors to a halt. But this management-mode response is not the only option open to Maria. Should Maria consider responding in the leadership mode? Why might this be a better option?

The management mode can be useful in curtailing the offending behavior. But when you intervene in the leadership mode, you encourage learning, which can yield additional benefits for the individuals involved and the group as a whole. So, assuming Maria really wants to understand what is going on with Ivan—because it might benefit not only herself and Ivan, but also the group, and possibly the organization as a whole—she might consider intervening in the leadership mode. How might she do so? Remember that leadership-mode interventions deal with contentious problems, which implies multiple perspectives. So, unlike in the management mode, we need to acknowledge the reality of those other interpretations.[8] Maria's challenge, then, is to inquire into Ivan's meaning while holding open the possibility that his emotional response may point to another, equally valid, interpretation of reality. It may be a sign of implicit-level thoughts and feelings that, in turn, may have relevance to the group's explicit goal of improving the way it functions.

Before considering how Maria might respond in the leadership mode, let us acknowledge that making such an intervention immediately, or soon after, an incident like Ivan's outburst would probably be difficult for most of us. We would probably be too upset or taken aback. So let us imagine that, later in the session, when emotions had cooled somewhat, Maria was able to intervene more in the leadership mode. Maria might have said something like: "Ivan, I'd like to go back to your suggestion that I lacked the guts to speak my mind. What is it you think that I've had on my mind that I lack the courage to speak up about. Also, your voice sounded angry. Was that so? If you were angry, what was behind that feeling?"

To make such an intervention clearly involves facing a considerable level of threat. Does the potential benefit outweigh the risk for Maria?

The potential payoff is that the ensuing discussion will surface material from the implicit domain that was otherwise inaccessible. This material is a resource to the group in building shared meaning. Consider, for example, Ivan's reply: "Yes I am angry. I'm angry because I think this is a covert bid for control of my area by several of you."

At one level, Ivan's response may give rise to even more threat and discomfort. Yet, at another, it opens up new grounds for exploration. The group has a stated goal of creating more openness; Ivan's strong words may be spotlighting some hidden tensions the group may need to process to achieve the change the chief executive envisages, and Maria supports. If the group has not been operating in a collegial manner, then some group members may need to shift their thinking. (This may or may not include Ivan.) A learning-inspired conversation, though perhaps awkward and uneasy at first, can expand to allow new insights and understandings to come through. For example, someone in the group might follow up with a question along these lines: "Tell me what leads you to believe that some people are seeking to gain control of your area?" This question may pave the way for the group to begin to talk about mutual perceptions and expectations in a way they had not succeeded in doing before. This is by no means a guaranteed outcome, but leadership-mode interventions enrich the quality of information available. Sometimes this can be the key to making progress on longstanding and difficult problems.

Three Guidelines for Safer Intervention

As Maria's story illustrates, intervening in the leadership mode involves some risk. Generally, we will be acting outside the norm, and that can be threatening to others and risky for us. How can we ensure that our interventions do not threaten people unduly and that they minimize risk to ourselves? To that end, I offer three guidelines for how to interact with others in undertaking learning-leadership work. They are:

- Work from observation;

- Attribute reasonableness; and

- Seek to act authentically.[9]

Following these guidelines can help us intervene in ways that are less threatening, thus creating more safety for others and ourselves.[10]

Work from Observation

Observations are the currency of learning-centered leadership. When we stay close to what can actually be observed, we stay grounded in shared reality. We avoid leaping to judgments or inferences, and confusing these with actual data. This is helpful to creating shared meaning.

We can observe two kinds of data. The first kind of data includes whatever you can see or hear directly in the external world. Linking back to the iceberg model in Chapter 2, this first category includes the data in the explicit domain, such as numbers and measures, the contents of documents, and observable behavior—whatever may be directly perceived. When Maria challenged Ivan, for example, she drew on her observation that this was the concluding session of the review process and that Ivan's was the only area that had not yet been reviewed. Our observations of the explicit domain can provide clues as to what might lie beneath the surface, in the highly-charged implicit domain—or at least identify areas for possible exploration. One such area of exploration might be the reasons—perhaps good reasons—for the non-review of Ivan's area.

The second type of observation refers to the contents of our awareness. Although much of what goes on in our minds is beyond our awareness, we can observe many of our thoughts, feelings, assumptions, and judgments. In terms of the iceberg model, any feeling, assumption, or thought that we are aware of holding is above the waterline to us, but below the waterline to others.

With respect to the contents of our own consciousness, we work from observation when we:

- Distinguish between what we perceive directly (that is, what we observe), and any conclusions or inferences we make *about* those observations;

- Make any pertinent conclusions or inferences (and other relevant thoughts or feelings) contestable by revealing them to others.

When we work from observation, we note any thoughts, feelings, and assumptions that arise concerning the problem at hand. We know that it is when these perceptions become hardened into judgment and certainty that problems arise, so we hold ours open to examination. In practice, we declare what we observe and any inferences we have drawn, in order to make our thinking contestable. We are in effect offering others a "window" into our thought processes. Declaring the basis for any judgments we make helps others feel more in control, which diminishes threat, and helps them be receptive to what we have to say. This is what Maria did when she stated that Ivan's voice sounded angry, then asked if that was so, and what was behind that feeling. (We shall delve more into practicalities of working from observation in Part 2, on the ARIES practices.)

Attribute Reasonableness

We need to begin any intervention with attributions of reasonableness. We start from the presumption that those we are dealing with are capable of acting in a reasonable, decent, and competent manner—and they are doing so, within their context. We also presume that their ideas are reasonable to hold. Regardless of whether we agree with their ideas, they make sense to them (though their application in this particular context may need to be examined). When we attribute reasonableness we acknowledge that everyone—even those we have difficulties with—has experience, knowledge, and insights that enable them to make sense of the world and can be the basis of a useful contribution. If their ideas are not clear to us, then the problem is largely ours to better understand them. I refer to this as the "reasonableness principle."

In our case story, Maria could apply the reasonableness principle to help her contemplate what kinds of factors might lead Ivan, as a person capable of reasonable thought and action, to be so reluctant about having his area reviewed. She could also apply it to help her make sense of his subsequent outburst. What might cause Ivan, a person capable of reasonableness, to react in such a heated way? Rather than leaping to conclusions, a learning-leadership perspective obliges us to hold such questions open, to explore them non-judgmentally.

When you practice the reasonableness principle you are likely to discover new dimensions of people. An additional benefit is that it encourages us to take an active interest in, and discover the value in, what people are communicating. When we behave this way we reinforce people's sense of self-worth. This creates greater safety because it is unlikely that they will feel threatened by our actions.[11] Conversely, when we hold negative attributions about people, we tend to fuel feelings of insecurity and lack of trust, which diminishes everyone's safety.

There are certainly circumstances where it will be very difficult, if not virtually impossible, to apply the reasonableness principle. (We caught glimpses of this struggle in the case of Alice and her efforts towards school change in Chapter 3.) Undoubtedly, there are some people who are motivated more by self-aggrandizement, or the exercise of power and control, than by serving others or working to a common good. Such people may not act in a reasonable manner.

The principle says to begin from a presumption of reasonableness, and prepare to step back as necessary. If you find yourself unable to adhere to the principle with some people, so be it. You do not have to be naive about human behavior, looking only for the positive. But in those cases where you cannot apply the principle, you will need to find an alternative to learning-leadership interventions.

Seek to Act Authentically

Most of us want to get the problem solved or the task accomplished, but we also want to maintain cordial relations with those around us and to be seen in a positive light. In doing so we can get caught up in all manner of pretences and ploys. We may tell people what they want to hear; we let others think "it was their idea." We avoid expressions of disquiet or frustration, and declare one objective while keeping others hidden. To talk more candidly would require getting into hidden, implicit areas, so we tend to steer clear of voicing our truest thoughts and feelings.

Maneuvers such as these are part and parcel of the modern workplace, and—as we saw earlier in the chapter—such practices tend to be reinforced by "underground rules." Such tactics enable us to get on with the work to be done.

But if *all* our relations with others in work settings are of this form, we will find accessing the leadership mode virtually impossible.

As we have seen, working relationally with others requires conversations about our deeply-felt aspirations, assumptions that we are perhaps only dimly aware of, and knowledge that in other respects we might see as too sensitive to divulge. In this work we are giving a lot of ourselves. We are inviting others to do the same. Safety is at risk for everyone concerned.

Authenticity is at the heart of this work. Our interventions need to reflect, and be seen to reflect, our deeper intentions. What we say needs to be a true, authentic expression of our thoughts and feelings on the matter at that time. If we are being disingenuous with those around us, how can we reasonably expect them to share what might be difficult or worrying to disclose?

How do we know that we are being authentic? An important test is to ask yourself whether your motives can be made explicit. If revealing your motives would be significantly threatening or embarrassing, then you know that—however well-intentioned you may be—you have allowed yourself to be caught up in a detached stance. For example, Maria could test her authenticity by asking herself about her reasons for raising the non-review of Ivan's area. She could ask herself questions such as: How much was she motivated by a desire for change in the way the business units interacted? How motivated was she by a desire to try out the learning-centered leadership communication skills she had been trained in? Was there a part of her that wanted to get back at Ivan over some past dissatisfaction, to show him up, or embarrass him?

Not only do your motives need to be capable of being made of explicit, you need to be prepared to make them so. Of course, having clear motives does not make you immune to attack, but it does afford a powerful source of self-protection for learning-centered leadership actions. If you are challenged, attacked, or misunderstood, you are then in a position to explain genuinely what you did intend, and what you did not. Authenticity is a strong place to speak from—and you may find that in revealing your intentions, further possibilities open.

Whenever we consider learning-leadership intervention, we can turn to the guidelines and ask ourselves questions such as:

Observation	To what extent am I basing my actions on what I observe, either in the surrounding environment or internally? Am I willing to make my observations explicit so they can be tested?

Reasonableness	Am I crediting others who have different views on this problem with reasonable intentions, interests, and capabilities?
	Am I holding negative attributions of others, but keeping this conclusion hidden?
Authenticity	What are my motives for intervening in this situation? To what extent can I make these motives explicit, contestable? Am I voicing my truest thoughts and feelings, or am I saying what I think people want to hear?

The detached style of operating tends to be the norm in most organizations, and the pressures to swim with the dominant current are strong. If we decide to work in accordance with these guidelines we should not diminish the significance of that choice.

Engaging with Risks and Opportunities, Mindfully

Anyone learning to ride a bicycle will probably fall off at some point. Even experienced riders can hit the ground. The same is true of learning-centered leadership. However consciously you follow the three guidelines, you will most likely "fall over" on occasion. For instance:

- A behavior that seems authentic to you in a particular situation will seem deceptive or disingenuous to others.

- Your attention to working from observation might be construed as operating from bias or prejudice.

- You may collide with people who are particularly adept at keeping their assumptions and feelings veiled, making joint exploration especially difficult, if not impossible.

- Perhaps you find yourself under attack, as Maria did. Or unanticipated issues reveal themselves, and you realize you are headed into uncharted territory, accompanied by feelings of fear, vulnerability, and possibly failure.

It is virtually impossible to predict with any certainty how your learning-leadership efforts will play out. This is in the nature of working with, and towards, change. As leadership and change theorist Michael Fullan puts it, "Change is a journey, not a blueprint. Change is non-linear, loaded with uncertainty, and sometimes perverse."[12] You never know quite what will happen in the exercise of leadership towards change, and this is as true of learning-leadership as of any other variety. Risk is unavoidable. Yet, just as most cyclists do not suffer permanent injury (or worse), you are not likely to sustain serious damage either. The most probable adverse results are "bruising" and lost confidence, though bleaker outcomes are definitely possible.

Sensing the hazards, some people will opt out of learning-centered leadership. "It's too dangerous," "There's no support," and "You won't get anywhere—why bother?" are typical rationales. At the other end of the scale—and less common—are those who will take a gung-ho approach, emphasizing "strong" and "decisive" leadership to get results. Neither is optimal. If we choose to work mindfully, as discussed in Chapter 3, we know what is in order: a keen assessment of the risks and opportunities presented by a particular situation. This is the first step in making an informed choice. Then, we also need to evaluate each potential action and its likely implications.

To make informed choices, you must be able to weigh risk against potential gain, both for the organization and yourself. Below are some pointers that will help you identify, assess, and cope with risk:

- Be alert to situations of heightened risk.

- Prepare well, without over-preparing.

- Adopt a learning attitude toward setbacks.

- See not only the risks, but also the possibilities and opportunities.

Be Alert to Situations of Heightened Risk Caution is warranted in situations where there is a strong emphasis on controlling behavior within narrow bounds. Symptoms are centralized decision-making and tight controls over the actions that people are permitted to take. Making learning-leadership interventions in such a setting can be construed as "not fitting in," or as "not being a team player." You are also in a risky situation if an individual or group sees your actions as inhibiting their ability to use power and influence to achieve their own objectives. The risks can be especially high if you are perceived to be mounting a challenge to someone who has line or other authority over you.

As a general proposition, undertaking learning-leadership interventions is likely to *least* hazardous when you have a relatively high degree of control. These relatively low-risk circumstances include practicing learning-leadership with a group that you are the head of, or with a project that is your responsibility. Many opportunities will not fall neatly into either of these categories; evaluate each on its own merits.

Prepare Well But Avoid Over-Preparing Good preparation diminishes risk. Preparation involves reflecting on questions such as the following: What is my own vision for change and how does this relate to visions that others may hold? What do I see as our current reality and how might the other interested parties view it? What learning-leadership interventions seem called for, and what consequences might flow from those actions? How can I best maintain a learning attitude in this situation? What are the outcomes that I need to avoid, and how might I prevent those outcomes coming about?

Of course, preparation is not always possible prior to making learning-leadership interventions. Sometimes opportunities arise in the spur of the moment, and there is little if any opening to think about possible approaches. In addition, while some preparation is important, it is not possible to anticipate every scenario. If you over-prepare, the temptation can be to stick with your plan when it would make more sense to respond to what is emerging in that moment. Being able to read the signs is critical. If your interventions seem to be attracting strong antagonism, you may be advised to step back and reconsider. Pushing ahead, without regard to the reactions of others, can invite serious adverse repercussions.

Adopt a Learning Attitude Toward Setbacks Sometimes, your learning-leadership interventions will not unfold as you would like. How can you recover and minimize any undesirable impacts? A first point is to reflect without brooding. A temptation can be to conclude, "These learning-leadership processes don't work," or to attribute the result to the shortcomings of others. A challenge here is to come back to the idea, from relational working, of placing yourself within the system seen to be problematic. A key question, again, is: "How might my own actions have contributed to the result I experienced?"

If you think your behavior could reasonably be seen as inappropriate in some way, or as having caused upset or offence to others, then own up to what you have done and be prepared to apologize. If you think your intentions were sound, but your execution was flawed, consider writing a short reflection piece about what you were trying to do and—without apportioning blame—where you think your intervention fell down. (It could be advisable to gain some feedback on your reflection piece from someone you trust before sending it to the other people involved.) Perhaps you are unclear as to where your intervention went amiss. In any event, rather than dwelling on what went wrong with your intervention, use the experience to help inform your future actions.

See Not Only the Risks, but Also the Possibilities and Opportunities Most of us working in organizations are highly sensitized to risk. At the explicit level, a myriad of controls, processes, rules, and systems are put in place to restrict the likelihood of people acting in unanticipated ways, or of errors occurring. (They do not always work.) Similarly, at the implicit level, we have "underground rules." These also tend to reinforce risk-averse behaviors. In short, disincentives to taking risks are all around us. On top of that, the institutional reinforcements for seizing and taking advantage of *learning* opportunities—or even for identifying and assessing them—are few and far between. (The organization may be adept at seizing specific business opportunities, however.)

To make an informed choice to act from a learning-leadership stance, then, we must see beyond this cultural conditioning, while at the same time being acutely aware of it. While there may not be obvious rewards or reinforcements in the beginning, we need to be confident that there is clear potential benefit down the road, and that this benefit makes the risk worthwhile.

When trying to evaluate opportunities, bear in mind that there is some truth to the old cliché that on the flipside of every problem is an opportunity. When we choose to see problems in that light, opportunities multiply. When we are trying to evaluate potential benefits, we must keep in mind that learning-centered leadership evokes emergent possibilities; it invites us to hold open the possibility of organizational and personal benefits *emerging* through the interventions we make. The challenge to us is to have sufficient patience to allow these benefits to emerge. This requires a belief in the latent capacity of groups to find their way through the messy problems they confront, a willingness to "hold" contention and work with it (rather than seeking to overcome or step away from it), and the resolve to exercise conscious choice in the kinds of interventions we make.

Choice is ever-present when we face a contentious problem and the prospect of change. Do we intervene at all? If we choose to, do we seek to contain and control the problem, or work towards change at deeper levels? If we elect the latter course, do we take a transformational approach (articulating and communicating a vision, and looking to align others with it), or a more relational orientation, such as we have been exploring? And, of course, choice is not to be exercised on a once-only basis. Insofar as we move between leadership- and management-mode interventions, we can potentially choose different intervention orientations according to what makes sense at a point in time. The choices we make, while not unconstrained, depend on our intentions and our confidence in being able to realize them. As we consider moving in the leadership-mode direction, it will serve us to pay attention to what we really want, and to ask ourselves how far we are prepared to go in pursuit of shared learning and change.

Chapter Summary

Our attention in this chapter was on the choices and consequences of intervening in the leadership mode as distinct from the management mode. We focused first on the challenges of so-called "underground rules." These are the unwritten organizational codes that people intuit about "how things get done around here."

By following these rules they minimize the prospect of harm for themselves and others. To function in the leadership mode, one needs to be aware of these underground rules and be prepared to bring them out in the open and scrutinize them; not in a blunt or confrontational way but in a manner that helps people talk more authentically about how they work together. We used a case story to examine two possible courses of action, one in the management mode, and another in the leadership mode.

We then looked into choice in the context of undertaking leadership- and management-mode interventions when others are behaving in ways we find difficult. In discussing the case featuring Maria and Ivan, we saw that management-mode interventions can have particular value in controlling or limiting a problem (in this case Ivan's aggressive behavior). Leadership-mode interventions, though, potentially give us greater traction in making sense of the problem from a variety of perspectives.

We saw that our learning-leadership interventions can be less risky for both others and ourselves if we follow these guidelines: work from observation, attribute reasonableness to others, and seek to act authentically. We also considered some pointers to assist in weighing up the risks and opportunities of possible leadership-mode interventions. These included: being alert to situations of heightened risk; preparing well, without over-preparing; adopting a learning attitude to setbacks; and recognizing the possibilities and opportunities for action, not only the risks.

Questions for Reflection

5.1 What implicit rules influence behavior in your organization?

5.2 Recall a difficult interpersonal encounter in your recent past, in which the way someone else behaved troubled you. Can you think of a) a leadership-mode intervention and b) a management-mode intervention for engaging with this problem?

5.3 What risks might you face in making a leadership intervention in the Question 2 scenario? What is the opportunity? How would you weight the two? How could you deal with these risks productively, while maximizing the potential gains?

PART TWO

THE ARIES FRAMEWORK—PRACTICES AND TOOLS

Preamble to **PART** TWO

Having teased out a perspective on leadership that is grounded in individual and group learning processes, and distinct from management practices, we now turn to giving practical effect to these processes. Enacting learning-centered leadership requires, in effect, that we recognize and work to overcome five sets of common behaviors. These behaviors all reflect the dominance of the management mode, with its emphases on the explicit aspects of problems and the accomplishment of tasks, and with its basis in authority. Each of the five ARIES practices—attending, reflecting, inquiring, expressing, and synthesizing—can be viewed as a response to one of the following clusters of behaviors:

- *Interacting with others and the environment around us in ways primarily oriented to achieving our own particular objectives*—When an achievement orientation is the norm, we increase the likelihood of failing to connect with the deeper experience that others have to offer us, and of missing or ignoring signals that might challenge our thinking. **Attending** is the practice of putting the quality of our perception ahead of task achievement. We do so in order to enable a clearer, more comprehensive, and cooler-headed sensing of all of the voices pertinent to a contentious problem (including our own self-talk), and to enable us to attune to the surrounding context.

- *Forming— and acting upon—judgments we make about what people with an interest in a problem think and feel*—We act as if we "know" how others think and feel, but we avoid testing our interpretations with them, as to do so gives rise to threat. **Reflecting** is the practice of contemplating—as a basis for testing—what stakeholders, ourselves included, might have in their minds, but keep unstated concerning a contentious problem.

- *Making limited use of questioning, and, in particular, avoiding asking questions that delve into the hidden or unspoken domain*—Commonly, questions are underutilized, used merely to search for a single "correct" or best answer, even when the problem might be better framed as contentious, involving multiple perspectives. **Inquiring** is the practice of asking questions relationally, so as to build shared meaning on a contentious problem.

- *Advocating our own views as if they were "the truth," and as if the challenge were to persuade others of this truth*—We tend to leave concealed our own assumptions, interests, feelings, and the more sensitive aspects of our knowledge. **Expressing** is the practice of stating our views relationally, including some of what we might ordinarily hold back, in order to build shared meaning on a contentious problem.

- *Dealing with disagreement by seeing it as something to be coped with or pre-vailed over*—We rarely see contention as a resource for enabling more productive engagement with contentious problems. More commonly, we might strive to reach a compromise, or to push through our own arguments. **Synthesizing**, in contrast, is the practice of working relationally with disagreement in order to create more integrated understandings of a contentious problem as a basis for action.

With the unrelenting pressures reinforcing management-mode behaviors in most organizations (as described in chapters 4 and 5), we need a structure to help us intervene in the leadership mode. ARIES is, effectively, an "engine" designed to help "pull this effort along," to support leadership-mode action in working with contentious problems.

Each of the ARIES practices is highlighted in turn in the following chapters. Please note that I use the term "practices" in preference to "skills." To speak of skills would seem to imply these are competencies that can be learned, assessed, and vouched for. In contrast, the ARIES practices are more akin to a discipline like piano or tennis, in which capability is progressively developed with intentional practice over time. Sometimes I refer to the ARIES "tools." The tools are specific frameworks, such as the Reflection Matrix in Chapter 7, the inquiring framework in Chapter 8, and the expressing framework in Chapter 9.

Treating the practices separately allows for consideration of the distinctive features of each. In application, though, the practices need to be blended in different combinations, perhaps within the space of a few moments. This is an inevitable consequence of the reality that leadership-mode interventions involve conversation: it is through thinking and talking together that shared meaning is established. Conversations, however, do not tend to follow orderly or predictable patterns. An implication is that we might see flashes of a particular practice for only a few seconds, before another comes to the fore. In this sense, we can think of the practices as "flowing into" one another, rather than standing as discrete behaviors.

ARIES is primarily a framework of conversational practices to help us develop our unique, personal voice. Though the spotlight is on conversation, the focus of the ARIES practices is on improving our own individual actions, not those of the people we are engaging with. By and large, we can choose how we interact with others; we cannot control how they relate to us. ARIES helps us deal with what we, personally, can take charge of: our own thinking and behavior.

For most people, the ideas behind the ARIES practices are not difficult to grasp, intellectually. At one level, this helps make application easier. At another level, it complicates things. People often assume that, because they can understand the practices, performing them will be easy. That is a bit like a non-golfer seeing a professional hit a birdie hole and thinking, "That's not too hard." In one respect, the ARIES practices are like the clubs in the golfer's bag. Their usefulness is dependent on your proficiency in using them. And that is largely a matter of practicing, reviewing your efforts, and continuing a cycle of practice and review. As we saw in Chapter 3, practice is more than a matter of just trying harder.

While the focus here is on workplace applications, the ARIES practices are potentially relevant whenever complex and contentious issues need to be faced, including at home or in other non-work settings. As you read, you might think of areas of your own life where these practices could be helpful.

And now, a note on the examples used in the following chapters: There is no intention to be prescriptive or to suggest there is only "one right way" to enact the practices. It is true that the leadership-mode concept implies that some behaviors are preferable to others. Nonetheless, you should feel free to express your individuality through your practice, and act in ways that feel right for you. Similarly, the actual words used in the examples are meant to indicate types of language that could be employed, not to prescribe particular forms of words. Again, speak in ways that sound authentic to you. Of course, it also pays to be alert to the possible meanings that your particular style and language constructions might convey.

Specific Acknowledgements

I would like to acknowledge a number of authors whose works provided inspiration and building blocks for the development of various aspects of the ARIES practices and tools:

- The tool for distinguishing observation and inference in Chapter 6 is a variation on tools developed and described by Chris Argyris.[1]

- The inspiration for the inquiring and expressing frameworks came particularly from two separate authors: Peter Senge and Bill Torbert, as well as their respective associates.[2]

- The synthesizing interventions described in Chapter 10 draw on my experiences over many years in facilitating, and training others in, dialogue. These experiences were informed by the writings of David Bohm, Peter Senge, and William Isaacs.[3]

- The framing of the transformational challenge concept, in Chapter 10, draws on Peter Checkland and Jim Scholes' work on transformation in relation to "soft-systems methodologies."[4]

We turn now to the practice of attending.

Chapter
SIX
....
Attending

Emily had been with the local government council for twelve months when her manager, a member of the organization's senior executive group, asked her to take on the role of overseeing a service integration project involving a group of small-town libraries. The strategy called for the libraries to be integrated electronically and to share books (which is hardly novel now, but it was at the time, particularly to the affected librarians). Emily was ambivalent about taking on this role. As an experienced project manager, she was not concerned about her skills. What did concern her, however, was the fact that this project had been a stop-start affair since well before the time she arrived at the council. In addition, the project had been on hold for the past several months. Emily was not sure of the reasons, but she had heard stories about the librarians resisting the changes. Emily wondered if she had been handed a poisoned chalice.

In this chapter we draw upon Emily's efforts at library change to illustrate and demonstrate the practice of attending. Attending concerns the quality of our perception. This practice asks us to put the pursuit of awareness ahead of the drive for task achievement.

We explore three aspects of attending here:

- Giving full attention;

- Perceiving holistically; and

- Differentiating observation from inference.

We also look into the proposition that the practice of attending necessitates centering ourselves in the present moment.

But first we need to ask: Why is attending a critical component of learning-centered leadership practice? And how is it different from what we do already? Sometimes people in workshops—particularly more senior executives—argue along the following lines: "Yes, paying attention is important. But you don't get to be a successful top executive unless you do this well. This is a presumed skill at this level. Can't we focus on something more directly relevant to our needs?"

One way to look at this argument is to notice how it actually reflects, and reinforces, the predominance of management-mode thinking. Recall that when we function in the management mode, our primary orientation is to the explicit aspects of problems and task action, with the legitimacy of those actions stemming from authority. Succeeding at higher executive levels requires—among other things—that you have your wits about you. You must be able to scan the horizon, listen to arguments, distil the essence of information coming at you, interpret it, and act decisively upon it. We might use the term "paying attention instrumentally," meaning that in paying attention in the management mode we are primarily focused on achieving our objectives. Paying attention, from this perspective, is bound up with us accomplishing what we are setting out to do.

Yet, to the extent that we have a laser-like focus on explicit factors, such as resources, products, or benchmarks, we are likely to be oblivious to the more subtle indications of intelligence lying beneath the surface. Insofar as our efforts are directed towards accomplishing particular tasks, how sensitive are we liable to be to expressions of disquiet or other feelings—perhaps only partly formed— relevant to the problems before us? How receptive might we be to faint signals that indicate a challenge to our assumptions? How open might we be to anyone who has a very different portrayal of the issue at hand?

Then there is the matter of authority. In Chapter 1 we considered some of the dynamics that tend to shut down the expression of dissenting opinion in hierarchical structures. How can we be sure that what we are hearing is a full and accurate account? If others believe that we are not really tuning in to them, they are likely to be more circumspect in what they tell us. Commonly, people at all levels declare that those at different places on the hierarchy "do not listen." Reflecting this, a common response—regardless of level—is for people to "just get on with the job"—dealing with tasks, focusing on problems at the explicit level and applying whatever authority is theirs. The management mode is reinforced.

Attending is essential for dealing with contentious problems because, inevitably, these entail multiple viewpoints, some of which will be at least partly hidden. To work through the problem requires developing a degree of shared meaning, and establishing shared meaning involves gaining access to—and learning about—the fullest possible range of perspectives on the problem. To do this we must practice attending, giving this a higher priority than the accomplishment of specific tasks. Attending enables the emergence of a clearer, more nuanced comprehension of the dynamics underlying a contentious problem.

In short, attending is different in kind and quality from paying attention instrumentally. Far from being "a presumed skill," as the executive in my workshop called it, attending sits center-stage as a key practice for learning-leadership work at all levels—and as a practice that needs developing.

CASE STORY Change in the Library System

Emily quickly discovered that the project's history went back nearly three years. Finding out just what had happened, though, was difficult; there had been extensive executive turnover and records were patchy. Even her manager was of limited help. She managed to get a briefing from him, but it was sketchy at best, as he had been with the council only slightly longer than Emily.

Emily's manager told her that the librarians were committed to their libraries, but they "like things very much as they are." He said their view was very insular, confined to their local surroundings and their profession, whereas the council had a more systemic outlook. "The bottom line is there needs to be integration; the chief executive expects it. Each library should be an entry point to the whole library system, rather than a freestanding operation as they all are now. Apart from this, there could be some room for negotiation about the precise form the integration takes."

One thing Emily discovered was that the librarians had been involved in a consultation process regarding the proposed integration model about a year prior to her arrival. As part of these consultations, the librarians had been assured there would be no job losses as a result of the integration, and that the desired outcomes were more in terms of service improvement than cost reduction. At that point, Emily knew she had to engage the librarians in the change process if it was to succeed. Yet this was to prove more difficult than she expected.

After speaking with a few people, including some representative librarians, Emily prepared a slideshow presentation that highlighted the benefits of the proposed integration, as she understood them, as well as a process she had developed for involving the librarians in the detailed planning. The presentation also outlined some of the more technical IT-related aspects. She arranged to attend a gathering of the librarians to explain the change process and the steps involved. Emily invited her manager along, but he phoned to cancel at the last minute, citing another commitment. He said to Emily, "You don't really need me there anyway. You will handle it just fine."

The session began well enough. Emily worked through her slides, speaking enthusiastically about both the proposed changes and the change process. She had planned to take questions at the end of her presentation but some of the librarians interjected. "What's the real agenda?" asked one. "There's no meaningful consultation," said another. A third commented, "No one's considering our workloads." Another remarked, "We have many decades of service between us—some of us have been here 20 years—but the council does not value that at all. The professional librarian will be a thing of the past in this region, if these changes go ahead." Emily looked around the room, trying to spot which speaker might pounce next. "I don't like the way this project has been handled either," said another librarian, addressing her colleagues. "But shouldn't we at least listen to what she has to say?" Emily said later she did not fully register this comment; instead, she had been intently focusing on what she took to be a concerted attack by the librarians. And the objections, mainly about the change process, had kept on coming.

Frustrated by what she saw as resistance by the librarians, Emily said in her concluding remarks, "Come on, don't be so negative. This will turn out to be good for you all." At the end of her presentation, the applause was, shall we say, muted. By this stage Emily's head was reeling. It was as if the librarians' negative comments were on automatic replay in her mind; all she wanted was to get away.

Not to be deterred, however, Emily arranged to meet two weeks later with a smaller group of librarians. She again suggested to her manager that he come along, but this time he declined by email, saying that he had yet another "unavoidable commitment," and adding, "I have full confidence in your ability to drive this important project through."

At this second meeting, Emily was determined to ask the librarians about their objections, as well as to present a strong case for the benefits of the integration plan. Unfortunately, the response turned out to be only marginally better than before. Emily found it hard to get past the librarians' obvious anger to discover much about their underlying concerns. One concern she did hear was that the librarians were worried that the changes would undercut the libraries' role in serving their local communities. As she divulged later, though, Emily spent much of the meeting grumbling in her own mind about the librarians' resistance, rather than listening to what they were actually saying.

As the meeting ended, one of the librarians came up to Emily and said, "Don't worry, it's not you personally we're against; it's the fact that the council has been trying to bludgeon us into toeing their line for three years now." But Emily was worried.

"I don't know what to do. This project is totally stalled—again, and I'm not sure why," said Emily to a colleague the next day over coffee. "My efforts to engage with the librarians just don't seem to be working. My manager cancelled again; he really isn't interested in being involved. The council's integration plan is not a bad thing, but I sure could use some top management support to help bring the librarians around. Without that, I could be sunk."

Giving Full Attention

In *Tuesdays with Morrie*, Mitch Albom recounts a series of conversations— "classes," as he calls them—with his dying sociology professor, Morrie Schwartz.[1] Morrie offers much wisdom on many of life's challenges, among them the importance of giving full attention:

> " I believe in being fully present," Morrie said. "That means you should be with the person you're with. When I'm talking to you now Mitch, I try to keep focused only on what's going on between us. I am not thinking about something we said last week. I am not thinking about what's coming up this Friday. I am not thinking about doing another Koppel show, or about what medications I'm taking. I am talking to you…"[2]

To be fully present means to center your attention on the person or group you are interacting with, and to open up to the richness of what they are communicating. This is not just a matter of hearing their words. To fully pay attention means you allow what the other is communicating to seep into you so that you feel the pain, frustration, excitement, or whatever they are sharing. It means you center your awareness on the experience, on the feeling and the intention behind the words.

While we might like to think of ourselves as being open and receptive to new inputs, it is a real challenge to demonstrate such openness in the moment, especially when we are interacting with others regarding a contentious problem. Can we recognize the perceptual filters that we routinely apply and perhaps open them a little? Can we notice and pay attention to views that might not correspond easily with our own? Can we let some of what is meaningful to others permeate and perhaps expand, or even modify, our own understanding? Can we deal with the vulnerability that such active attention in the immediate moment implies?

Emily appears to have some way to go in mastering this particular aspect of learning-centered leadership practice. In her first meeting with them, the librarians said things like: "There's no consultation," and "This meeting is a waste of time." Each statement potentially expresses a rich combination of knowledge, thought, and emotion. Even if she caught the words spoken, there is little sign that Emily engaged receptively with the librarians. Her responses seemed to be driven more by a desire to ward off threat than an intention to learn about the librarians' experience. Emily's challenge—and ours—in the practice of attending is to be alive to the fullness of what is being conveyed. We must learn to avoid the temptation to judge harshly and to refrain from attributing explanations that have the effect of closing down our perceptions.

For many of us, the experience of paying attention fully in the way Morrie Schwartz describes is probably a rarity. It is easy to allow distractions to interfere, as when we allow a stream of internal chatter to flow unchecked while we participate in a conversation. In fact, we take pride in our ability to multi-task, such as checking email while someone speaks to us. When our mind is alive with activity, our attention is fragmented, and so we diminish our capacity to learn from others.

Sometimes, the stream of chatter concerns those with whom we are currently engaged. Maybe we are judging their behavior, as with Emily's silent "grumbling" about the librarians in their second meeting. Perhaps we are anticipating their next point, or figuring out a solution to their problem. If we stop to analyze it, we might see that we are devoting only a small portion of our mental energy to listening and paying attention, while most of our mind's effort is assigned to judging, categorizing, and strategizing. As a workshop participant once put it, "Of course this activity is going on in my head. I can't just turn my mind off."

It is true that the mind has a tendency to be very active, but we do have some control over it. A challenge is to "catch ourselves in the act" of letting our attention wander, and to then gently bring it back to where it needs to be at that moment. There are no sure-fire ways of doing this, though we shall consider some ideas later in the chapter.

Perceiving Holistically

We learn from an early age that paying attention means to concentrate. If you think back to your days at school, a teacher telling you to "pay attention" probably meant to stop talking (or whatever else you were up to), and focus on the task at hand. Paying attention, in this sense, suggests a converging or narrowing of focus. But there is a danger in concentrating intently in one direction, and that is that we may fail to perceive signals coming from other directions. In the story, for example, Emily's attention was so intently directed towards spotting which of the librarians might "pounce next," that she did not catch the words of one of them urging others to listen.

In the ARIES framework, the meaning of attending is broader and more holistic than we traditionally associate with paying attention. Attending is the active process of being aware of one's surroundings and one's self; it is about allowing ourselves to perceive more fully, more completely, the action in which we are presently engaged, and all that surrounds it. It means keeping one's antennas up, one's eyes and ears open. It means being alert to the *whole context* in which you are operating, rather than fixing only on the more tangible, readily visible aspects.

Perceiving holistically does not preclude concentrating. Both are necessary. When perceiving holistically, we can still place our attention primarily on a particular person, or interaction, or object—but at the same time we have a wider field of view. Some of our attention, even if a small portion, is actively registering what is taking place in this wider field. This is a *dynamic* form of awareness (not to be confused with a more static concept of self-awareness, as with having an appreciation of one's strengths and weaknesses). Moving between concentration and a broader awareness implies a shift of attention, akin to the way a camera can alter focus by zooming in and drawing back. In our story, for example, if Emily detected a quieter voice from the back of the room in one of her meetings with the librarians, she may have had to concentrate keenly in order to make out what was being said. But—ideally—she would still have maintained a sense of the whole field.

Perceiving holistically implies a kind of peripheral perception; you are noticing and registering a range of information, including background information, which may or may not turn out to be significant. Taking note of such signals does not mean processing, thinking about, or evaluating them. Rather, you hold them in your consciousness without judgment, trusting that you will be able to access and act on them if the need arises.

Emily's case story provides some examples of background information that may (or may not) turn out to be significant. In her first meeting with the librarians, she might have noted the following: the consultation process had been going on for nearly three years; Emily had been in her role for twelve months; some of the librarians had been in the job for twenty years; no one else from the council had accompanied Emily to the meeting.

If you find yourself resisting this aspect of attending, you may be thinking that your mind is full with information already, so the last thing you need is to jam it with more. Remember, though, that all you are doing is registering information, making a mental (or perhaps written) note of it. You do not necessarily need to process, think about, or evaluate it straightaway. That can come later. Just noticing is what is important at this stage.

You might also be asking the question: How can I know what information is actually relevant? The technique I recommend is to call upon the "invisible observer," mentioned in the Chapter 3 discussion of working relationally. The invisible observer is a construct intended to reinforce that we are *within* the sphere of the problem we are concerned about, not independent of it. As we saw in Chapter 3, keeping yourself in the frame is vital; it is key to working relationally.

Use this device to help you discover the most relevant information. Ask yourself: What might an informed, but impartial, observer regard as potentially significant here? Another question to ask yourself is, What do I notice about my own actions that might be significant? In Emily's case she might take note that she spoke "enthusiastically" about the change process in her first meeting with the librarians. Again, this is something to be calmly noticed, not judged or evaluated.

Distinguishing between Observation and Inference

Think back for a moment to the case story of Emily and the librarians. What details come to mind? When I ask workshop participants to do this, a typical response is, "Emily's manager is not interested in working with the librarians." Emily herself made a similar interpretation, telling her colleague that she thought the manager "really isn't interested in being involved."

This is an inference, not an observation. We know from the case description that the manager did not attend the two meetings, citing other commitments; this was observable. But as to any other reasons for his non-attendance, we have little firm information, just possibilities. It may of course be true, or partly so, that he did not want to work with the librarians. But perhaps he is simply busy and content to rely on Emily, as he says. Or, conceivably, Emily's manager just does not recognize the importance of his involvement.

Being clear about the distinction between observation and mere conjecture helps guard against the culturally reinforced tendency to make rapid-fire diagnoses and come up with quick-fix "solutions" to multi-faceted problems. Of course, many people in managerial, technical, and professional roles take considerable pride in their ability to quickly assess and resolve problems. Such abilities also tend to be strongly reinforced in organizations where the management mode is dominant. People who are good "problem-solvers" are held in high esteem and the ongoing pressures for task achievement and short-term results ensure that these capabilities are in continual demand. When the problems are technical, these abilities are obviously valuable, but contentious problems call for a different mindset.

The orientation toward high-speed problem assessment and solution generation is so ingrained, that we should not be surprised when people set about applying technically oriented problem-solving skills to contentious problems. Many will find it hard to step back in order to disentangle what it is that they observe directly from what they generate through the application of their reason and experience.

Yet, stepping back does matter. If we do not, our deeply ingrained habits, assumptions, and practices can take effect without our being aware. We might make an observation, perhaps unconsciously draw conclusions as to its meaning, and then act as if our conclusions were necessarily true, without testing their validity. In turn, the results of our actions tend to confirm our assumptions. The whole process can become a closed, self-reinforcing loop.

But how do we step back and introduce more awareness into the way we approach problems? When you are faced with a difficult situation, and your wish is to intervene from a leadership-mode standpoint, a useful exercise is to write down what you think is directly detectable and then—separately—list any possible inferences that might be drawn from these observations. A two-column format works well. Record your observations on the left. Then write down any plausible inferences on the right—not just the first that occurs to you. This exercise encourages disciplined thinking by helping you to separate observation from inference. In addition, it encourages you to identify a *range* of possible inferences, not just the one that comes into your mind first. This helps open up your thinking. Another benefit is that the very process of writing down these observations and inferences slows you down, and encourages you to make a more considered assessment than you might have otherwise. Once again, adopting the invisible observer perspective is critical; it also supports you in registering what others might see as significant about your own behavior.

Let us apply this two-column technique to review some observations and possible inferences from the library change case story. In Figure 6.1, you will see some observations have been recorded in the left column, and possible inferences in the right. Of course, we are restricted here in that our observations can be drawn only from the information provided. Moreover, this is only a sampling of the observations and inferences based on the case; you may be able to spot others—and you may want to question some of the inferences suggested here. [3]

FIGURE 6.1 Separating Observation and Inference in the Library Change Case Story

OBSERVATIONS	POSSIBLE INFERENCES
In the briefing session with Emily, her manager said the librarians "like things very much as they are."	The manager believes the librarians would be opposed to pretty much any change in the existing arrangements. The manager believes that he understands the librarians' thinking.
In her first meeting with the librarians, Emily spoke "enthusiastically" about the changes and a process for involving the librarians.	Emily sees the problem as having to "sell" the changes to the librarians. She regards the benefits of change as self-evident. She believes that the librarians should recognize these benefits when the benefits are communicated to them.
One librarian was suspicious, asking, "What is the real agenda?" Another said, "no meaningful consultation." Applause was muted.	The librarians believe the council has an agenda it is not sharing with the librarians. The librarians believe the council has made up its mind what it wants to do, and is not really interested in what the librarians might say.
Emily remarks, "Don't be so negative."	Emily may be frustrated by the librarians' lack of enthusiasm for the changes, especially if the benefits are apparent to her. Emily thinks the librarians should view the change positively. The manager sees change as straightforward.
Her manager refers to Emily "driving the project through."	He believes that change requires a "push" approach. He expects Emily to achieve the change without significant involvement from him.
One staff member remarks, "It's not you..."	At least some of the librarians may be amenable to working with Emily. The librarians may have difficulties with other individuals at the council.

One way to conduct this exercise is as a quick self-assessment. When used this way, it will help you distinguish what is observable and real in a problem situation from the products of your own mental processes. A team or group can also use the exercise as a reality check on how clearly they are seeing an issue without their various predispositions getting in the way. In a simple yet powerful manner, this process can help us become more aware of the tendency to jump from observation to inference, and more adept at just seeing, just paying attention, before leaping to conclusions about what those observations might mean.

Attending to the Present Moment

In this chapter we have looked at three aspects of attending: giving full attention, perceiving holistically, and separating observation from inference. Each is difficult enough to put into practice in its own right, but a deeply attentive stance implies that we need to do each of these things *simultaneously*.

When the conditions are supportive, it is easier for the three to come into play together. By "conditions" I mean our frame of mind more than the external circumstances. We need to develop an attentiveness that is at once receptive to what is being communicated, alert to the wider context, and sufficiently relaxed, so that our mind is not constantly rushing off with distracting thoughts.

Some readers may wonder whether this is about to become a discussion of "spiritual" aspects of leadership. That is not my intention. The challenge I am addressing is a very practical one. As we saw in Chapter 4, many factors come together to propel us along a management-mode path, such as the pressures to maintain and improve operations, to deliver results, and to avoid actions that could give rise to threat and embarrassment. Under these conditions our attention tends to be fleeting; it darts all over the place as we struggle to stay on top of what others expect from us. In such circumstances, how can we possibly muster the kind of attending this chapter says is critical for engaging effectively with contentious problems? How can we make the practice of attending an actuality rather than just a concept that is "nice to have," but completely unrealistic?

Much of the time, we may be well-served by our attention zooming from one thing to another in order to glean new information, appraise the signals coming in, and figure out how to deal with technical problems. But at other times, when circumstances call for us to engage with a contentious problem, we need to be able to find that little bit of quiet. At those times, we need that brief period of relative stillness in which we can just "be" with others, a moment when we can go to a deeper level, and learn more about the reality they see. When these moments are called for, it is preferable that we not be thinking, planning, or strategizing. It is more appropriate that we just be quietly receptive to the people we are with and to the surrounding environment. Our attention is directed to the present moment.

The question of how to achieve a greater degree of in-the-moment awareness is one I have often discussed with participants in my workshops. I recall one woman saying that, when she recognized she needed to pay special attention—such as when talking with a staff member about a sensitive work performance issue—she would hold her left thumb and the index finger of that hand lightly together. Now, this little device may have no value at all for others, but for her it was a continuing reminder to pull back, to not push her own agenda so vigorously, and to create space for others to express what mattered to them.

Paying attention to one's breathing is another approach that some find helpful for bringing their attention to the present moment. Again, there are many different approaches to this, ranging from simple exercises to advanced yoga-based methods. Timothy Gallwey, whose ideas on the telling self and the doing self we discussed in Chapter 3, describes an approach he has used as a professional tennis coach with his players. Gallwey speaks of the need to stay concentrated in the present moment between points in a tennis game, that being a time when attention is likely to wander.

"My own device, and one that has been effective for many of my students, is to focus attention on breathing. Some object or activity which is always present is needed. What is more here and now than one's breathing? Putting attention on breathing simply means observing my breath going in, going out, going in, going out in its natural rhythm. It does not mean intentionally controlling my breath."[4]

Gallwey is speaking about paying attention in the context of tennis. But what relevance do these ideas about breathing have for leadership? Amanda Sinclair, professor at the Melbourne Business School, offers this view in her book, *Leadership for the Disillusioned*.

"What is needed in leadership may be simply stated but is hard to give: the capacity to not react impulsively from our own immediate needs; to be really present for others; to relinquish our need for control or mastery to the requirements of the challenge in front of us. Breathing consciously supports a leadership that steps back to reprioritise and reframe. Conscious breathing provides a connection to constancy, but supports these sometimes subtle but difficult changes."[5]

Attention to breathing is one approach among many for bringing one's awareness to the here and now. Others in my workshops have spoken of using the quiet repetition of a particular phrase or word to help them be more receptive in particular instances. The key to such approaches—which I have personally found useful—is not to force the repetition of the phrase or word, but just allow it to repeat gently in the back of your mind, while allowing the main focus of your intention to be directed externally, to where it needs to be at that point. If you find your mind filling with distracting thoughts, gently return to repeating the phrase, and bring your attention back to the person or group you are interacting with.

It must be said that arguments—including my own—about the relative effectiveness of various techniques for bringing your attention into the moment often spring more from personal experience and anecdotal accounts than any scientific research or evidence. Some argue that such exercises, in so far as they require a level of concentration, simply dull the senses and get in the way of the kind of attention we are seeking. The philosophical thinker and writer on awareness and related matters, J Krishnamurti, had this to say:

" There are systems which say, 'Watch the movement of your big toe, watch it, watch it, watch it;' there are other systems which advocate sitting in a certain posture, breathing regularly or practicing awareness. All this is utterly mechanical. Another method gives you a certain word and tells you that if you go on repeating it you will have some extraordinary transcendental experience. This is sheer nonsense. It is a form of self-hypnosis. "[6]

As you can see, this is a highly contested area! My argument is that techniques such as we have discussed can help you to ground your attention in what is happening in the moment. This happens because placing some of your attention on your breathing, a word, or whatever, enables some of the relentless activity of the mind to subside, at least temporarily. This phenomenon is what we might call a paradox of attention: by focusing a portion of your attention on one small thing, you enable an internal sense of quiet that allows you to embrace more of the fullness of what is occurring.

Different people find different approaches helpful; others try out various techniques but find nothing at all that helps center their awareness; still others think this whole area is a waste of time. There are obviously no universal remedies. If you are interested in trying any such techniques, then you need to be prepared to experiment, to find out what works for you and what does not. If a particular technique does not help you, discontinue it—but perhaps try it a few times first. Then, make a judgment once you have overcome any initial awkwardness in using the method.

The practice of attending is at the heart of learning-centered leadership and leadership-mode interventions. Working relationally with others, and paying mindful attention to both current realities and emerging possibilities, requires attending. We must carefully notice what is occurring around and within us, without leaping to judgment. Attending informs all of the other ARIES processes, yet it is difficult, and so must be considered problematic. Techniques for improving our practice of attending can help. But sometimes, no matter which method we apply, we find that we get sidetracked into our own thoughts, needs, wants, priorities, and impulses. When that occurs, the challenge is to notice what is happening, and make a conscious choice to re-center our attention. With practice, and over time, we might get better at attending, but it is unlikely that we will ever to be able to declare that we have "mastered" this practice.

Chapter Summary

Drawing on a case story of change in a library system, we considered attending, the first of the ARIES practices. Attending has three facets: giving one's full attention, perceiving holistically, and differentiating between observation and inference.

Giving full attention is a matter of being present with others without allowing distractions to get in the way. We tend to be only partly attentive to those we are communicating with, as our attention moves from one thought, idea, or fantasy to another, with the constant mental activity reinforced by the pressures of keeping on top of day-to-day demands.

Perceiving holistically refers to practicing a wider, contextual awareness, rather than a narrowly framed concentration. This facet is highlighted because of the ease with which we can become entrapped in a restrictive or "hard" concentration, characterized by a "screening out" of signals that might distract or interrupt our focus.

The need to differentiate observation from inference reflects a common tendency to apply technical problem-handling skills to problems in which multiple realities are at play. Rather than trying to rapidly diagnose and "solve" contentious problems, the need is to first truly take in "the data" before thinking about possible interpretations.

We also discussed means of achieving a greater degree of centeredness when intervening from a learning-leadership stance, including through breathing more consciously. Such practices may help avert the mind's tendency to wander, enabling our attention to stay directed to those we are interacting with and the surrounding context.

Questions for Reflection

6.1 Bring to mind a conversation in which someone was conveying something that mattered very much to them, but where you found yourself not paying full attention. What got in the way of your paying attention? Is this typical?

6.2 Think of a discussion you have been involved in where some disagreement occurred. Try to recall some observable details that might have been apparent to a third party observer—including observations about your own behavior. Create a two-column table and list the observable details in the left column. In the right column, for each of those observations, write down one or more plausible inferences that you or others might draw.

6.3 What behaviors might you cultivate that would help you exercise greater attentiveness when dealing with thorny problems?

Chapter
SEVEN

Reflecting

The word reflection means different things to different people. One person might think of reflection as mulling over the day's events while traveling home from work or chatting with colleagues. Another might connect reflection with religious or spiritual practices such as contemplation, prayer, or meditation. For yet another, reflection might denote an extended process of deliberation about an important question in life, such as why a significant relationship ended. Reflection has a collective aspect, too. In many organizations, groups can be asked to engage in reflection. These exercises can vary widely; they can range from an informal discussion about, say, why a particular procedure is causing problems, to one-off organized events, such as an executive retreat, to more formalized project review processes. While not necessarily carefully structured (or productive), all of these are called reflection. In addition, the importance of reflective practice has long been recognized as important to professional development in fields such as education, social work, architecture, and medicine. In short, reflection is increasingly being valued, but there is no shared understanding of its meaning, nor what constitutes doing it well.

In the ARIES framework, we use the term "reflecting" and assign to it a particular meaning: it is the process of making sense of the various stakeholder perspectives, including our own, that are manifest with respect to an issue, thus making it a contentious problem. Reflecting is the process of recognizing, understanding, and contemplating those differing perspectives. In our framework, reflecting is the reciprocal of attending. As we discussed in the previous chapter, attending focuses on perceiving clearly; it involves paying heed to signals from the external environment, as well as the contents of our own awareness. Reflecting, on the other hand, is the practice of making sense of, or interpreting, what is perceived.

At one level, the distinction between reflecting and attending is something of an artificial separation. Ideally, these processes come together as a seamless whole: we notice what is happening within and around us; we consider a variety of possible meanings; then we take action to test those interpretations. Such attending and reflecting in the moment is, however, something of a "gold standard"; it is an ideal we aspire to, not a reality achieved regularly in everyday life. Among the factors that make reflecting difficult are the pressures considered in chapters 4 and 5. There is ongoing pressure to achieve short-term results, to focus exclusively on the tangible rather than implicit aspects of problems, and to avoid actions that could generate threat or defensiveness. These pressures reflect the dominance of the management mode.

Reflective practice does have a place in the management mode, but it has a different character. In the leadership-mode (ARIES) context, reflecting is the process we use to make sense of multiple perspectives on a contentious problem. In contrast, the place of reflection in the management mode is in helping us to *achieve present objectives, through drawing upon, and contemplating, past experience.* Imagine the situation of a top executive who has been told her area's budget is to be reduced because of difficult business circumstances. She decides to restructure the area. As she thinks through possible models for the new structure and plans for implementation, she reflects on her own past experience with restructurings—as well as on other change efforts she is familiar with—in order to learn how she might successfully bring about this reorganization. Reflection in the management mode implies focusing on the tangible aspects of a problem (e.g., the budget cut, possible models for a new structure), and contemplating how what went before can help us in achieving our current task objectives. Management mode-reflection is important in enabling us to learn from past experience and the experience of others. When problems are contentious, however—as a restructure might well be—we need to reflect from a leadership-mode perspective, often in conjunction with management-mode reflection.

In the leadership mode our focus is particularly on making sense of *present realities* on a contentious problem.[1] By definition, contentious problems involve a multitude of unreconciled perspectives. These multiple perspectives hold the key; they are the seeds of collective wisdom. Therefore, to make progress, it is imperative that we sort through them. It is through recognizing, understanding, and contemplating these that we come to a higher-level of understanding about the problem. This is the essence of reflecting in the ARIES context.

Contentious problems present us with a bit of a paradox, however. In order to deeply comprehend that full range of perspectives, we need to be able to enter into and appreciate the realities that others see. Yet, much of what others assume, think, feel, and know sits—as we saw with the iceberg model in Chapter 2—below the waterline, in the implicit domain, largely obscured and undeclared. Our own perspective is part of the range that we need to consider, too. While we may be inclined to think that we are fully aware of our own perspective, it is probable that we bring to the problem assumptions, interests, feelings, and knowledge that we are only partially aware of.

Clearly, to facilitate reflection, we need a tool that can help us gain access to more of the implicit domain, both others' and our own. In this chapter we introduce such a tool, the Reflection Matrix. The Reflection Matrix is designed to aid our understanding of what might "really be going on" with a problem. It helps illuminate what is going on for each of the individual stakeholders as well as the dynamics between them. The result is an effective analysis—based in reflection—that can be used as a basis for testing understanding with various stakeholders. Drawing on the library change case from Chapter 6 for illustration, we show how the Reflection Matrix can help make sense of a problem from multiple standpoints, including our own. While our illustration focuses on a change effort, the Reflection Matrix process can be applied in any organizational context where a contentious problem has a strong human dimension (that is, where the contention does not simply concern differing technical perspectives).

Shifting Perspectives with the Reflection Matrix

The Reflection Matrix provides a window to the inner realities of the various interested parties. It helps us to draw forth the implicit or hidden dimension. "Hidden" here refers to relevant content that is not stated or declared either because it is being intentionally concealed, or because it is not within their conscious awareness. We can think of the implicit side of the iceberg as comprising four hidden aspects, as shown in Figure 7.1.

FIGURE 7.1 Four Aspects of the Implicit Domain

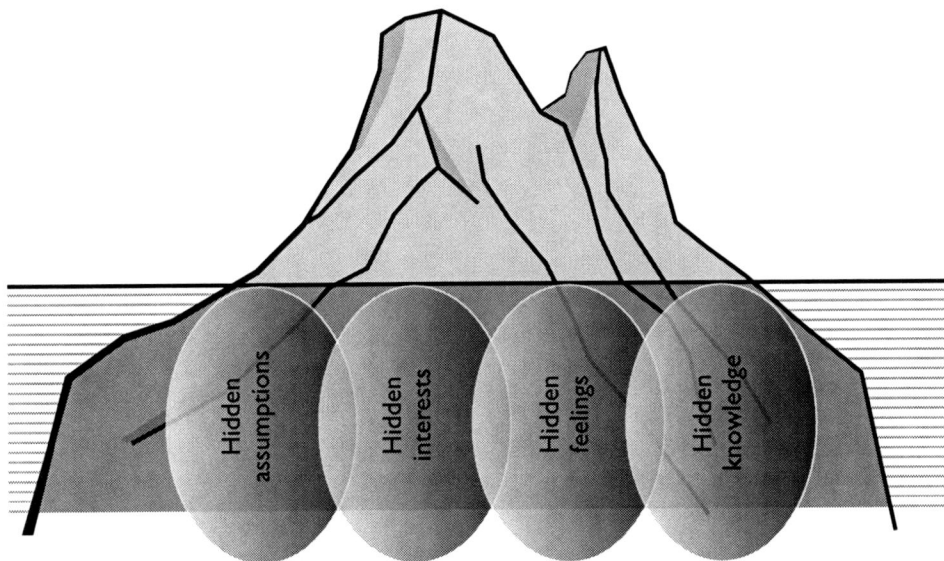

Working through the Reflection Matrix involves contemplating what you have seen and observed and then, based on that data, recording what you suspect might be important and relevant content in each of these hidden domains for each of the major stakeholders, including yourself. You would record:

Hidden Assumptions	What particular stakeholders appear to take as given or true in relation to the problem;
Hidden Interests	What we think they would value and hold as important; what the evidence says really matters to them, not just what the stakeholders assert as significant;
Hidden Feelings	What unsurfaced emotions the evidence suggests stakeholders may be experiencing, such as disappointment, optimism, frustration and anger;
Hidden Knowledge	What we imagine stakeholders know—due to their professional training, for instance, or because of their experience in work and life.

As shown in Figure 7.2, the Reflection Matrix includes the four hidden domains in columns and the major stakeholders in rows.

FIGURE 7.2 The Reflection Matrix

	Hidden Assumptions	Hidden Interests	Hidden Feelings	Hidden Knowledge
	What assumptions might this stakeholder make?	What is likely to be important to this stakeholder?	What might this stakeholder be	What relevant experience or knowledge might this stakeholder have?
Stakeholder 1				
Stakeholder 2				
Stakeholder(n)				
Self/own group				

Completing the Matrix prompts you to "drill down" below the surface and consider possible explanations for stakeholder comments and behavior, especially some you might not otherwise consider. It asks you to "stand in the shoes" of each stakeholder and *imagine* what might be in their mind, but has not been made explicit. This is never a matter of judging other stakeholders, but of applying the reasonableness principle as described in Chapter 5. What hidden assumptions, interests, feelings, and knowledge could reasonably lead to the behaviors we have observed?

This exercise is appropriate for both individuals and groups. An individual who is seeking to better understand the concerns and motivations of stakeholders—as well as the dynamics unfolding between them—might use the process to aid reflection off-line. After completing the Matrix that individual would then be more prepared to intervene from a learning-leadership perspective. A group, such as a management team, could also use the Reflection Matrix to better understand each member's perspective and those of other interested parties. In that case, the process might take the form of a facilitated "live" session. In both cases, it would be preferable to be assisted by a coach (or a colleague) who is skilled in learning-leadership to help open up other ways of seeing.

The Reflection Matrix process is especially valuable when the group seems stuck, when progress on an issue seems blocked, and the reasons are unclear or in need of review. It is easy to be lax in our thinking when we are dealing with complex issues and have a lot on our minds. The Matrix can help us to achieve greater clarity in our assessments of others' positions and what might be driving them. Using this tool enables us to get our evaluations of others' statements or behavior—as well as our own—"out of our heads" and into an organized framework where we can review them. The output is a systematic and carefully considered appraisal of multiple perspectives on the current realities. A clear benefit is that we can use this analysis to inform our choices about whether and how to intervene. It can also lead to a major shift in our—or the group's—perspectives, as we uncover possible explanations for others' apparent behavior.

The contents of the resulting Reflection Matrix involve supposition, and therefore the output should be regarded as a set of hypotheses that require testing. We must always bear that in mind. Conducting the Reflection Matrix exercise is not a substitute for talking with people; rather, it is a resource for informing subsequent conversations and action.[2] It is through the subsequent testing that major shifts in perspective, or insights, can occur.

Applying the Reflection Matrix with the Library Change Case

Recall from Chapter 6 that Emily was a project manager in a local government council, tasked with better integrating some local library services. On one hand, the librarians appeared to be resisting the change effort. On the other hand, her council's senior management—in particular, her own manager—were providing little support. Emily told her colleague that "this project is totally stalled," and that she did not know what to do. Here we draw on Emily's case to look more closely at the Reflection Matrix tool. The starting point is a page, or pages, drawn up as per the graphic in Figure 7.2.

Deciding on Stakeholders for Inclusion

How many stakeholders should be included? Your choice about how many stakeholder categories to include can influence the sensitivity of the analysis. Building in more stakeholder categories can result in a finer-grained, more accurate analysis, but completion is likely to require more time and effort. There is a trade-off. A rule of thumb is to keep the number of stakeholder groups low at first. Then, as you work through the Reflection Matrix you may find that you need to add others in order to capture and reflect upon all the relevant stakeholder comments and behaviors. In our library case, "top management," for instance, might be put in as one category. However, if there were, say, two camps within this group with substantially different views, then it would make sense to include two separate groups. As it stands, three stakeholder categories will be used in the illustration: the librarians, the council's top management group (as we have no information about any differences within the group), and Emily herself.

Emily's inclusion is critical. The person (or group) with the primary interest in conducting the analysis—referred to as the case owner—should always be included. It can be tempting for that person to believe that "I know my own stuff," and that the need is to shed light on the viewpoints of others. However, this raises the danger of compromising the central tenet of relational working: the notion of oneself as an integral part of the system of concern. To work relationally implies the willingness to leave one's views open for inspection. Reviewing one's own assumptions, interests, feelings, and knowledge can also be a powerful source of personal growth and learning.

Completing the Actual Matrix

How can we identify the assumptions, interests, feelings, and knowledge of other parties when they do not make these apparent and they appear unwilling (or unable) to articulate them? The essential process involves considering one stakeholder (or stakeholder group) at a time and asking questions of oneself, particularly the following:

- What assumptions might this stakeholder make?
- What is likely to be important to this stakeholder?
- What might this stakeholder be feeling?
- What relevant experience or knowledge might this stakeholder have?

The example, in Figure 7.3 on the following pages, shows Emily's assessment of the implicit domain for, firstly, the librarians, then—going down the table—the council's senior management, and finally, herself. Note that the assumptions, interests, feelings, and knowledge included are meant to be indicative rather than exhaustive. The first column in Figure 7.3 shows some of the assumptions Emily thinks the librarians (and then other stakeholders) might hold. The second column sets out some interests Emily considers might be important to them, and so on.

When filling out the Matrix, how do you determine what to include? Rather than just picking points "out of the blue," consider points for which there is clear supporting evidence. For instance, one of the interests Emily credits to the librarians (in Figure 7.3) is "maintaining their self-image, status, and skills as competent professionals." Her supporting evidence is a remark by a librarian in a meeting with Emily: "The professional librarian will be a thing of the past in this region, if these changes go ahead." The key is to be clear in your own mind as to the rationale for including each point. If you are unable to articulate the thinking behind an item, it is probably better left out.

Applying the reasonableness principle in completing the Matrix is critical. This does not mean you must sugarcoat or put a positive spin on your assessments. Rather, the reasonableness principle helps ensure that any attributions you make are potentially testable; testing is an essential component of the reflecting process. In effect, this means you want to be able to put the attribution to the other party and seek their response. As an example, Emily includes in her Matrix the assumption that the librarians see their primary role as managing separate local libraries. Others, in particular, the council, would most probably not agree with that assumption. But the key question is whether Emily could test this assumption with the librarians directly. Could she state this assumption and ask the librarians whether they held it? Of course, there is no way of predicting with great confidence how the librarians would react to such a question. But if her assumption credits the librarians with reasonableness, an adverse reaction is less likely.

Let us suppose that you have entered onto the Matrix some assumptions, interests, feelings, and knowledge for each group. How can you tell if the Matrix is sufficiently worked-up? The point is to generate a useful Matrix, not a comprehensive one. Avoid getting caught up in trying to "perfect" the analysis. A more effective approach is to register, fairly swiftly, some thoughts that come to mind under the various headings in the structure. If you get stuck, for instance, in trying to identify possible feelings for one group and nothing springs to mind, do not agonize over it. Move on. The Reflection Matrix exercise is not an end in itself; it is an aid to understanding problems and to informing conversations.

FIGURE 7.3 A Reflection Matrix for the Library Change Case

I. THE LIBRARIANS Emily's assessment as to what might be in the implicit domain for the librarians

Hidden Assumptions	Hidden Interests	Hidden Feelings	Hidden Knowledge
Emily thinks the librarians—or at least most of them—might assume that:	*Emily thinks the librarians' interests might include:*	*Emily thinks the librarians might be feeling:*	*Emily thinks the librarians might have knowledge regarding:*
The role of the individual librarian is to operate a separate local library facility The council wants to impose change top-down, without regard for the librarians' views The council does not understand or value the librarians' experience and expertise The council will not act in the librarians' interests	Maintaining their self-image, status, and skills as competent professionals Maintaining a level of independence such as traditionally associated with each library's "owning" its own books Individually, to ensure high levels of service for their own local library users Not being burdened with unreasonable additional workloads as a result of change	Frustration and anger—at the council's stop-start efforts at change, and at what the librarians see as insufficient involvement in the change process Fear—regarding possible loss of value for present skills, difficulties in gaining new skills, and about what the future may hold Despondency—from a lack of confidence that their interests will be looked after	The needs of library users and what they value The impacts of past change initiatives, especially past efforts to integrate the libraries

2. THE COUNCIL'S SENIOR MANAGEMENT Emily's assessment as to what might be in the implicit domain for the council's senior management

Hidden Assumptions	Hidden Interests	Hidden Feelings	Hidden Knowledge
Emily thinks the council's senior management might assume that:	*Emily thinks the council's senior management's interests might include:*	*Emily thinks the council's senior management might be feeling:*	*Emily thinks the council's senior management might have knowledge regarding:*
The council can see the bigger picture; has a more comprehensive view	Achieving high levels of service for the population of library users in the area served by the council	Frustration at what is seen to be self-interested action by the librarians and about lack of progress on the integration project	The parameters for this project, including the level of integration that must be achieved and what aspects are negotiable

An integrated library system would be more "rational"	Being able to demonstrate improved performance and efficiency of the library system overall	Annoyance that she (Emily) is not making more progress	The performance of the library system currently—possibly in comparison with benchmarks from elsewhere
The librarians are resistant to change	Being able to demonstrate advancement on the integration effort, after three years of delayed progress		
Emily should be able to overcome this resistance and "drive" the change process herself			
The librarians have had adequate opportunities to be involved			

3. EMILY HERSELF Emily's assessment as to what is in her own implicit domain

Hidden Assumptions	Hidden Interests	Hidden Feelings	Hidden Knowledge
Emily admits to assuming (at earlier stages of the project, not currently) that:	*Emily sees her own interests here as:*	*Emily admits to feeling:*	*Emily has relevant knowledge including:*
The benefits of integration are self-evident—when explained, the librarians will recognize them	Achieving a result that meets the needs of the council (as my employer) and, desirably, the needs of the librarians as well	Dispirited—at the librarians' lack of enthusiasm for the project and at the council's lack of active support for the change effort	A (developing) appreciation of the complexities of the change effort, of the perspectives of the stakeholders, and of the dynamic between them
If I can communicate the benefits effectively, change should flow smoothly	Not becoming caught in the middle of a battle between the council and the librarians, where I may become a "sacrificial lamb"	Disempowered—unclear as to what action I can take that will progress the change effort	
Emily's current assumptions include that:		Vulnerable—that if either party wishes to scapegoat me, I could end up sidelined from the project	
Achieving meaningful integration will require finding common ground between the parties			
The council expects me to achieve change with little extra support			

Interpreting and Utilizing the Completed Reflection Matrix

The Reflection Matrix process can assist us in making sense of a problem at two levels. First, it helps us appreciate how the problem might appear to individual stakeholders. Second, it helps us better understand how the perspectives of the different stakeholders intersect with, and impact on, one another.

Learning to appreciate how the problem might appear to an individual stakeholder involves weaving together the various entries concerning that stakeholder in order to arrive at a composite picture. The Matrix will enable us to gain a more nuanced, differentiated account of how this stakeholder conceives of the problem than we would otherwise. Reflecting upon this more textured account should lead to increased awareness, even insight.

For the librarians in our case study, the Matrix in Figure 7.3 points to a range of factors that could help explain their apparent lack of enthusiasm for the integration project. The evidence suggests they hold assumptions such as that the council does not value their expertise and will not act in their interests. It indicates that their interests include maintaining their professional status and not having their workloads increased, and suggests they may be dealing with largely unexpressed feelings of frustration and despondency. In addition, the librarians may possess valuable knowledge that is very relevant to the change effort: namely, they understand their customers' needs and expectations. As the change process has been going on for several years, it is likely that these aspects of the hidden dimension have intensified with the passage of time.

Looked at from the council's perspective, however, a somewhat distinct set of assumptions, interests, feelings, and knowledge emerges. The evidence points to their holding different assumptions about, for instance, the role of individual libraries (and librarians) within the library system, and about the librarians and their willingness to change. Their interests appear to concern the need to demonstrate improved system performance and achievement of some form of library integration. With respect to feelings, it is likely that they are experiencing frustration about the perceived lack of change preparedness on the part of the librarians. Their hidden knowledge likely includes actual system performance measures and parameters for the change process.

Emily, too, carries her own assumptions, interests, feelings, and knowledge. When she first met with the librarians she assumed that the benefits of integration were virtually self-evident, and that her role was to communicate those benefits. That assumption has since given way to an assumption that the challenge is more one of finding some common ground between the librarians and the council. Emily's primary interest lies in achieving a result that is satisfactory for the two other parties, without becoming trapped in the middle of a battle between them. She acknowledges that she feels, or has felt, dispirited, disempowered, and vulnerable. However, she does bring particular insights to the problem. Because of her role, and her efforts to practice learning-leadership, she is increasingly able to take a high-level view and thus see the interactions between the parties, including herself, in a larger context.

The second level of interpretation of the Matrix considers the interplay, the dynamic interaction, between the various stakeholder viewpoints.[3] If we look at the overall Matrix in the library change case, what emerges is an apparently mutually reinforcing pattern. Leaving Emily out of the picture for the moment, the major stakeholders—the librarians and the council—can be seen as making negative attributions toward each other. The librarians apparently regard the council as insensitive to their experience, needs, and concerns. The council appears to see the librarians as resistant to change and focused on their own interests. Each party is caught up in a self-referential process in which the other is viewed in unflattering terms; they are not testing their attributions, but acting as if the attributions were true. I use the term "attribution dynamic" to describe this pattern. The pattern resembles two gears in an engine that do not connect; they just keep spinning independently.

We shall return to Emily's situation shortly; but first, a more general comment on attribution dynamics and the Reflection Matrix tool. Attribution theory in psychology tells us that, when things are going well, people and groups tend to see themselves as responsible for the result. When things are not going so well, they tend to apportion responsibility elsewhere. The latter is generally the prevailing situation where contentious problems arise. It follows that we are most likely to use the Reflection Matrix in situations of inter-group (or inter-personal) conflict, since we are generally using the tool to better understand a messy problem rather than a success story. So, it is no surprise when we find patterns that point to stakeholders' holding unfavorable views of each other. What is of interest, though, is the specific form that such patterns take. If we have taken sufficient care in preparing the Matrix, we should be able to step beyond generalized perceptions to gauge more precisely where the concerns lie.

Our reflective analysis suggests that, while the concerns of the librarians and the council are different, they are not directly opposed in all respects. The librarians' concerns appear to center on the role and contribution of the local individual library, and their role in running that library, as well as on process aspects such as a lack of consultation. The council's focus appears to be more on the structure and performance of the overall library system, coupled with frustrations regarding the perceived resistance of the librarians. Emily's manager has indicated there might be room for negotiation as to the precise form the desired integration takes. The implication is it might be possible to build a bridge between the two groups—if the librarians can be encouraged to adopt more of a system-wide view, and if the council can be similarly assisted to pay more attention to the local perspective.

Such bridge-building calls for leadership-mode interventions, with Emily applying the range of ARIES practices. As she consciously designs her interventions, Emily knows she can potentially switch tack and intervene in the management mode whenever appropriate. As the process unfolds, certain tasks might call for a more conventional approach. An example might be when she sets about preparing and gaining approval of a change management plan based on the agreements made by all parties as to the strategy for achieving library integration.[4]

Insofar as she elects to act in the leadership mode, Emily needs to test the content of the Reflection Matrix with the respective stakeholders. She needs to check in with the librarians regarding the assumptions, interests, feelings, and knowledge she has attributed to them, and to do the same with the council management.

One way Emily can test her analysis is to inquire opportunistically. That is, she can take advantage of chance opportunities to ask the librarians or council management about particular items in the Matrix. For example, she might say to the librarians, "I'm wondering about something that relates to the proposed integration project. How important it is for you to maintain a level of independence in your individual libraries, such as you enjoy now?" Or she might ask the council management (perhaps via her own manager), "I presume you regard the librarians as having had sufficient opportunities to be involved in the change process. Does this preclude the possibility of creating more opportunities, if it looks like they would be valuable?" (Questioning processes are essential to learning-leadership, and they are covered in more depth in the next chapter, on the practice of inquiring. In particular, see the section on "testing questions.")

Alternatively, Emily might regard the analysis she has prepared as a draft for her own purposes, and as only one view of the puzzle. She might decide that it would be beneficial for each of the stakeholder groups to develop their own versions of the Matrix.[5] She could then work with one or both of the groups—separately—taking them through the exercise. Say, for instance, that she decides to lead the librarians through the Matrix. She might begin by explaining that the process is intended to help those involved in a change process to develop a more differentiated appreciation of the perspectives of the various stakeholders. Using an outline of a Matrix (based on Figure 7.2) on a whiteboard or flipchart, Emily could then ask the librarians about the assumptions, interests, feelings, and knowledge they would attribute, firstly, to the council management and, secondly, to themselves.[6] Of course, she would need to emphasize the reasonableness principle. If Emily had previously done her own draft, she could then test any differences between her own analysis and that of the librarians, again using the inquiring processes described in the next chapter.

The potential benefit of using the Reflection Matrix with groups is that it helps the parties to stand apart from their own views. This helps them appreciate other realities. If people can see that their view of the problem reflects just one line of logic amongst others that are also reasonable, they may become more receptive to those other views. This process can help foster useful, reflective conversations about perceptions, particularly where stakeholders have been reluctant to explore what is underneath their own positions, or to engage productively with other views.

How might you use the Reflection Matrix tool in your own work? You might prefer to go through the exercise privately, preferably with a coach, using the process outlined earlier. The advantage of beginning in this way is that it is low risk, yet there is a good likelihood you will gain fresh insights. Once again, the critical point is to test your findings rather than taking them as "the truth."

When you are familiar and comfortable with using the tool, you might consider involving other stakeholders in the exercise, as described above.

Reflecting in, or Close to, the Action

Earlier, reflecting in the ARIES context was defined as making sense of stakeholder perspectives, including our own, on a contentious problem. The Reflection Matrix process is a relatively formal, structured way of making sense of those different perspectives. Often, however, the situation calls for a form of reflecting that is more spontaneous, more informal and unstructured. This form of reflecting is closer to the action. It can occur at the time action occurs—for instance, in contemplating what someone says during the course of a meeting and how their viewpoint seems to imply different assumptions to our own.[7] Reflecting can also occur after the event, as with thinking later that day or the next about what transpired.

As stated earlier, reflecting in the ARIES framework is the corollary of attending. Attending deals with noticing or perceiving what is occurring, including within us. Reflecting entails making sense of, or interpreting, what we notice. The two practices can almost fuse together. Being able to reflect implies the ability to attend.

Here we shall reconsider a segment of the library change case. In Emily's first meeting with the librarians, she gave a presentation about the proposed changes and the change process. However, during the presentation some of the librarians interjected. Emily felt frustrated and, in her closing remarks, said to the librarians, "Don't be so negative. This will turn out to be good for you all."

Let us imagine that Emily has some ability to reflect at the time of that session and afterwards. What behaviors might we expect to see?

First, Emily is practicing attending, so during the meeting she becomes increasingly aware of her own mounting frustration and the accompanying self-talk. She notices that she has been labeling the librarians as resistant and self-interested. And she recognizes that in doing so, she has moved from simply observing—noticing that the librarians are interjecting, and that their voices are raised—to inference.

Now, the reflecting component of learning-leadership asks Emily to contemplate what factors might be driving that which she observes—with respect to both the librarians' behavior and her own actions and thought processes. Emily's reflecting is likely to be most productive to the extent that she can apply the guidelines from Chapter 5 regarding working from observation, attributing reasonableness, and seeking to act authentically.

Questions such as those featured in the Reflection Matrix process might be useful to Emily here, as informal prompts to aid her thinking: What assumptions might the librarians be making? What assumptions is Emily herself making? What interests are important to the librarians? What interests does Emily seek to protect? What might the librarians be feeling? What is Emily feeling herself? What knowledge or experience might the librarians not be stating? What knowledge and experience is Emily herself unaware of or holding back?

Reflecting when close to the action has an individual aspect and a collective, or social, aspect. The individual aspect is in evidence when we quietly mull over events and ask ourselves what might account for what is unfolding. As always, we need to keep in mind that the actions of the various stakeholders are reasonable to them.

Obviously, a high quality of reflecting is difficult to achieve in real time, given how quickly conversations often move. On occasions, though, opportunities present themselves. There might be a break in the discussion. Perhaps a new topic is introduced that you are personally not as involved in, enabling you to "pull back" for a few minutes to think and perhaps make a brief note. Or, your individual reflecting might take place some time after the event.

Reflecting takes on a more social complexion when we declare our interpretations and invite others to respond, or when we invite others to tell us what they perceive regarding a problem and how they account for those perceptions. In the library change case, Emily would invoke the collective aspect of reflecting by giving voice to her interpretations and seeking to test those with the librarians. Collective reflection is vitally important to learning-leadership, with its accent on developing shared meaning. In the ARIES context, individual reflecting is necessary, but alone it is insufficient.

We can assist—or possibly hinder—reflection by individuals and groups through the choices we make about how we interact with them. We can state our own interpretations definitively, dogmatically, or we can state them in ways that invite inquiry. In seeking to examine others' views, we can presume that their analysis is flawed, and seek to expose those flaws through our questioning. Or, we can query others with a view to mutual learning; we can ask them to tell us about their framing of a problem and about what leads them to see the problem in the way they describe. This is the skill of inquiring, the subject of the next chapter.

Chapter Summary

This chapter explored the ARIES practice of reflecting, which involves making sense of observations and experience. A tool, the Reflection Matrix, was introduced as an aid in appreciating and analyzing the various perspectives bearing on a contentious problem by looking at four facets of the implicit domain. The tool, illustrated with reference to the library change case from Chapter 6, involves asking what hidden assumptions, interests, feelings, and knowledge seem to be implied by the actions of the various stakeholders. The Matrix exercise can be conducted as a private reflection, preferably with the assistance of a coach or skilled colleague. It can also be conducted "live," in a group setting, to assist a stakeholder group in better comprehending the differing perspectives that make the issue contentious.

The preparation of a Reflection Matrix helps us develop a testable account of what appears to be going on for individual stakeholders, as well as a picture of the interplay or dynamic between the stakeholders. This reflective process can help circumvent superficial analyses or knee-jerk reactions, such as attributing the problems to one group. We also looked at how the kinds of assessment undertaken in the Reflection Matrix process can be incorporated into more informal forms of reflecting.

Questions for Reflection

7.1 When considering a contentious problem, to what extent do you tend to recognize, and reflect on, the assumptions implicit in your particular interpretation?

7.2 Think of a contentious problem that is important to you currently, or that recently has been. List one assumption, one interest, one feeling, and one piece of knowledge that you are aware of holding in relation to this problem, but that you have not declared to the others involved.

7.3 How might you apply the Reflection Matrix to a problem in your own organization? Would it be best to do this privately or publicly? If you were to use the Matrix in a more public forum, what risks and considerations would you need to be alert to?

Chapter
EIGHT

....

Inquiring

" It troubles me. This battle has been going on for several months now. It's like a low-level war is taking place. What really gets to me, though, is the effect it's having on the other people. They are progressively becoming aligned with one or other of the warring duo, and the group environment is slowly becoming poisonous."

Helena, a middle manager, is describing to Brian, the newly appointed executive she reports to, the difficulty she is experiencing with a rift between two of her team leaders. (Brian had observed tensions between them at a get-to-know-you meeting with Helena and her group.) In this chapter, we utilize Helena and Brian's conversation and other examples to examine and illustrate inquiring in the leadership mode.

Building on the leadership-mode definition from Chapter 2, inquiring means asking questions in a *relational manner* with the intention of building shared meaning in order to effect deep-reaching change. Good questions—particularly those that stretch people's thinking—have great power. That power lies in the possibility of moving the way people conceive of issues. Not only does that movement release energy for change, it often also reveals new pathways for action.

Inquiring is core to each of the learning-centered leadership processes of exploring current realities, clarifying preferred futures, and harnessing energy for change. Well-crafted and timely questions can shed light, for the parties in a conversation, on how each frames the issues currently. Such questions often contribute to the reframing of problems, thereby opening up new opportunities for action. Inquiring can also help us find common purpose and shared vision. Through asking good questions, and listening appreciatively, we can come to know what others aspire to for the future. Inquiring also helps us dig down into the implicit or veiled territory of assumptions, interests, feelings, and knowledge. Uncovering hidden mental resources often generates new ways of conceiving of a topic. Thus, a good question can be a powerful catalyst for releasing energy for change.

But what makes for effective inquiring? As with the other ARIES practices, inquiring is not a matter of mechanically following a series of steps or applying straightforward techniques. Nonetheless, an element of structure can make it easier to get started and develop your practice. In this context, we consider a framework of five question types: Checking, Gathering & Clarifying, Exploring, Testing, and Futuring. The intention behind the framework is to help you in making considered choices about the best type of question to ask in a particular instance. We also review some ideas—about preparing and fostering safety, in particular—to help you improve your practice of inquiring.

As potent as inquiring can be, it remains a largely undeveloped practice. Partly, this is because performing it well requires discipline, skill, time, and continued application. Some people experience inquiring as almost counter-intuitive. It can seem to go against the grain, to be at odds with what they see as "natural" tendencies to look for an answer or solve the problem. But perhaps the perception of inquiring as being out of the ordinary is more a reflection of the social and cultural biases that reinforce the importance of tasks, outcomes, and "things." As discussed in chapters 4 and 5, these biases favor management-oriented action over leadership. The pattern continues when it comes to the use of questions: inquiring in the leadership mode tends to be largely neglected compared to what we might term result-oriented questioning.

Result-Oriented Questioning: A Common Default

Let us see, in the context of the story with Helena and Brian, how a result-oriented questioning process might unfold. First, Brian makes some initial observations about conflict in her group. After Helena responds—including with her "low-level war" reference—Brian follows up with a series of questions:

Brian	"Have you tried talking with the team leaders about their conflict?"
Helena	"Yes, I've spoken with each of them individually. Each blamed the other for being uncooperative and neither was willing to take any responsibility. This is typical of them. I think it's really a matter of a personality clash; maybe these two people just shouldn't be in the same place at the same time."
Brian	"What about bringing in a third party to mediate?"
Helena	"We had a session with an outside mediator but one of the team leaders objected to the mediator's style. It didn't go any further. I always seem to hit a wall in dealing with this issue. It's really discouraging."
Brian	"How about shifting one of the team leaders to another area?"
Helena	"I would rather not do that if I could avoid it. They both have a lot of specialized expertise that would be hard to replace. I would prefer to hang on to them both if possible."

As the name implies, result-oriented questioning is directed toward arriving at a solution to a problem. As this exchange exemplifies, the person asking the questions typically has identified in their own mind possible solutions or remedial actions for addressing the problem. Then, they use questioning to progressively work through these prospective solutions. One workshop participant described the application of result-oriented questioning as resembling the "grid search" undertaken when a boat is reported missing at sea. The search authorities map a grid encompassing possible locations for the vessel and progressively hunt through the sections of the grid.

We can see this approach in Brian's questioning of Helena.

Each of Brian's questions seeks Helena's response to his ideas. In a manner similar to grid search, Brian appears to be identifying potential "locations" for the answer in his mind, i.e., that Helena needs to talk with the people concerned, engage the services of a mediator, or shift one of the team leaders. Then, he "searches" them via questions to see if they hold "the answer." When one does not, he moves on to another possible "location." Though Brian does not state this directly, an implication is that he is seeking to analyze the problem and come up with a solution for Helena. It appears he assumes that the problem is largely a technical one, meaning there is a correct answer and, if his questions cover the various possibilities, a solution should present itself.

We do not know Brian's intent, or how Helena feels about the questions. Yet, the way they are framed—with Brian seeking Helena's response to his ideas—suggests that he sees himself in the intellectual driver's seat in this conversation.

While result-oriented questioning can often meet the perceived needs of the person asking the questions, it can be a frustrating experience for the person on the receiving end. Helena may well have already thought about the various ideas that Brian is putting to her. If so, she could be expending energy responding to his questions without gaining much benefit. Brian's questioning would likely be of more value to Helena if it expanded her thinking, or opened up new areas for consideration.

When dealing with technical problems, result-oriented questioning is necessary and useful. We go astray, however, when we unthinkingly apply this method to a contentious problem. Result-oriented questioning practices tend to short-circuit the joint sense-making that such problems require.

With its focus on explicit and task aspects, result-oriented questioning is an intervention in the management mode, particularly when applied in the context of an authority relationship, such as Brian occupies as Helena's manager. That said, result-oriented questioning can be a useful complement to leadership-mode-oriented inquiry processes. For instance, once a grounded appreciation of the underlying problem has been achieved, result-oriented questioning can help clarify specific action strategies. Care is needed, though, in order to avoid enacting result-oriented questioning while believing that you are functioning in the leadership mode.

Establishing inquiring as part of your learning-leadership repertoire requires that you recognize how easy it is to slip into result-oriented questioning and that you make conscious choices about the types of questions you ask, particularly when you are dealing with contentious problems.

Inquiring in the Leadership Mode

Whereas result-oriented questioning is geared to finding a specific solution, leadership-mode inquiring is oriented more towards enabling learning in relation to a contentious problem. Inquiring can serve many purposes, such as helping another person think through a problem at deeper levels, helping a group make joint sense of a problem, or learning more yourself about different ways of conceiving of a problem.[1]

Inquiring was described earlier as asking questions in a *relational manner* with the intention of building shared meaning in order to effect deep-reaching change. As we said, the potential power of the process—when enacted well and in conjunction with the application of the other ARIES practices—lies in the possibility of bringing about movement in the way people conceive of issues. And that movement often reveals new pathways for action.

Consider this example: a group of executives from different Australian schools were discussing a plan by one of them to establish a separate middle school structure within his school. The executive described the intended structure, covering school years five to eight, and outlined some of the issues he faced, including physical space limitations and reluctance by some of the teachers in the senior school to teach in the proposed middle school, apparently fearing that this might compromise their career prospects. Then one of the group members asked a question that led the executive to reformulate his problem: "Tell me more about what leads you to see the problem as one as establishing a suitable middle school *structure?*"

This question, and the conversation ensuing, enabled the executive to discover that his problem was not primarily one of structure at all; it was more about establishing what the group members referred to as an "appropriate stage-specific pedagogy" which—for those of us who are not trained teachers—essentially denotes a teaching and learning framework and environment that supports the needs of students at different stages of their schooling. That realization, in turn, prompted him to explore strategies that placed more emphasis on the processes rather than structure, including teaching practices designed to meet student needs at different stages.

As the example might suggest, good inquiring can sometimes appear to be a matter of just asking the right question for a particular moment. There is more to it, of course, as implied in our discussions of threat and defensiveness. The story of Helena's and Brian's conversation indicates the ease with which one can slip into a management-mode style when it may not be called for.

Once again, intention is critical. It is vital to think clearly about what you are trying to achieve—immediately, and in the longer term—as well as about how you regard those with whom you are working. Before you begin the process of posing questions to others, it may be helpful to ask yourself some questions, such as the following: To what extent *in this particular instance* do I genuinely hold an intention to work alongside this person, to discover more about their world and their perceptions of the current issue? How well am I able, at this time, to set aside whatever beliefs I may hold about the people I'm working with and the particular topic they're addressing? Can I adopt an attitude of openness and curiosity toward whatever they might tell me? To what degree am I able to treat the views they express as reasonable to hold, even when I might personally disagree?

The relational aspect of inquiring is pivotal. Working relationally also implies a need to pay attention to the role you are taking in a particular intervention. Are you putting yourself in the "intellectual driver's seat," as Brian did? In the Brian and Helena case story, we saw Brian—Helena's manager—effectively just launch into a series of questions regarding whether Helena had talked with the team leaders and so on. If you wish to intervene more from a learning-centered leadership standpoint, then consider indicating your intention in a suitable way and inviting reactions, particularly if you have formal authority over the others involved. For example, Brian might have said something to Helena like: "I'm wondering how I can best help. Perhaps I could ask you some questions to help tease out the underlying issues? Tell me what would best help you."

Even when your intention is primarily to help someone else reflect more deeply on a problem, the concept of working relationally (from Chapter 3) implies the need to remain open to learning yourself. For instance, if Brian is amenable to learning himself at the time he questions Helena about the team leader conflict, he may discover something that will contribute to his own leadership and management effectiveness. Relational working does not require you to suppress your own needs and concerns when asking questions; rather, it asks you to be attuned primarily to what is occurring in that moment, and to frame your questions accordingly.

From the discussion of mindful working in Chapter 3, attentiveness to your use of language is critically important to the way others experience your questioning. For example, simply asking "why" a person holds a particular belief may be interpreted as a demand that the person justify their actions. This can be threatening. Asking someone to share more of their thinking with you—or to help you understand more about their thinking—is less likely to put that person on the defensive.

This is not a case of "sanitizing" your speech or playing manipulative games, but rather of seeking to build safety for all parties in the conversation.

Tone of speech is as important as the actual words used. Consider, for example, the following question: "What do you regard as the key factors that contributed to the delay in the project?" Depending on the inquirer's tone and purpose, the question might be interpreted as either seeking to apportion blame for delays or as genuinely aiming to uncover, in a low-threat manner, ideas as to how further delays might be averted. It is critical to place yourself in the position of the person being asked the questions and to anticipate how they might experience the question, even as you are thinking about the wording of the question. Obviously, this is not easy to do, but this is what inquiring requires, and it can be done.

The Chapter 3 discussion of mindful working also emphasized the importance of process, including the processes unfolding in the moment. A process perspective requires paying attention to the manner of your questioning as well as to question content. In particular, fostering learning for ourselves and others implies that we pay close attention to the other, to listen for the deeper meanings in their responses, and then to ask questions which extend, deepen, and—sometimes—challenge those responses.

In the Helena and Brian story, Helena commented that she thought the problem between the two team leaders came down to "a personality clash" between "two people who shouldn't be in the same place at the same time." Brian followed up by asking about the possibility of bringing in a third party to mediate. This might seem like a reasonable question; yet, if Brian had been more attentive to the process dimension, he might have sought to explore what Helena said. Her statement about the personality clash suggests she is assuming this is the cause of the problem. Brian might seek to deepen the analysis here, perhaps by asking Helena what leads her to the think that the problem is one of a personality conflict. The challenge is to stay in the learning process by asking questions that are in touch with what the other is expressing at that point, as distinct from imposing whatever is on your mind at the time.

Inquiring for Learning: a Framework of Question Types

As we all know, contentious problems often present as a big "mess" (perhaps like the forest where the Wollemi Pine was discovered). They are likely to remain in this state unless one or more people exercise leadership to help the group (or individual) find their way out of the forest. Finding the way requires having faith—in the innate, not-yet-evident, latent intelligence of the group as well as in the emergent nature both of solutions and of energy for change. Being able to hold open the possibility of insight and some coherence of thought and action coming out of the apparent messiness is critical; so is being willing to probe, in the belief that there is more beneath the surface. Through the use of well-chosen questions, the process of inquiring helps elicit the wisdom and the "oomph" needed to move towards clarity of direction and a sense of progress.

While there is no set formula for effective inquiring, this book offers a framework of question types as a "structural support" for inquiring with contentious problems.

The framework comprises five question types, each serving a particular function. *Checking questions* are to make sure that we are interpreting people correctly. *Gathering and clarifying questions* enable us to add to our understanding with extra information and to clarify meanings. *Exploring questions* help us reach down into the implicit domain to gain insights into others' assumptions, interests, feelings, and knowledge. *Testing questions* let us investigate the reactions of others to propositions and information that we put to them. *Futuring questions* are for clarifying what the future might bring in relation to this topic, both in terms of what we *want* to happen and what *could* happen.

FIGURE 8.1 Inquiring Framework: Five Types of Question

Checking	Verifying your understanding of what is being communicated
Gathering & Clarifying	Seeking more information to expand or flesh out understanding and/or to clarify intended meanings
Exploring	Delving into underlying thoughts, feelings, beliefs, interests, and assumptions
Testing	Scrutinizing claims that others make by putting forward new information or observations and seeking their response; examining the inferences we draw from others' words and actions
Futuring	Seeking to clarify what the future might hold in relation to the topic of inquiry.

Like the other frameworks in this book, the question types do not represent hard and fast categories. Some questions do not readily slot in. Examples include rhetorical questions—"You don't like to eat, do you?" when asked of a person taking a second helping of food, and requests—"Could you please copy this report to marketing?" Other questions will cut across two or more categories rather than fitting neatly into one.

Checking Questions

By definition, there is always more than one interpretation of a contentious problem. You may be confident that you understand what others who have an interest in the problem are communicating to you, but can you be sure? Checking questions enable you to find out how well your interpretation reflects what the person communicating had in mind. Such questions are particularly useful in group conversations when a variety of people weigh in on an issue in a short time. To make sure that valuable information is not lost, it can be useful to check with the other(s) to make sure the group as a whole grasps the essentials of their argument or concern.

Questions of this type involve a statement of what you think the other party intends to convey, and a request for confirmation or correction. From the case at the beginning of this chapter, Brian could ask Helena something like:

"I understand that you're troubled by a long-running conflict involving two of the people that report to you, and that you're particularly concerned about the effect the conflict is having on others. Am I hearing you correctly?"

Checking questions help us guard against the possibility of misconstruing the speaker's intent. Such misconception should be considered at least reasonably likely, given the unique frame of reference we each apply in making sense of our interactions with others. Checking questions also encourage attentive listening. It is difficult to confirm your interpretation if you have not really been paying attention. (Let me emphasize that checking here is about confirming understandings, not about testing inferences or challenging what others say. Those functions fall under "testing" questions, later.)

This next example is based on the case story in Chapter 2, in which Bernardo sought to focus more of his executive colleagues' attention on innovation. One of his colleagues might check along the following lines:

"Bernardo, I understand that your main concern is about what you see as the split between what we say we're on about, with respect to the organization's stated value of supporting innovation, and what employees think is the reality, as expressed through the survey results. Is this correct?"

Asking checking questions is especially important when others are sharing a great deal of what is on their mind. Often, people will circle around a subject rather than getting to the crux of the matter, and it can be difficult to discern what really matters to them. Sometimes it may help to ask the speaker to pause briefly, at the risk of interrupting their train of thought, while you recount to them the essence of what you are hearing, and seek their reaction.

As important as checking questions are, they are rarely asked. We may want to avoid the possibility of appearing silly or inattentive, and not having understood correctly. We may assume that we have discerned the speaker's intent and message accurately. Or, we might have been so preoccupied with what *we* want to communicate ourselves that we have not taken the trouble to listen carefully.

Making a practice of asking checking questions is a useful strategy for strengthening one's proficiency in the leadership mode. Such questions help to establish a receptive stance towards others and an open frame of mind.

While checking questions are used relatively rarely in my experience, questions in the next group tend to be over-worked, at least from a learning-leadership standpoint.

Gathering and Clarifying Questions

In learning-centered leadership work, gathering and clarifying questions are asked in order to help prepare the ground for moving the understanding of the problem to deeper levels.

Earlier in the chapter we introduced the idea of result-oriented questioning, which is more in keeping with management-mode interventions. Gathering and clarifying questions are actually a mainstay of result-oriented questioning, as the responses can provide much of the data through which potential solutions are identified.

That said, gathering and clarifying questions can also support learning-leadership. Gathering questions can help establish a mutual sense of what is going on, and clarifying questions can help elucidate others' meanings, such as what they intended by particular words or phrases. The purpose of these questions, however, is not for the questioner to gather enough information or clarity to solve the problem him- or herself. Rather, the purpose is to spark learning about the situation such that something new emerges. When rendered skilfully, these types of questions often lead to insight—including by alerting us to previously unexplored aspects of the implicit domain.

From a leadership-mode stance, then, the main problem with using gathering and clarifying questions is the tendency to ask *too many* of them. This is a sign that we have likely fallen back into result-orientated questioning, which is the default for many of us. Frequently, practitioners are surprised to find they have reverted to trying to solve the other's problem. "But that's what I'm used to doing," is a common response.

With these cautions in mind, let us return to the case of Helena and Brian. If Brian is seeking to use learning-leadership processes to help Helena to think through the issues in the team leader conflict, he does not need to acquire large amounts of information about the problem. He simply needs enough background in order to pose questions that help Helena reflect on the problem's underlying dimensions.

Examples of gathering questions he might ask include:

- Where does the conflict happen; in what kinds of circumstances is it played out?

- What does the conflict "look like"; how do the two protagonists behave towards each other?

- Can you tell me more about the impacts on you and other members of your group?

Helena likened the rift between the two team leaders to a "low-level war." Clarifying questions could lead to a new insight about how to respond. Brian might ask, "Can you tell me what you mean by a 'low-level war'?" Or, "What kinds of behaviors are occurring that prompt you to regard the clash between these people as resembling a low-level war?"

In other cases, we ask clarifying questions to probe generalized statements, to make them more specific. Again, we do so to stimulate insight. Consider this example, again involving Brian and Helena:

"Meetings involving the two team leaders are always unproductive," says Helena.

"In what ways are the meetings unproductive?" asks Brian.

"They just keep attacking each other."

"Can you give me some examples of how they do that?" inquires Brian. He adds, "Are there exceptions, any productive interactions between them?"

There are no prescriptions as to what sorts of gathering and clarifying questions one should ask. The key is to ask as few such questions as necessary, consistent with establishing a basic understanding of the problem, its circumstances, and impact. (You can always ask more such questions later if needed.) If you find yourself asking many questions of this type at any point, you may have unwittingly wandered into the management mode. If you think this may be the case, ask yourself: What objective am I seeking to serve through my questions?

Exploring Questions

Exploring questions "delve down" into perceptions of reality, seeking to draw out more of others' deeper thoughts, feelings, and experiences relevant to the topic at hand.

A gardening image can help in differentiating exploring questions from those of the gathering and clarifying variety. The latter effectively involve "dragging in" information laterally to a central point; they are akin to raking leaves. Exploring questions are more like digging the garden. These questions enable learning about the contents of other people's implicit or unspoken domain—and perhaps your own as well.

An exploring question is an invitation to others to share with us more about what they see, and about what leads them to see things as they do. The concept of exploring questions reflects an assumption—building on the iceberg concept and the idea of the hidden domain from Chapter 2—that most people have much more to contribute than they are inclined to volunteer. That silence, or—at the very least—a tendency to hold back, is a default condition in many workplaces.

In Chapter 7, in the context of discussing the Reflection Matrix, we considered the implicit domain as having four hidden dimensions: assumptions, interests, feelings, and knowledge. Exploring questions can be framed to inquire into any of these dimensions, as the examples in Figure 8.2 suggest. (The examples are based on the case involving Helena, Brian and the team leader conflict.)

FIGURE 8.2 Examples of Exploring Questions, for Brian and Helena Case

AREA OF HIDDEN DOMAIN	ILLUSTRATIVE QUESTIONS (Brian inquiring of Helena)
Assumptions	"You say the problem between the team leaders comes down to a 'personality clash.' Can you explain to me what leads you to focus on a personality clash as the key factor, rather than something else?"
Interests	"What matters most to you in dealing with the difficulties between the team leaders? What is especially important to protect?"
Feelings	"You mentioned that the conflict between the two team leaders 'troubles you.' Please tell me more about how the dispute is affecting you?"
Knowledge	"Is there some other factor, in your experience, other than what you have mentioned so far, that might help account for the tensions between the team leaders?"

Whenever we ask exploring questions (indeed, whenever we intervene in the leadership mode), we need to be alert for any signals or clues—perhaps subtle or indistinct—that may indicate hidden assumptions, unquestioned beliefs, unexpressed feelings, or tacit knowledge that is not being brought to bear on the issue. Remember, the things that are hidden or undiscussed are often the greatest resources.

We noted in the previous section that gathering and clarifying questions are the mainstay of result-oriented questioning. Exploring questions fulfill an equivalent function for leadership-mode inquiring. These are the principal vehicle for inquiring into what is otherwise unspoken. Such questions are potentially extremely powerful in helping achieve breakthroughs on contentious problems. A well-framed exploring question can encourage a "rattling" of a person's (or group's) assumptions, as they grapple with the question's implications. A degree of shaking up of assumptions is to be expected if learning of a deep order is to occur.[2] Moreover, those asking the questions can find their own taken-for-granted views are being challenged, just as can those being asked.

While exploring questions are critical for leadership-mode work, they tend to be infrequently asked. This is perhaps not surprising. Such questions, especially if not carefully framed, can generate high levels of threat, both for those inquiring and those being inquired of.

The person asking might worry about embarrassing others if, for instance, her questions lead to new revelations about the problem. Another concern is that of appearing disrespectful, particularly in asking a person of high status or recognized expertise to make explicit the thinking behind something they have done or said. There might be a fear about appearing too clever, smart, or ambitious. On the other hand, people being asked can worry that they are being called to account for their views, that flaws in their thinking might be exposed, or that they might be pressured to disclose something they are uncomfortable with revealing.

A challenge, then, is to learn how to ask such questions to enable learning by all involved, while at the same time minimizing the risks of adverse reactions. Later in the chapter we shall consider some ideas for effective and safe use of exploring questions, as well as of other question types.

Testing Questions

It can be tempting to take shortcuts in our thinking with contentious problems. For example, we sometimes conclude that others are "wrong," that they have misunderstood the issue, or they are uninformed. The difficulty is that we often come to these conclusions because of avoidance of threat, anxiety, time pressures, or other factors; we settle on these views without testing them.

Testing questions have essentially two functions in learning-leadership. First, they enable us to scrutinize claims that others make, by putting fresh information or observations to them and seeking their response. Second, these questions allow us to examine the inferences that we draw from others' words and actions. In serving both of these functions, testing questions help raise the collective intelligence that can be brought to bear on a contentious problem.

A testing question invites us to hold open the possibility that what may appear to us as an error of judgment or misinterpretation by others is instead a matter of their seeing things that we cannot, or their having access to information that we do not. We need to allow that the problem could be more ours than theirs. For example, an executive in your organization speaks about morale being positive when, to you, the indicators suggest widespread employee dissatisfaction. It might appear that the executive is captive to particular assumptions or deluding herself in sticking with a version of the truth that feels comfortable, no matter what the evidence says. The discipline of using a testing question requires that you put to one side this negative attribution and keep open the possibility that there is more to the matter than you are aware of.

A question to the executive on the morale matter could take the following form:

"I hear you say that morale here is positive. Yet turnover over the past twelve months has been high, at twenty five percent, and the recent employee survey showed a drop on the satisfaction index of ten percent. Do you have other information that leads you to see morale as positive?"

The next example comes from the library change case in Chapters 6 and 7. Emily, the project manager, has heard her manager criticize the librarians for resisting change. Yet she has also heard the librarians expressing frustrations of their own regarding the change process. One testing question Emily could ask her manager is:

"You say the librarians 'like things the way they are,' but they are saying to me things like 'the council has been trying to bludgeon us into toeing their line for three years.' How do you reconcile this difference in perceptions?"

Journalists, for example, often use testing questions when interviewing politicians—though not necessarily with the same stance towards learning encouraged here. For instance, a politician being interviewed about the likely outcome of a forthcoming election says, "We're in a strong position to win." The interviewer asks, "How do you account for the latest poll results, published this morning, which show the other party is now favored by sixty percent of electors?"

We make inferences or interpretations based on what others have communicated. Here, the problem is that we might settle on one meaning when others are possible. Testing questions can help us examine the validity of those inferences and interpretations.

In the library change case, for example, Emily was troubled that her manager did not attend either of two meetings with the librarians. Emily concluded that he was not interested in being involved in the project, which presented a difficulty for her as she believed she needed support from higher-level management.

To test that assumption, Emily might ask:

"When you declined to attend the two meetings with the librarians, you said in different ways that you had faith in me to drive this project through. Should I infer that you expect me to handle this project fully by myself—without active involvement from you or other senior management group members?"

The next example comes from the case of Helena and Brian and the team leader conflict (this chapter). In listening to Helena's description of the conflict between the team leaders, Brian might read into Helena's words that she is experiencing a level of stress in relation to this problem. A question to test this inference could be:

"I've heard you describe this problem as extending over several months, and with the team environment 'slowly becoming poisonous.' I imagine you must be experiencing quite a bit of stress in dealing with the problem. Is that so?"

As with other aspects of inquiring in the leadership mode, the key is to maintain a learning stance in concert with paying attention to the guidelines (observation, reasonableness, authenticity). A question like Brian's can enable learning to the extent is that it is posed to help reveal another factor for consideration, rather than to entrap or outpoint the other person. Thus, it is critically important to remain open to the possibility that there are other valid interpretations besides your own.

Testing questions can be especially confronting because they commonly convey an implication that something is "not quite right." Others may interpret your asking such questions as an attack, no matter what your actual intentions. Accordingly, testing questions should be used sparingly.

Futuring Questions

As the name suggests, these are questions that stimulate people to think creatively and constructively about the future: about their *preferred* futures (what they would like to see happen and bring about); about *possible* futures (what might actually happen, including unintended consequences); and about ways of acting to increase the prospects of the preferred future being realized.

Sometimes, asking a person (or group) about their aspirations early in a conversation can foster imaginative thinking. This is particularly the case when people seem to be overwhelmed by a problem and at a loss as to how to approach it. In our story, Helena admits to being "troubled" by the team leader conflict, which has been going on for some months. To help her shift out of this mindset, and stimulate her creativity, Brian might ask her something like:

"Tell me, what outcome would you most like to see, say six months from now, from this conflict between your team leaders?"

As with all the other question-types, there are some cautions here as well. While asking questions about vision early on might prove fruitful, there is a danger in focusing on action strategies before the underlying issues are clarified. Failure to truly engage with the deeper problem can lead to further problems. Let us say that Brian asks Helena what strategies she has in mind, and that Helena replies that she intends to discontinue the regular team leader meeting, and meet with the members individually instead. Shortly after initiating the individual meetings, however, she finds the two team leaders are now rallying their respective team members against the other team. In short, the problem has not gone away, but "morphed" into another form. The lesson is that focusing on solutions, strategies, and actions has its place, but clarity about the problem is still essential.

FIGURE 8.3 Examples of Futuring Questions

| Preferred futures | What would be a good result for you? |
| | What would you like to see happen? |

Possible futures	What do you think could happen that you might not expect?
	In what ways might things turn out differently from what you intend?
Ways of bringing about preferred futures	What do you see as the options you have?
	Which strategy do you think would result in the best outcomes?
	What might be a good place to start?

Improving Your Proficiency in Inquiring

Preparation

When you face a potentially difficult conversation, consider taking a little time beforehand to consider some good questions you might ask. Possibly begin by asking some questions of yourself, to help clarify your own thinking. Suggested questions include: What is my purpose in this conversation? What do I really want to learn here? What aspects do I need more information or clarification on? What deeper topics need to be opened-up? What propositions might I usefully test? Which topics might provoke intense reactions? Insofar as I need to explore these topics, how can I do so while minimizing the likelihood of aggressive responses (whether overt, in the sense of attacks or covert, in the sense of withdrawal or shutting down)?

In preparation for asking questions to foster learning and change, Juanita Brown and her colleagues in *The World Café* recommend writing down several questions with a colleague and then reviewing them, to see which ones are more compelling than others.[3] Brown suggests experimenting with a question's scope and construction, as well as reflecting on what assumptions are contained in it. She suggests noticing the impact of the questions that you hear, read, or introduce into your own conversations as a means of strengthening your proficiency in using questions well.

The question-type framework introduced in this chapter can also be used as an aid to preparation. This involves coming up with a list of proposed questions and then reviewing each of your questions to identify their question type. Do you have a mix of gathering and clarifying, exploring, and futuring questions, for example? The benefit of this exercise is that it will help you frame different *types* of questions thereby avoiding the risk of asking too many questions of the same type—particularly gathering and clarifying questions. This will assist you in avoiding the common bias toward result-oriented questioning.

One obvious caution is to avoid coming up with a pre-set list of questions and then attempting to work through them in a real conversation; this will seem mechanical at best. Any questions you identify in advance of an actual conversation should be thought of as no more than possibilities. You can ask (or adapt) these questions if they seem timely, but it is more important to maintain your attention in the present moment, and ask a question that seems apt at that point.

Asking a Good Question for the Moment

The practice of inquiring is inextricably related to that of attending, in that the suitability and power of your questions depends heavily on your capacity to pay close attention to, and "be with," the people with whom you are communicating. This requires listening closely and staying alert to what is occurring at that moment, rather than letting your mind race ahead, perhaps to anticipate answers and generate further questions or ideas.

A question appropriate to the moment connects in some way with what the speaker is communicating, rather than primarily suiting the needs of the questioner. Your question might encourage the speaker to extend or deepen their thinking. It might challenge something they have said. It might acknowledge what they have said and then jump to a new topic. Such a question also has regard to your own needs, but it does not place these above what is unfolding in the conversation.

While workshop participants nod sagely when I emphasize the need to stay with the speaker, most of them—when they actually practice inquiring—fall into a result-oriented questioning pattern. This will probably happen at some point in your own practice of inquiring, as it has in mine. The mindful practice of inquiring requires being conscious of both your *intended* and *actual* purpose in asking questions. It is when we lose this awareness that the default management mode tends to come into play, and we find ourselves practicing a grid-search style of questioning, asking mainly gathering and clarifying questions. If you become aware of doing so, you might reflect on which mode you are actually functioning in at the time, and look for opportunities to incorporate other types of questions: checking, exploring, testing, and futuring.

Maintaining Safety in Inquiring

Sometimes a question triggers an unexpected response: the person reacts in a hostile or angry manner or withdraws from the conversation. Say, for example, that when Brian asks Helena what leads her to see the team leader conflict as a personality clash, Helena seems to shut down; she is quiet for a minute or two. The challenge, if you are in Brian's position, is to avoid reacting defensively yourself, such as by saying something to fill the silence or changing the subject. You need to be able to step back from the interaction and pay attention to the unfolding process.

Our three guidelines from Chapter 5 can help in dealing with such difficult circumstances. "Work from observation" tells us to look for what is observable in the situation, what can be directly discerned. Brian has asked what led Helena to see the problem as a matter of personality conflict; Helena has gone quiet. The "attribute reasonableness" guideline reminds us to ask what might cause someone capable of reasonable behavior to act as we have observed. Perhaps Helena thinks Brian is overstepping the mark; that he is "wearing his manager hat," and making a judgment about her handling of the problem. "Seek to act authentically" prompts us to act from our truest and most honorable intentions. This enjoins us to avoid taking unprincipled or questionable shortcuts in an attempt to settle the problem. This would be the case if, for example, Brian had decided to speak directly with the team leaders without telling Helena.

On the other hand, if Brian were able to respond in a manner suggested by the three guidelines, he might describe to Helena, without judgment, what he observed about the situation, including his own question and her response. He might talk about what he did and did not intend, and acknowledge how Helena could have interpreted his question, which was as a judgment on her ability to handle the problem. He could then ask for her response to his assessment, conceivably with a question in a form such as the following: "This is what I have observed (describes), and this is how I have interpreted the interaction (describes). How does this fit with what you see?"

Of course, there is no guarantee that such an intervention by Brian will ameliorate Helena's concern, but it is a step in the right direction. The skillful application of the three guidelines can reduce the likelihood of your efforts at inquiring being undone by others' attempts to shield themselves from perceived affronts.

You can minimize the threat generated by your questions by providing some context for them. Specifically, you might anticipate how others—acting reasonably—might react to a question and openly declare the thoughts and feelings you have that seem relevant at the time. For instance, if you are hesitating to ask a particular question because you are worried about causing embarrassment (as the question might seem too personal or suggest fault on the other person's part), then you can give voice to that concern. State your concern as an introduction to your question. A key is to make the relevant contents of your own consciousness explicit and testable. Sharing some of what is in your mind—and what you think may be in the mind of the other person—indicates that you are making an effort to connect with their experience. The more you can do so, genuinely, the more others are likely to reveal what they would otherwise keep to themselves.

Inevitably, there will be times when your inquiring does strike a raw nerve and you will be unable to recover effectively. In these circumstances, you might find yourself moving into a more controlling mode; this is especially easy to do if you are under pressure. The challenge is not to give up or criticize yourself unduly. It is preferable to observe what happened and reflect, with a cool head, on how you may have contributed to the problem and on what you can learn from the experience to inform your next effort at inquiring. Thinking of every inquiring session as both a substantive intervention and a trial run for the next time is vital to building your effectiveness with this practice.

In this chapter we have considered the practice of inquiring in relative isolation from real conversation. Obviously, this is artificial. The intention is that, armed with this understanding, you will be able to incorporate inquiring into your exchanges with other people. Care is needed, though. If asking questions in the context of a conversation seems "natural," it may be that you are engaging in result-oriented questioning while believing that you are inquiring. Inquiring in the leadership-mode needs special attention if it is to become a well-utilized hallmark of learning-centered leadership.

Chapter Summary

With the aid of a case concerning a manager's handling of a conflict between two team leaders, the chapter differentiated inquiring in the leadership mode from result-oriented questioning, which is an expression of the management mode. Rather than being oriented towards finding a "solution," the purpose of inquiring is to enable learning in relation to a contentious problem in order to generate deeper insights and fresh understandings. Reflecting the relational nature of leadership-mode work, the person asking the questions also needs to be open to learning.

A typology of questions was presented to aid in the practice of inquiring: *Checking*—for confirming interpretations; *Gathering and Clarifying*—for seeking information and establishing meanings; *Exploring*—for drawing out deeper thoughts and feelings relevant to the matter at hand; *Testing*—for examining responses to information and inferences; and *Futuring*—for thinking about "where to from here."

We considered ideas to improve your practice of inquiring. These centered on the need for preparation; on paying close attention so that questions are timely and that they build on what the other person is communicating; and on utilizing the three guidelines from Chapter 5 (work from observation, attribute reasonableness, seek to act authentically) to minimize threat and maintain safety when asking questions.

Questions for Reflection

8.1   Recall a time when you were genuinely interested to learn from another person. How would you describe your stance towards them?

8.2   Think of an important issue where someone you know takes a different position to you. What might be an exploring question you could ask, to better inform your understanding of how that person sees the issue?

8.3   Which of the question types, in the framework presented, would you be most comfortable in using? How might you practice developing your comfort with some of the other types of questions?

Chapter
NINE

....

Expressing

"

They just don't get it. This board includes some very successful business people. They have a lot of experience. I have tried several times, using every way I can think of to present the numbers to the board, but most of them seem incapable of seeing the writing on the wall."

Michael, the treasurer and a director of a long-established metropolitan golf club, is telling his friend, Bill, a retired executive and now a business coach, about his frustrations in trying to get his fellow directors to appreciate the precariousness of the club's financial situation.

"Today I gave them the long-term projections. I told them about the consequences, just as I've told them many times before. I put it to them directly: the club will be out of business within two years unless we can turn our financial situation around. But the other directors aren't listening. They don't want to know."

Sometimes it seems people are unable, or unwilling, to see the obvious. They seem to be shutting down to what we recognize as real, perhaps because their assumptions are being challenged, their perceived interests threatened, their fears raised, or all three. It could be they do not understand the significance of what we say. Perhaps they disagree with our analysis, or do not respect our judgment. They might be preoccupied with other concerns. Most probably, they are viewing the problem through a different lens. It could also be that something in what we say, or the way we say it, contributes to our experience that the others "just don't get it." Perhaps the result is, at least partly, a product of our own actions.

Expressing in the ARIES framework refers to the practice of stating our views—and declaring the thoughts and feelings behind those views—in a relational manner. That is, we express when we give voice to our views in a way that indicates that we are connected to the problem (rather than standing apart from it), yet we are also open to other viewpoints. Expressing is directed towards seeking a more encompassing truth that is built from the contributions of multiple voices. For this reason, attention to process is as important as attention to content. To express effectively, we need to be simultaneously alert to how we frame and how we present whatever it is we wish to communicate to others. This is different from the type of communication that is commonly known as advocacy.

Conventionally, to advocate is to represent the interests of an individual or group, as when a lawyer pleads on behalf of her client in court, or when a youth worker makes appeals for improved recreational facilities to benefit young people. Advocating can also refer to speaking up for a cause, as in campaigning to reduce carbon emissions, or to improve public transportation. The conventional concept is that the advocate exerts influence on others in order to further a particular interest. The goal is to win, or at least gain a decent outcome.

In terms of our framework, to advocate is to intervene in the management mode. The explicit problem might be the "cause," such as improved public transportation, and the task component to persuade others. Authority often comes from the advocate's role as a representative of the interest group concerned. It appears that Michael, at the golf club, has also been acting in the management mode: the explicit problem being the financial plight of the club, and the task element being Michael's efforts to get his co-directors to "see the light." Michael's authority on the matter derives from his role of treasurer.

Advocating in the management mode implies seeking to have your views prevail over others. This behavior is common on many executive and professional teams. As one general manager put it, "We each argue our point of view and, at the end of the day, one argument prevails. That's okay, as we all have a win from time-to-time."

With contentious problems, however, a fundamental difficulty is that what may seem straightforward and relatively non-problematic to us, can be loaded with different meanings for other people. If we want to engage those other people in working on such problems, we need to recognize the inevitability of a variety of interpretations, and reflect this recognition in the way we put forward our own arguments.

Whereas advocacy is oriented towards "winning," expressing (in the ARIES framework) is directed towards seeking a more holistic truth, one in which your own views form one part of a composite picture. Obviously, seeking to influence and win others over has its place. Michael wants his fellow directors to recognize the financial warning bells that he hears. But the spirit of expressing—as with the other ARIES practices—is to be attentive to other ways of seeing. This spirit is at the core of the practice, not just of secondary importance.

The presentation in this chapter takes on a practical edge by providing a framework to assist you in speaking up on difficult issues in ways that model and promote learning. The framework, illustrated with reference to the golf club case story, is designed to help you prepare and express your views in situations that are both difficult and important, situations where you want others to appreciate more deeply what you think and feel, while remaining open to learning yourself.

The Practice of Expressing

Expressing involves putting forward one's thoughts and feelings in a relational manner so as to build shared meaning on a contentious problem, and contribute to creating a context where deep-reaching change can occur. The story of the Curve Ball ride in Chapter 3 illustrated the dangers of confusing our sense of reality with any absolute truth. When we assert, "We are right," we may be correct within the confines of a particular set of assumptions. But this truth does not preclude other constructions. Yet, commonly, we act as if those other truths did not exist.

In their book, *Difficult Conversations*, Douglas Stone, Bruce Patton, and Sheila Heen of the *Harvard Negotiation Project* make the case that "we typically begin inside our story. We describe the problem from our own perspective and, in doing so, trigger just the kinds of reactions that we hope to avoid."[1]

When Michael says the other board members "aren't listening," perhaps that is true—at one level. A question for Michael, though, concerns what he is missing. Are the other directors seeing something that he does not? Michael is speaking from inside his construction of the problem; he is objectifying his own view and discounting others. However, it could be that when Michael starts speaking about the club's financial problems, something about the content he presents—or the manner of his delivery—sets off a reaction amongst his colleagues, a reaction that Michael fails to recognize. Perhaps some of them think, "Here we go again," and stop paying attention. They might also think that Michael "isn't listening" to something they see. And their switching off could be prompting Michael to try even harder with his presentation.

Michael's challenge is to adopt a more encompassing standpoint, one that incorporates his own place as part of the system that he sees as problematic. Recalling the advice that Alice, in the Chapter 3 case, received from her coach, Juanita, Michael might benefit from stepping back to look at what an "invisible observer" might perceive.[2] From such a standpoint, Michael might be able to observe not only the "hard" data about the club's financial position, but also the reactions of the other directors when he presents his analysis and tries to get them to "see the writing on the wall."

The discussion of mindful working in Chapter 3 called our attention to the way we use language; this discussion is very pertinent to the practice of expressing. Enacting learning-leadership means that we reject generalizations in favor of more nuanced interpretations and steer clear of conveying certainty where different interpretations are possible. To follow these guidelines, we need to be discriminating in the way we use language to express ourselves. A practical way to work towards this is to practice communicating provisionally, non-dogmatically. The use of this kind of language is relational, and is essential to the practice of expressing.

Speaking provisionally, by using expressions such as "I find," "in my opinion," "what I notice," and "as I see it," demonstrates to others that you recognize that what you are saying is only one expression of reality: your reality. It also helps reinforce that concept in your own mind. (Of course, this assumes that you are using such qualifications genuinely, not just because you are trying to create the impression of openness.) In a similar vein, when we are making learning-leadership interventions we need to refrain from using language that indicates either judgment or certitude. Example statements would be: "They are wrong," or "This is definitely the best option."

Provisional language is not always viewed positively. Some people might mistakenly associate the practice of expressing with an insipid, watered-down type of speaking. Recall, as an illustration, the case in Chapter 5 in which Ivan attacked Maria, saying that she was using "fancy talk ... but it's really just word play. It's sanitized language." People who take this view see the use of provisional language as evidence of a failure to deal directly with what matters. On the contrary, however, the practice of a less judgmental form of speaking often makes it possible for more people to speak up about sensitive matters—making it more likely that the matter will be dealt with effectively. In this way, the practice of expressing enables the examination of contentious issues that might otherwise be stepped around or completely suppressed.

Others object to the idea of speaking relationally because they see it as hampering their ability to assert their beliefs strongly. "My beliefs are important to me," said one workshop participant. "I want to be able to state them clearly, forcefully, unambiguously." There is no argument here against holding or expressing one's *core beliefs* firmly. However, from a learning-centered leadership standpoint, it is important to differentiate your *views* on particular issues from *beliefs* that you hold as a matter of faith. This is a crucial distinction. If you confuse the two, you could be at risk of construing disagreement with your views on issues as an attack on your person. When this occurs, you are likely to respond defensively, possibly by attacking, thereby escalating any contention. You may resort to defending certain positions because you "believe" in them, rather than being open to inquiry into those positions. In sum, the learning-leadership stance allows us to express our core beliefs with strong conviction, but asks that we express our views in ways that convey they are provisional and open to inquiry. This is in recognition that there may be other valid views.

There is another aspect of mindful working, from Chapter 3, that is equally pertinent here: attention to process. When we pay mindful attention to process we are actively aware of how a conversation is unfolding; further, we tend to the nature, as well as the content, of our own contributions. We ask ourselves questions, such as: To what extent am I speaking up about matters that are deeply important to me? How successfully am I making explicit my assumptions, as well as the thinking behind them? To what degree am I authentically voicing what I feel? Am I able to explain the relevance of those feelings to the issue at hand? How much am I sharing my relevant knowledge rather than holding back? How effectively am I allowing space for others to contribute, rather than dominating the conversation?

No matter how skilful your practice of expressing, chances are that you baulk at speaking up on occasion, perhaps frequently. Sometimes, the potential hazards seem to overwhelm the benefits. You might think your boss is wrong on an issue you feel strongly about, but whenever the issue is mentioned his body language seems to scream out, "Don't argue this one with me." Or you need to raise a difficult matter with a colleague but somehow you both seem to continually avoid the topic.

A practice-based perspective invites us to work from the following proposition: If something needs to be said, it can be. The challenge is to find words that allow you to speak authentically and fully, while at the same time being receptive to other views. The biggest barrier to speaking up is generally our fear of what could happen. We saw the impact of such fears in the story in Chapter 3, in which Alice avoided confronting the school principal. Alice was concerned that the principal would think she was failing in the change effort she was responsible for. In turn, the principal thought that if she spoke up, Alice would regard her as interfering. In other cases, it is not so much that we are fearful, but that we are skeptical. We tell ourselves that, "They won't listen," "Raising this issue again will be a waste of time," or "There's no chance of getting through." If you find you are giving yourself pessimistic messages, it may help to draw on Timothy Gallwey's advice from Chapter 5 before making an expressing intervention. Just take a moment to notice your self-talk, without making any judgments about it. Pay attention to your breathing, perhaps. Then begin. Later, find time to reflect on the experience. Continuing to work intentionally on your practice over a period, with careful reflection following each expressing effort, is a good way to become more adept at saying what you think the circumstances really call for.

Expressing — A Framework

Most of us probably know of situations where we wish to speak up and be heard, but sense that doing so could be difficult. Perhaps you have a viewpoint that you think others would disagree with regarding a contentious problem under discussion. Or, you have an idea that you think is valuable, but which others would likely oppose. You might want to raise a previously undiscussed matter, as Bernardo did in the innovation story in Chapter 2. The following framework, comprised of five elements, provides a structure to help in precisely these kinds of situations.

FIGURE 9.1 Expressing — A Framework

Introducing	Describe the context Preview the content you wish to cover Establish your purpose, and your stance on the topic
Asserting & Supporting	Put forward the main propositions of your case and the key arguments and evidence that support them
Illuminating	Offer illustrations, stories, and/or examples to support your ideas and engage your audience
Disclosing	Name and describe your relevant but previously unspoken assumptions, interests, feelings, and/or knowledge
Inviting	Create opportunities for others to engage with you on specific aspects.

The expressing framework is a tool for preparation and rehearsal. It is designed to help you put together the elements of a short presentation. This is an *outline* of what you might say; it is *not* the intention that you prepare a script and then read it (or speak it) word-for-word to your audience.

The five elements in the structure serve both as a reminder and a prompt; an effective, relational presentation should include attention to each of these key areas. In particular, people often pay insufficient attention to introducing (giving information about the context, the topic to be covered, and their intentions) and disclosing (giving voice to what is otherwise unspoken).

The framework is flexible, not mechanical or linear. When working through the exercise, for example, you can order the elements in the framework as you see fit. For instance, you might choose to commence by telling a story (illuminating), or naming an assumption (disclosing). The key is to cover all five of the elements. It is also important to keep your expression succinct; as you complete your outline include only a few key points under each element. [3]

Of course, conversations happen in "real time," and many situations are such that we can only make brief inputs. But, even then, the expressing framework can be useful as a mental prompt. If the situation is such that you can only introduce a point, for example, you can draw on the framework to help you think how you might express it so your meaning is clear. Or, if the situation seems to call for more frankness and openness, you might use it as a prompt to think through a question such as, What assumptions might I disclose here?

While we are treating the expressing practice here in isolation, in actual application it needs to be interwoven with inquiring and the other ARIES practices.

"The other directors are just not seeing it, Bill," said Michael. "I've given them all the analyses, including comparisons with other clubs, and the forecasts. But no matter how often or how strongly I tell them, they still don't get it."

"It sounds like they've really got their heads in the sand," said Bill.

"They have, and the problem is likely to become terminal if we don't act soon. Two years ago—well before I joined the board—the club spent nearly all of its $2 million reserves on a redesign of the course. The club then took on a loan to cover its 'short term' operating needs, but without any strategy for managing the debt over time. Up until recently—and I mean very recently, including at yesterday's meeting—I've been hammering the other directors about the club's lack of financial discipline, and telling them that we need to raise our membership fees or apply a levy. Our fees are currently the lowest in the region.

"The lack of any kind of financial discipline is mind-numbing. I asked the head greenskeeper the other day about his three-year budget forecast for maintaining and improving the course. He said he 'didn't have a clue.' He'd never been asked that question before. No one here plans beyond the next twelve months. It's crazy.

"It's becoming clear to me, even as we speak, that the issue is sustainability. I've played here for fifteen years. I feel loyalty to the place. I'd like to think the club will still be here when my grandkids are old enough to join—but it will be a different club from the one we know today. I certainly don't want it to die while I'm a director; I take that responsibility seriously. But if I can't get some serious action at board level—and I haven't announced this yet—I intend to resign from the board and just get back to enjoying my game."

"I can understand your wanting to do that," said Bill. "But there's one thing I can't figure out. You've said some of the directors are successful business people. Presumably, they're not stupid. Why don't they get the message?"

"Some of those directors have been on the board for many years. They've seen the club go through tough times before and survive. They probably don't think this time is going to be any different. A few of the directors do recognize a serious problem—although they didn't when I first raised it. I think they see the solution as one of shaving costs, such as cutting back on course maintenance. I've been telling them this won't work. If we cut back on maintenance, we risk destroying our most important asset, the course itself. But I think there is scope to raise fees or apply a levy. I don't think many of our members would walk; they'd still be getting an attractive deal compared to the other clubs in the area. We could also generate significant returns from leasing out part of the clubhouse. But we need to think even more broadly than that."

"Could part of the difficulty be that you're suggesting solutions?" asked Bill. "Could that be distracting the directors from thinking about what's at the heart of the problem?"

On his way home, Michael thought about Bill's questions. Perhaps he (Michael) had been preoccupied with his own analysis and solutions, and had not given enough attention to what the other directors were saying. In particular, he might have pushed too hard on the matter of raising fees. This idea seemed to really antagonize some of the other directors.

Michael needs to get the other directors to engage with the problem of financial sustainability; he needs to do so while remaining alert to his own unspoken thoughts and feelings, as well as to how the interaction is developing. Michael's challenge gives us an opportunity to examine each of the elements in the expressing framework more closely. We will illustrate the use of the framework by working through *one* version of what Michael could say at a future board meeting.

Introducing

The function of *introducing* is much like that served by the introduction to a book. It provides a high-level overview; it sets the scene, gives an indication of the ground to be covered, and outlines your purpose. Careful attention to the introducing element helps reduce the likelihood that others misconstrue your intended message.

As we saw earlier in the chapter, part of the challenge of the expressing practice is to speak from "outside" your point of view, indicating that you are aware that your view is just one perspective among others. One way of doing this, as we saw with the reference to the book *Difficult Conversations*, is to adopt more of a third-party perspective. This involves speaking as someone who can see different formulations of the problem. Stepping outside your view does not mean you must abandon it and adopt a "neutral" stance, or that you cannot speak with passion or conviction. All these are acceptable; the primary requirement is just that you refrain from conveying certainty, and that you indicate openness to the possibility of other interpretations.

Let us imagine that we are working with Michael to identify some key points for his presentation to the board. In his introduction, it is important for Michael to:

- Set the context for his remarks (as following earlier discussions which may not have reached the core issues);

- Preview the topics he wants to talk about (focusing on building a sustainable future; but not at this time reviewing the financial situation in detail); and

- Establish his purpose (to reach agreement on an understanding of the issue).

Drawing on the concerns he expressed to Bill—and the outline he prepared—Michael's introductory remarks might be along the following lines:

- I want to speak with you about building a viable future for the club.

- I have spoken several times recently about our finances and the shape they're in. I don't intend to go over those details here again.

- But there's an issue that's concerning me that I don't think we have spoken about directly.

- It has to do with our financial sustainability, about our ability to remain viable as a club over the longer term. I see that as hanging in the balance now, with the gap between our revenues and costs.

- I don't think that we've engaged with this issue squarely.

- I acknowledge that some of you see the problem differently. For example, perhaps you think this is not terribly concerning as the club has weathered other tough periods before.

- I think it is critical that we need to reach an understanding of the issue that we all feel comfortable with, or at least can go along with. From there, I think we would be well-placed to develop some strategies.

In acknowledging the other directors' views, such as that the club has survived other difficult periods, Michael helps establish his intervention as a relational one; he makes it clear that he sees realities other than his own, and that he is willing to take these into account.

Critical to Introducing well is the need to be conscious of your stance on the topic—the frame, or interpretive lens, through which you approach it. Michael has told his friend Bill that he had been "hammering the other directors about improving our revenue situation and raising fees," but that he is now seeing the issue as "about sustainability." Even a subtle shift in the way you frame an issue can have a significant bearing on how others interpret and respond to what you say. Making explicit the choices you have made in constructing the issue—making it clear that you have chosen this interpretation rather than another—helps others appreciate your stance on the problem.[4] Revealing the thinking behind your choices also promotes understanding.

Asserting and Supporting

The next element of the structure involves presenting one's ideas, and the arguments and the evidence that supports them. Generally, people feel relatively comfortable with this aspect of expressing. "Yes, I can do that," said one workshop participant. Managers, professionals, and other workers in knowledge-related fields are commonly expected to be able to make clear and cogent arguments. Even children are taught these skills in the early years of schooling.

Asserting and supporting your argument involves making choices about what aspects to include, what to emphasize, and what to leave out. I suggest beginning by identifying the few most critical points you wish to convey. Then, think about what information you need to back those points up, and assemble the evidence. As you do so, it is critical to remember that these are *your* key points, not *the* key points.

Now, let us return to the case story to exemplify this element. Building on his introduction, Michael might then decide to elaborate on the topic of sustainability, arguing why it is relevant. The next point he asserts might be his view that the board has the responsibility to engage with this issue, but has not. If he chooses this tack, he must then present supporting evidence. (In the interests of brevity, we shall assume that he has provided an overview of the club's financial situation and outlook, but will leave that aside from our consideration.) Michael's argument might go something like this:

- By sustainability I mean our ability to function as a successful, independent, and viable entity that is able to meet our obligations in an ongoing way and to meet the needs of members at the same time.

- Our sustainability is at risk, in my assessment, because:

  —We have been borrowing to cover operating expenses;

  —We don't have a plan for repaying our debts;

  —We lack a sound financial management and planning strategy to take us forward; and

  —Based on the analysis I presented earlier, the current estimate says we have only about eighteen months—two years at the outside—in which to turn the situation around.

- I am concerned that, as a board, we are not adequately facing up to the significance of the issues we face:

  —When I have sought reactions and feedback from board members about the seriousness of our problem, there has been very little response. No one has taken up my invitation to discuss these concerns with me.

  —I acknowledge that some of you have been looking into ways of reducing costs.

  —My worry is that we might worsen the situation by cutting costs, as we may reduce our attractiveness to current members.

—I have repeatedly offered possible solutions, such as increasing fees and leasing out part of the clubhouse, but my so doing so may have distracted us from coming to a shared understanding of the underlying problem.

—One way or the other, though, it seems to me we must deal with the imbalance between our costs and revenues—and do this in a way that supports our ongoing viability.

• I would like us to agree today on a definition of the problem we face—which I believe has to do with sustainability—and start work on building a strategic approach to dealing with the problem.

The key to getting your argument across is focusing on a few key points and providing evidence supporting those points. Here, for example, as evidence for his proposition that the board is not facing up to the issues, Michael states that no one has responded to his invitation to discuss the issues. Another important key to asserting and supporting your ideas effectively is—once again—to do so relationally. Here, we see that Michael locates himself within the problem sphere when he acknowledges that his continuing to push for solutions may have actually distracted the board away from dealing with the issue.

I offer some tips to help you in preparing an expressing presentation of your own. It is particularly important to avoid getting so caught up in the content of your argument that you lose sight of the process dimension. You know this is the case when you see yourself embellishing your arguments with detail upon detail, as if this is what will convince others of the merit of your case. When this happens, it is likely that you are functioning in the management mode. Look for signs such as the following: You are emphasizing the more concrete side of problems (including the "facts and figures"); you are focusing narrowly on a task, such as convincing others; you are drawing on your authority, as Michael was drawing on his authority as the golf club treasurer. It is a challenge to stay in a more relational process and to work jointly with others to appreciate the problem at a deeper level, rather than operating on them to achieve your own objectives.

Once you have identified what you think are your most critical points, consider stepping into your audience's shoes, and reviewing the points from their perspective. What assumptions might they detect? What might they see as missing or requiring further information? What criticisms might they make?

Illuminating

A presentation based in reasoned analysis goes only so far in helping others to understand your viewpoint, especially if the ideas you are attempting to convey are at all abstract. The people you are interacting with are likely to disengage if they find your presentation dry, and remote from their experience. Apart from that, others will make sense of what you say through their own frames of reference, and will most likely draw meanings quite different from those you had in mind. Supporting your ideas with illustrations—examples, stories, and anecdotes—can help to spotlight the points you wish to emphasize. They will also engage your audience.[5] Well-chosen illustrations help others to see your ideas in more concrete terms, see them more vividly, and connect them with their own experience.

To illuminate his concerns about the lack of financial discipline, Michael might tell the board about the conversation in which the head greenskeeper said he "didn't have a clue" about a three-year budget for course maintenance and improvement. This story clearly illustrates the lack of financial discipline at the club, which is one of Michael's key concerns. This story might be much more illustrative of the issue than Michael's speaking to them again about the need for financial planning and management. The power of a real-life story is that it might prompt the directors to consider the implications of what the head greenskeeper is saying.

While your stories, anecdotes, and examples should highlight—illuminate—the points you wish to emphasize, they should not be so prominent as to become the main focus of attention, to the exclusion of your central ideas. They should support your story, not *become* the story.

Disclosing

In the expressing practice, *disclosing* means revealing relevant content that lies in our own implicit domain. These are the pertinent assumptions, interests, feelings, and knowledge that we hold—perhaps only formed to a degree—but have not, as yet, openly declared. (And sometimes it is the act of speaking that helps us become more aware of what we assume, value, feel, or know.) As we have emphasized, working productively with contentious problems requires that we delve into the hidden domain in order to extend and deepen the range of intelligence applied to the problem. Disclosing material from our own implicit domain is essential to learning-leadership. If we were to only inquire into the implicit domain of others, without disclosing any content from our own implicit domain, we could be seen—quite legitimately—as operating on others to our own advantage. This is not in keeping with the relational quality of learning-centered leadership.

Disclosing is perhaps the hardest part of the expressing practice. It requires that we face our fears and vulnerabilities, and avoid the temptation to downplay or sugarcoat what really matters to us. Disclosing, however, is not a matter of "letting it all hang out." Discretion is called for. The challenge is to strike a balance: to reveal the relevant content in our implicit domain and describe its significance, without going too far, and sparking defensiveness in others. Talking to others about such matters requires that we speak from a deeper place than we are perhaps accustomed to. To do this, we need to ground ourselves in the present moment, and speak about what is real to us then and there.

What hidden content might Michael want to disclose to his board colleagues? In Figure 9.2 there are examples of statements that Michael might make to reveal his implicit assumptions, interests, feelings, and knowledge. In practice, of course, it is not always necessary to disclose content from all four categories of the implicit domain. These are simply examples, pointing to possibilities.

FIGURE 9.2 Examples of Possible Matters for Disclosure (Golf club case)

Assumptions	I've spoken many times to the board about the state of the club's finances. I've assumed the problem is essentially a technical one, meaning it's about financial management or the lack of it. There is an explicit fact here—we are in financial difficulties. But perhaps there is a deeper dimension that I don't yet understand. When no one appeared to respond to my earlier presentations, I assumed that you just weren't "getting it." It could be there were some things I was not getting as well—such as that you saw me as lecturing you, or as obsessed with raising fees.
Interests	I want this club to succeed. I've been playing here for fifteen years, and I'd like to think the club would be around when my grandkids are ready to join. I have a sense of my responsibilities as a director—as I'm sure you do. I don't want the club to fail while I'm on the board.
Feelings	I feel a sense of loyalty to the club. I expect that's something we all share. While I've been going on about financial management, I've been frustrated that you, the other directors, haven't seemed to share my assessment of the seriousness of the situation. Presumably, you have been similarly frustrated at my repeatedly pushing the same things.
Knowledge	From past experience in other organizations, I can see that we're really very close to the edge. We haven't named this directly, but I think we need to. And then, my experience tells me we need to take strong action. One thing I haven't mentioned is that I heard of a rumor this week, on the course, that I have been (supposedly) trying to railroad the board into accepting my financial reform agenda. Maybe my emphasis on putting strategies in place to deal with the gap between our revenues and costs has been interpreted this way.

Disclosing, like asking exploring questions in the inquiring practice, involves intentionally reaching down into the implicit domain. That is threatening. Few of us have been schooled in making our assumptions or interests explicit. Few have much experience in talking about how we feel in a work-related or business context. Few have much experience in sharing implicit knowledge. We are stopped by concerns that it may not be our place to bring this information to light, and that by doing so we might threaten or embarrass others, particularly those with greater status. A common worry is that making explicit our undeclared thoughts and feelings might enable others to take advantage of us. Some people worry that they will "say too much," or "become too emotional." For all these reasons, it can seem easier and safer to confine our comments to the explicit aspects of problems—if we say anything at all.

Yet, despite the risks, it can be extremely satisfying to speak more fully, more truly, and to say more of what really matters to us, even as we take care not to create undue hazards for others or ourselves. The more we do so successfully, the more we become role models for others.

Inviting

Inviting in the ARIES context means making a request of others to respond to what you have said. When you choose to practice expressing you are probably doing so because you believe there is something important at stake—and some action must be taken. Your presentation has an intention. Your presentation might be a pitch to launch a new idea, or a plea intended to re-orient an existing conversation. Whatever the intention, a presentation generally seeks a response. When we practice inviting, we make that intention explicit. How do we invite a meaningful response?

When we make ourselves vulnerable by speaking about what matters deeply to us, it is more than reasonable to want to hear others' reactions to what we have said. When seeking a response, it is best to refrain from an open-ended invitation, such as, "Tell me what you think." It is generally more productive to ask people to engage with something specific. In the golf club case, for instance, Michael might want to hear what the directors think about his views regarding the seriousness of the club's financial problems, and the need to focus on sustainability:

> " I'd like to hear your reactions to what I have said. I'm particularly interested in what you think about my assessment that the future of the club is in the balance, and that we need to deal with the imbalance between revenues and costs as part of a wider move to put the club on a sustainable financial footing. If your assessment is different, please tell me—and the other directors—what the problem looks like to you. "

Note that, in this invitation, Michael focused his request directly on what he sees as the main problem. He invited responses to this assessment, allowing that others may define the problem differently.

Inviting a response may not seem like such a difficult thing to do. But, in practice, how often do we call for feedback on the views we express? More often than not, we are operating in the management mode; we are trying to solve problems and get things done. When we are in that mode, we want others to accept our views, not to tell us where they disagree. Disagreement can be threatening, and we do not want to get derailed. But feedback is critical if we are to intervene productively in the leadership mode. When we actively seek reactions to the views we express, we improve our ability to understand the specific points of contention surrounding the problem. Feedback about others' reactions to what we say also provides useful input; it can inform our future learning-leadership interventions.

The most powerful leverage for improving your own expressing comes from incorporating the lesson Alice learned (Chapter 3) following her experience on the Curve Ball ride: recognize that your views are only one way of seeing. To take this a step further is to build this recognition into your expressing. This important and challenging step requires that we be able to hold our views on issues separate from our core beliefs and our concept of self. To the extent we can do that, we stand to be more able to put our views in a wider context, to give voice to relevant content from our implicit domain, to accept disagreement by others, and to reflect on our own contributions. These capabilities are at the heart of expressing skillfully.

Chapter Summary

Expressing was differentiated from advocacy on behalf of a point of view, party, or cause, in which a premium is placed on communicating "to win." In contrast, expressing is directed towards seeking a more encompassing truth which is built from the contributions of multiple voices.

As with the other ARIES practices, a relational orientation is critical. Expressing attaches importance to presenting your views in a way that:

• Recognizes your own connection to the problem of concern;

• Demonstrates your receptiveness to other viewpoints; and

• Gives voice to assumptions, interests, feelings, and knowledge that might be otherwise concealed.

To express effectively implies being attentive to how you are framing and presenting the problem, idea, or opportunity to others. Attention to the process of communicating with others is critical; expressing is not about being consumed with the "truth" of one's own viewpoint.

A framework was presented to assist you in preparing to express your thoughts and feelings on contentious matters. The framework comprises five elements:

Introducing Describing the larger context, the topic, and your purposes in raising it;

Asserting and Supporting Stating your key propositions and providing supporting evidence to back them up;

Illuminating Offering illustrations, stories, and examples as to how your ideas could work out in practice;

Disclosing Declaring relevant but previously unspoken assumptions, interests, feelings, and knowledge; and

Inviting Creating opportunities for others to engage with you.

This chapter featured a story concerning financial problems at a golf club to illustrate the application of the framework and the practice of expressing. The intent of the expressing practice is to enable us to give a well-rounded account of our thoughts and feelings that is both fine-grained and nuanced.

Questions for Reflection

9.1 Recall a time when you spoke up successfully about something important to you, and where you gave voice to aspects you had previously kept to yourself. What was it in your handling of this episode that enabled you to succeed?

9.2 Think of a contentious issue where you would like to express a point of view with which colleagues probably disagree. How might you introduce the topic to make it more likely that you would be heard?

9.3 What unhelpful behaviors—such as not disclosing sufficiently or going into excessive detail—do you think you would need to guard against in your own efforts at expressing? How might you avoid acting in these ways?

Chapter
TEN

....

Synthesizing

Julia, a human resources manager, was in the process of presenting her business case for a new, expanded employee retention program to her division's senior management team. The proposed enhancements included much greater flexibility in working hours. As Julia was outlining the potential benefits of her proposal she noticed a couple of the group members exchange knowing glances. Then one of them, Ed, interjected: "What about the business? No one from HR seems to care much about the business."

Another of the group members, who had previously worked in the company's HR department, spoke directly to Ed: "That's not fair," she said. "If you look closely at this proposal, you might find real business benefits." At that point, another group member brought up a valued employee who had been on a flexible working arrangement; this employee had suddenly resigned. An argument broke out about the circumstances surrounding the individual's departure. Ed remained quiet. The verbal scuffle continued for a few moments until it was interrupted by a knock on the door. The division head's assistant entered to give him a message.

Once the assistant had left, Julia—visibly shaken—continued with her presentation.

Most of us have experienced situations where group conversations unravel. Sometimes, the group splinters along differing sides of an argument. On other occasions, there are no readily discernable "camps," but those involved speak from their own worldviews with little regard for other perspectives. Group members commonly experience such conversations as unproductive or "going around in circles." When these rifts occur, much of the intelligence potentially available to the group goes untapped. At these moments, learning-leadership interventions can help the group re-orient and come together in a way that enables that latent intelligence to be brought to the fore. This is when synthesizing interventions can be most effective.

Synthesizing in the ARIES context refers to a set of interventions that enable stakeholders to understand their current realities from fresh or more developed perspectives. These interventions tap the groups' latent intelligence, combining apparently disparate views in new ways to achieve fresh understandings.

Synthesizing interventions also encapsulate current reality, and crystallize a vision of the group's preferred future in a form that energizes discussion. They focus the group on the learning-centered leadership work that is needed to achieve deep-reaching change.

Before looking more closely at synthesizing interventions, let us consider what commonly happens in situations where contention surfaces; that is, where people disagree and do so strongly. We have said that the management mode is characterized by emphases on the *explicit* aspects of problems and on task attainment, with authority providing the underpinning. We have also said that the management mode predominates in most organizations. The emergence of contention, however, signifies that the *implicit* level is involved: there are unspecified assumptions being made, undeclared interests being advanced, and unnamed feelings (such as anger or frustration) being acted out. As well, group members are probably suppressing or holding back knowledge and experience that might be very germane.

When contention arises in a group, people often experience tension, discomfort, and perhaps some anxiety. To get rid of the tension, they may feel the need to "get a decision made," to "move on," and make action happen. As a result, we commonly see what might be termed a "rush to convergence," which can have the effect of controlling, containing, or diluting (if not removing) the causes of the contention. This rush to convergence can manifest in various ways, such as:

- The group focuses on "the arguments," but the discussion is curtailed when the contention is assessed (implicitly, by someone in authority) as being too great. That same authority figure makes a decision that the group needs to "move on," which means determine some strategies for taking action. (If this does not happen, some might see the "solution" as more effective chairing of the meeting.)

- A compromise is reached; the parties most centrally involved are accommodated in some way.

- The issue is moved to another arena. It may be assigned to a task force or working group, or deferred to another time.

These are management-mode responses. They deal only with the explicit domain; they are task-oriented, and authority-based. Generally, the implicit domain is ignored entirely. This is because the management mode not does have adequate mechanisms for engaging directly with the implicit aspects that are coming to the fore, as this book has emphasized. When the implicit domain is not addressed, we greatly hinder our ability to deal with the fundamental aspects of contentious issues. When we rely exclusively on the management mode to deal with contentious issues, the problem may appear to be solved, but in reality, it merely goes underground, only to surface again, later, usually in a more virulent form. The management-mode response has this adverse effect because it encourages us to:

- *Look away from uncomfortable aspects of the present*: In today's business climate, there is an ever-present temptation to focus on the future, and not look too closely at some of the discomforting aspects of the present. This can be a defensive strategy as well as a control mechanism, especially for those in senior roles. In learning-leadership, however, we have emphasized the need to clarify current realities, which necessitates acknowledging the uncomfortable aspects of the present in order to move forward.

- *Focus on task activity:* When the focus on tasks is all-pervasive, as it tends to be in the management mode, we seriously impair our ability to do the deeper work, such as establish current realities, build shared vision, and harness energy for change. In short, we neglect the learning-centered leadership work. Learning-centered leadership work is about building shared meaning. It is emergent and relational. It cannot be done as a task; it cannot be broken down into a series of steps or identified as a set of deliverables in a project plan.

- *Lose some of the intelligence that could potentially be brought to bear on the problem:* When we are in the management mode, we often deal with an issue by "arguing it out." When that happens, the voices most likely to be heard are those of people who are comfortable in speaking out, who speak from authority, or who have a command of relevant technical perspectives. Less likely to be heard are those who are quieter, who do not have relevant technical knowledge, or whose views are out of the mainstream. In any event, as the major players jostle to gain the upper hand, some potentially significant thoughts may not make it into the argument. To some, this is just the way it is. A danger, though, is that these overlooked or unvoiced thoughts have the potential to transform the way the group understands the issue. In contrast, learning-leadership attends to those contributions, as we shall see in this chapter.

- *Miss out on opportunities for achieving creative integration*: As we have said, the rise of contention often signals a need to dig beneath the surface and to process undeclared assumptions, interests, feelings, and knowledge associated with different viewpoints. Because this work can be threatening, it is very unlikely that it will occur when the management-mode predominates. Therefore, the integration of views is unlikely. In contrast, it is exactly this kind of joint exploration of the implicit domain—undertaken in order to achieve a creative integration of viewpoints—that is the essence of learning-centered leadership.

To this point, we have described why the management mode is insufficient for dealing effectively with contentious problems, and the consequences of relying upon it. These inadequacies point to what is needed in these situations: an intervention that recognizes the implicit level is involved, and helps the group integrate the contentious material so that it can regain coherence and move forward with a greater degree of shared understanding. This is the role of synthesizing in the ARIES context. Here, I use *synthesizing* as an omnibus term referring to a range of interventions that can help a group creatively weave together the thoughts and feelings being expressed by those who have an interest in a contentious problem, and also crystallize the learning-leadership challenges the group faces.

In this chapter we look into four types of synthesizing interventions:

Connecting Interventions   Through the practice of attending, learning-leadership practitioners can see the value in contributions that otherwise might be dismissed. We make connecting interventions when we weave those comments back into the discussion in a way that enables the group to take them in and, as a result, possibly see the issue in a new light.

Integrating Interventions   These interventions tap the groups' latent intelligence by combining two or more apparently disparate views in new ways to achieve new understandings.

Transformational Challenges   These interventions attempt to distill the range of views being expressed about current reality and vision, and frame them in a single statement that encapsulates the change that needs to occur to realize the vision.

Relational Challenges   These interventions frame the relational work that stakeholders need to do in order to establish shared meaning on a specific contentious matter.

The first two describe interventions made in real-time, within the context of a particular conversation. The second two interventions involve stepping back to see the bigger picture, and then naming specific challenges for the group to address. All four of these synthesizing interventions help a group pull together and learn together by building upon and integrating the diverse contributions of its members.

"Connecting" Interventions

Sometimes it is the stray comment or the left-field observation that, although not recognized immediately as significant, turns out to be critical in helping a group frame its understanding of an issue. We make a connecting intervention when we notice, and bring back into the group, a contribution that we think has the potential to contribute to building shared meaning but which—in our assessment—has not been fully processed.[1] A connecting intervention can be in the form of a statement or question; it refers specifically to an earlier contribution, and weaves it back into the conversation in a way that enables the group to build upon it.

As learning-leadership practitioners, we consciously seek to pick up on the loose threads of the conversation, identifying those we think may contain unrecognized significance. Connecting interventions are most effective when we combine synthesizing with learning-leadership principles (and draw upon the other ARIES practices). Consider this example.

After Julia finished her presentation—and after the argument about the departed employee had subsided—the group discussed the implementation of the expanded retention program. Ed, who had made the "What about the business?" comment remained quiet. One of the group members, Martine, noticed that while Ed's comment had sparked some argument, no one had sought to tease out the thinking behind the comment. She thought Ed may be alluding to issues that needed dealing with if the retention program implementation was to be successful.

Martine said to the group:

" Earlier Ed suggested that HR doesn't care about the business. I think we need to understand more about this view if we are to successfully put the retention program into action. Perhaps Ed or someone else could tell us what it is about HR's proposal that leads to the view that HR is not concerned about the business? "

What makes Martine's contribution an effective *connecting* intervention?[2] She has:

- Recognized and given voice to a contribution from earlier in the conversation—Ed's remark—that she thinks warrants more attention.

- Made explicit her understanding of that earlier contribution: "that HR doesn't care about the business." (Others may have interpreted Ed's statement differently, and if so, they can disagree.)

- Created an opening for group members to build upon the earlier contribution. In this instance, she has put a question to the whole group inviting Ed or others to reveal more about the thinking underlying the statement.

- Made her intervention without judgment, reflecting the reasonableness principle from Chapter 5. (We would need to hear her tone of voice to be certain.)

Martine's intervention questions the thinking behind Ed's statement. This is one type of connecting intervention; there are others. We can introduce a story, an anecdote from personal experience, or an illustrative example to support an earlier contribution. We might extend a previous comment by expanding upon the original idea, or by raising possible implications. We can even use an earlier contribution as a springboard for introducing a new topic or perspective. All these are connecting interventions.

Figure 10.1 shows examples of different types of connecting interventions that could be made in relation to Ed's comment about HR lacking interest in the business.

FIGURE 10.1 Examples of Connecting Interventions

FUNCTION	DEFINITION	EXAMPLE
Extending a contribution	Further developing a line of argument or raising implications	"Ed says HR's proposal indicates a lack of interest in the business. To the extent that is true, I see it as raising some troubling implications, such as how much is HR pushing its own agenda rather than actively partnering with business areas."
Deepening a contribution	Encouraging exploration of an underlying issue or assumption	"I've heard Ed suggest that HR's proposal is out of touch with the needs of the business. I think there's an underlying issue here about how HR and the line areas communicate. I'm interested to hear other thoughts as to whether this is an issue."
Challenging a contribution	Questioning or disagreeing with the contribution	"I'd like to take issue with Ed's proposition that HR's proposal indicates some kind of disregard of what the business needs. It seems to me…"
Supporting a contribution	Providing evidence or examples	"I'd agree with Ed's analysis that HR is not 'on the case' with the needs of the business. I've seen that in quite a few instances myself. For example…"
Leveraging a contribution	Using the contribution as a bridge to a related or different topic	"Ed's point about whether HR has factored the needs of HR into its proposal has prompted me to think about the converse: How well do we in the business areas assist HR in getting its job done?"

The concept of the connecting intervention reflects an underlying premise of learning-centered leadership (from Chapter 2): that viewpoints on contentious issues should be regarded as of potentially real value. The comment that goes unnoticed or is quickly dismissed may contain critical information or insight. Suppose, for instance, that Ed's "What about the business?" comment had been ignored. If the team did not process Ed's view, it could "bubble up" again at a later time, threatening to thwart (or otherwise complicate) the implementation of the revamped employee retention program.

In practice, it may not be possible for all views to be heard, if only because of time considerations. And, if a group is dealing with a relatively technical matter, or an urgent decision is required, connecting interventions might even be a distraction. Further, the act of re-connecting earlier contributions back into a conversation is no guarantee of productive interaction. Yet, through picking up and working with earlier contributions, connecting interventions aid in weaving the various strands of conversation into a coherent whole. And a coherent conversation offers much better prospects for developing shared understandings of current realities and future vision.

"Integrating" Interventions

An integrating intervention attempts to bring together two or more contributions in a creative synthesis in order to generate a new insight or understanding. Through offering a framing that combines or integrates the perspectives of group members, these interventions help establish shared meaning, a concept vital to the leadership mode.[3]

Formulating an integrating intervention involves stepping back from the specifics of the conversation and contemplating how these might be placed in a larger context. It involves asking oneself (or the group) the following question: What might be a definition of the problem that would include each of these contributions, and provide a window onto a larger whole?

Here is an example: During Julia's presentation about the employee retention program and the subsequent discussion, one of the group members, Jo, sat quietly; listening, observing, and thinking. Then, she made an integrating intervention.

"I've been trying to get a sense of the views being expressed in response to Julia's presentation. It seems to me there are two main lines of argument being put forth. One line is concerned with employee productivity, as reflected in the "What about the business?" comment and the discussion on that point. The other is emphasizing the importance of retaining skilled workers through better enabling them to balance work and outside-work commitments.

"Somehow we have been treating these two perspectives as if they are incompatible, mutually exclusive. I think we would get farther by recasting the problem as one of a tension between the competing needs of productivity and flexibility in work practices. We need to reconcile the tension to achieve both."

An integrating intervention might take the form of a fuller articulation of a concept or idea that has been emerging in the group, but until now has been only partly formed. It may reframe a problem that group members have been grappling with, giving rise to a different way of understanding and a shift in perspective. Jo's intervention is more an example of the latter. Whether through "turning the ideas around" or adding additional ingredients, the group is enabled to see the problem in a different light. An element of new knowledge, insight or understanding comes into being. In that sense, making an integrating intervention is a creative act.

The difficulty of making effective interventions of this type should not be underestimated. For one thing, pulling back sufficiently from the specific content of a conversation in order to imagine the whole can be challenging. An inductive process is required; we must move beyond the specific inputs to "imagine the whole." Devising a suitable problem definition that integrates other perspectives is essentially an exercise in imagination. There is no way to logically deduce such a definition by working from particular inputs to the conversation.

We are more likely to be able to view a problem holistically when the mind is relatively quiet, when we are not pushing our own view, or searching for a solution. In moments of relative stillness, there is more scope for mentally "playing around" with different formulations of the problem; we are better able to hold them in our mind and look at them from different sides. For these reasons, making successful interventions of this type calls for the application of the other ARIES practices: attending, reflecting, inquiring, and expressing.

Such interventions, when made skillfully, can be invaluable in helping a group to get closer to a grounded definition of the problem that all can agree to or, at the very least, accept.

The Transformational Challenge

A transformational challenge is a statement that frames a description of current reality with that of a preferred future so that the essence of the shift to be made between the two states is clear. The intention is to integrate the variety of stakeholder perspectives on a contentious problem by creating a frame around them so that the opportunities and problems in moving between them can be contemplated.

The statement can be expressed in a "from—to" form, capturing movement "from" an initial set of conditions "to" a desired set of conditions.[4] This format is illustrated in the following example from the Chapter 3 case involving Alice and her quest for school change. The example shows one possible way in which Alice might frame the transformational challenge the school faces in relation to its teaching and learning processes, as an input to her discussions with the teachers and/or the principal.

FIGURE 10.2 Defining the Transformational Challenge for a School

FROM
A school which has committed teachers and which achieves good results, where teachers view their primary role as subject experts, where leadership responsibility resides solely in the executive team, and where there is a difference of view between the teachers and the school executive team about the most suitable teaching and learning model.

TO
A school which fosters learning at all levels to meet the needs of all students, where committed and knowledgeable teachers guide and support students' learning and actively participate in improvement activities, and where leadership comes from all levels.

This framing of a transformational challenge attempts to articulate the deep-reaching change that is required to achieve the preferred future; it articulates the changes in underlying attitudes, mindsets, and/or patterns of thinking and interaction that are necessary to achieve the vision. It is the focus on the deeper, subtler, implicit level of change that makes this challenge "transformational."[5] In addition, because the statement attempts to capture the essence of the overall change to be achieved, it includes any tangible changes as well.

The framing of the "from" statement is key. Having a clear and truthful (in your assessment) statement of present circumstances is particularly beneficial because it helps people stay involved in the change process. Candid statements about present conditions help people feel that "this is real," so they will tend to stay alert to more of the complexities and subtleties associated with the process. In particular, such a statement can provide a counterweight to the tendency to focus on the possibilities and intentions of the future while ignoring current difficulties. Even when productive conversations have occurred about vision and current reality, groups can quickly get into an action mode, thus losing sight of the more difficult, underlying issues. The focus shifts to "moving forward" by setting goals and determining strategies and measures, with little reference to process or resolution of the underlying issues. The transformational challenge helps a group maintain a focus on what is difficult or unsatisfactory about the present that needs to be overcome through change.

Another benefit of the transformational challenge is that it can be used as a reference point. Because it defines an initial point for a change effort (or for a renewal of effort), as well as a desired future state, we can use it to help gauge the success of the effort along the way (in concert with more conventional management-oriented tools such as milestones and performance indicators).

Note that a transformational challenge does *not* specify a strategy for achieving the vision. The intention is to provide a framing of current reality and vision so that prospective strategies can be discussed with both in view. With current reality and vision expressed in succinct statements together, we are better placed to assess proposed strategies in terms of their likely effectiveness in enabling movement towards the vision. A key question becomes: "How well would this proposed strategy help us move from our current reality, as described, to our vision?"

Nor is the framing meant to be definitive. In keeping with our relational stance, we frame the challenge knowing it is meant to be contestable. As the shared vision becomes clearer, the statement can be revisited and redefined.

When considering making this type of intervention, consider timing. While a statement of the transformational challenge can be prepared at any time, such a statement is likely to be of most value when it caps conversations that have already occurred regarding current reality and vision. If a statement of the transformational challenge is imposed on a group or prepared prematurely, a risk is that it will be disregarded. In addition, when developing (or assessing) the framing of a transformational challenge, the following guidelines can be useful. Before putting it before the group, ask yourself how well the statement:

- Integrates relevant perspectives;

- Describes current reality accurately, in ways likely to resonate with stakeholders, without glossing over points that may cause some discomfort;

- Expresses a clear vision that reflects the expressed aspirations of stakeholders, and yet is achievable;

- Captures the essence of the shift required from a present state to a preferred state;

- Does not incorporate any strategies or "how-to" elements; and

- Frames the challenge in such a way that it can be tested with all stakeholders (that is, it does not imply negative attributions toward any concerned group).

The transformational challenge defines the "bookends" for the change effort; it is a statement of where we believe we are now and where we want to go. Defining the transformational challenge does not directly light a path ahead. Nor does it provide a guarantee against simplistic interpretations of what needs to be done. Yet, this tool can help foster more thoughtful appraisal of what is really needed to achieve a desired change.

While the transformational challenge provides an overall framing of the change needed, we also need to clarify the difficult leadership-related work to be faced along the way. This is the purpose of relational challenges.

Specifying Relational Challenges

We frame a relational challenge when we specify an area where—in our view—the group needs to achieve shared understanding in order to overcome a contentious problem. The act of naming a relational challenge provides a counterpoint—and complement—to the task-orientation common to conventional planning processes. Specifying relational challenges can help us avoid becoming preoccupied with tasks. Articulating the relational challenges we face both elevates the attention we give to learning-leadership work and increases the prospect of our bringing about the changes we aspire to.

Because there is contention, a degree of threat is involved. The act of specifying a relational challenge helps to minimize the likelihood that this work will be avoided or put off because of its threatening nature.

Consider the case story with Michael, the golf club treasurer in Chapter 9. He can see that the club is facing a serious financial problem. He and the other directors appear to be making varying assessments of the severity and causes of the problem. Michael knows that he wants the club to survive; he wants his grandchildren to be able to join. He thinks the challenge is to focus on sustainability, but beyond this he does not appear to have a clearly formed vision in his own mind. And the directors as a group appear well short of being able to articulate a common view of what they want for the club in future.

In Chapter 9 (in the context of our discussion of the expressing framework), Michael was preparing to meet with the board for the presentation. As part of his preparation, Michael might frame a relational challenge for the group of directors along these lines:

As a board we face the challenge of coming to a shared understanding of the club's present financial circumstances, including a joint assessment of the severity of those circumstances as well as the factors driving our current situation. This is necessary to inform our thinking about what we aspire to in the future, and how we might achieve those aspirations.

Obviously, naming a relational challenge is only a first step. Nevertheless, identifying the particular relational work to be done is an important act in itself.

Let us consider another example.

In the Chapter 2 case story, Bernardo is concerned about a gap between company statements about innovation and employee survey results, which revealed that many employees do not see the company as particularly innovative. He has observed that the Corporate Strategic Group (or CSG, of which he is a member) has not discussed this issue, though they have dealt with other matters arising from the employee survey. Bernardo wants the company to become more innovative, and for the CSG to deal with this issue.

As he prepares to make a presentation to the Corporate Strategic Group, he might find it useful to specify—both for his own benefit and the CSG's—the relational challenge the CSG faces at that point. Bernardo might frame the relational challenge along the following lines:

To develop shared understanding among the Corporate Strategic Group about the existence of a gap between employee perceptions and company declarations about innovation, about the significance of that gap for the company and employees, and about the factors that give rise to the gap.

What makes this a *relational* challenge? We can identify three features:

- First, in line with the concept of relational working from Chapter 3, it is relational because it *defines a problem that we are part of.* Bernardo describes evidence that points to a problem (the employee survey results), and says why this problem concerns him (he wants the company to be more innovative). He then invites the CSG members to join with him in thinking about the nature and causes of the problem; that is, to develop a shared understanding about it. He does not claim that he has a privileged view of the deeper nature of the problem, nor does he imply that the problem involves others, but not himself.

- Second, *the actual form the shared understanding might take is left open.* We do not know at this point how the development of that understanding will—or should—unfold. We are not intending to persuade others to a particular viewpoint; we are remaining open to what emerges in conversations. Neither do we specify how to proceed. Again, this is something for the group to determine (though the person framing the challenge might be well-advised to give questions of process some prior thought).

- Third, a relational challenge is *stated candidly; it involves no hidden strategies or tactics.* The intention is to declare the challenge openly, and to hold it as contestable. Others may disagree with the framing, and want to propose an alternative, or suggest completely different priorities. In either event, the act of posing the relational challenge has furthered the discussion.

In sum, the purpose of identifying a relational challenge is to focus others (and ourselves) on the importance of reaching a shared understanding about a contentious matter. This need can arise before or after we frame a transformational challenge; the relationship between the two types of challenges is complementary and iterative.

The core capabilities for undertaking relational challenges are the kinds of practices we have examined in this book. They include: attending deeply to the others around us, to the surrounding environment and to our own thoughts and feelings; reflecting on the deeper meanings of what we perceive; inquiring into other views to foster learning; expressing our own views in ways that hold those views open to other perspectives; and framing syntheses that enable stakeholders to understand a problem from fresh or more developed perspectives.

While each of the ARIES practices contributes to the leadership-mode work of building shared meaning, it is the synthesizing practice that most directly "pulls together" different perspectives. The importance of this practice stems from the difficulties we face in finding common ground on contentious problems when the management mode is dominant—as reflected in our trying to force convergence prematurely. The four types of intervention discussed in this chapter offer potential antidotes to these unhelpful behavior patterns, increasing our capacity to realize the power of shared meaning.

Chapter Summary

We began by noting some of the potentially adverse consequences of our over-reliance on the management mode when dealing with differing viewpoints on contentious problems. These consequences—which flow from a tendency to rush towards convergence—include losses to the group intelligence, as it does not benefit either from hearing quieter voices, or from those advocating views outside the dominant standpoints. The group's ability to achieve creative integration of diverse viewpoints is restricted because it has difficulty facing any uncomfortable present realities and there is an over-emphasis on task-based work.

The practice of synthesizing was offered as a range of four types of interventions that can help us.

The first two types, connecting and integrating interventions, are undertaken within a particular conversation. Connecting interventions pick up on salient thoughts and feelings that members have contributed, but have not been given sufficient attention by the group. These interventions weave these contributions back into the conversation in a way that fosters coherence and reduces fragmentation of thought. Integrating interventions build on two or more contributions in a conversation by proposing a way of mixing and/or reframing those contributions in a way that shows the problem in a different light. Integrating interventions enable group members to gain fresh insights and new knowledge—critical to building shared meaning.

The second two intervention types, transformational and relational challenges, frame the leadership-mode work to be done. The transformational challenge is an overarching definition of the problem a group faces, incorporating an expression of both current realities and a vision of a preferred future. A transformational challenge is our interpretation of how the different viewpoints of group members might be interwoven to provide a framing of present circumstances and the desired future. We offer it so others can contest it, adopt it, or build upon it, as the case may be. This challenge serves as a reference point; it helps establish where the group stands in relation to the overall challenge of change. The transformational challenge assists us in considering the problems and potentials in moving between the present and future states.

Relational challenges name specific contentious matters on which we need to establish shared understanding with particular stakeholders in order to advance the intended change. We specify relational challenges to focus the group and ourselves on achieving those critical joint understandings.

The benefit of defining transformational and relational challenges is that they help us avoid the trap of over-reliance on management-mode-oriented planning processes, such as identifying strategies, actions, and measures, to the detriment of the more subtle, but necessary, learning-leadership work.

Questions for Reflection

10.1 Think about your own contributions to discussions involving a group to which you belong. What might you need to work on to better help the group achieve integrated understandings on difficult issues?

10.2 Recall a change effort that you have been involved in where a shift in perspective by some or all stakeholders was required. How would you define the transformational challenge for this change effort? Frame your answer in terms of a movement "from" (the current state of affairs) "to" (a preferred state).

10.3 What is (or was) an important relational challenge for you in working towards the change referred to in Question 2? What capabilities do you need to strengthen in order to better deal with similar challenges in future?

EPILOGUE

What implications arise from our exploration of this distinct form of leadership? There are implications for the development of leadership capability at the individual level, and also at the level of the organization or larger group. This concluding discussion considers both, but first we review some of the book's main themes.

Our concern has been with leadership in the context of dealing with contentious problems. We recognized, in the Introduction, that overcoming such problems requires dealing with both their explicit and implicit sides. Leadership is needed to discover the group's hidden resources: its latent intelligence, experience, and wisdom. Through learning-centered leadership, these resources can then be delved into and combined with other, explicit, data to help the group gain a clearer sense of their present reality, jointly envision a preferred future, and foster the necessary energy to bring about change.

Dominant conceptions of leadership, though, inhibit our efforts to work through contentious problems in this way. In particular, we identified four assumptions that tend to hamper us: that leadership is equivalent to leaders; that leadership is the exclusive province of those in roles of considerable authority; that leadership is based in influence; and that there is little value in attempting to distinguish between leadership and management.

In Chapter 1, such assumptions were likened to vines in a forest, tightly wrapped around the other growth, representing the many books, frameworks, concepts, and tools generated on leadership over the past fifty years. These assumptions render largely invisible an alternative view of leadership, based in learning. To see what it can offer us, we must look at leadership afresh. This requires "pulling back the vines." We must set aside the identification of leadership with leaders, influence and authority. We do not have to reject these ideas outright, but we do need to put them on hold.

Pulling back these particular vines reveals two prospective benefits from pursuing a learning-oriented approach to leadership. First, we stand to gain considerably by expanding the pool of potential contributors to leadership. People who do not comfortably put themselves forward as "leaders" often have much to offer in the *practice* of learning-centered leadership. When such people come into the circle of learning-leadership practice they make it possible for a greater range of expertise, knowledge, and understanding to be applied to the handling of contentious problems.

Second, we gain access to a greater *depth* of intelligence, which should also help in working through such problems. The approach to leadership presented in this book emphasizes practices that foster safety and minimize the risk of defensive responses—including our own—when examining contentious matters. These practices make it possible for people to bring to the table more of what they might otherwise leave unsaid, thus increasing the group's intelligence.

The concepts and actions that characterize learning-centered leadership were discussed in Chapter 2, with a case story involving Bernardo and his efforts to build a truer focus on innovation in his company. The "learning" in learning-centered leadership was seen to involve social processes, with people jointly making sense of multiple perspectives on reality. The emphasis on joint "meaning-making" implies that learning-centered leadership requires relational forms of interaction: processes of joint thinking and action are treated as prior to considerations of task; and value is placed on individuals and group members recognizing, surfacing and holding open to question assumptions, feelings, and beliefs as they relate to the problem at hand.

I proposed that learning-centered leadership needs to be viewed through two lenses. We can consider this form either at some remove, where we concentrate on a "higher-level" view—on processes as they need to unfold over a period—or we can look through a "close-up" lens, at specific individual actions at points in time. The higher-level processes involve establishing current realities, clarifying preferred futures (purpose and vision), and harnessing energy for deep-reaching change. The processes revealed in the close-up, more immediate, view involve specific interventions (such as asking a question or making an observation), which are made relationally to contribute to the current reality and vision-building processes. Undertaking these specific interventions is what is meant by acting "in the leadership mode." (The term "learning-centered leadership intervention" has the same meaning).

Three overarching concepts inform interventions made in the leadership mode: relational working, mindful working, and a basis in practice, as discussed in Chapter 3.

Relational working implies seeing oneself not as removed from the problem and as applying strategies towards it but as located at least partly within the system deemed to be problematic. Critically, relational working denotes not only being actively receptive to other ways of seeing, but being able and willing to invite and accept inquiry into one's own views. Drawing on the case story with Alice and her efforts toward school change, we canvassed some of the practicalities of working relationally—including doing so with people with whom you have difficult relationships.

Mindful working was presented as involving attentiveness to both the use of language, and to process. In relation to language, working mindfully implies seeking to understand others, and expressing ourselves in nuanced, differentiated ways. With respect to process, we work mindfully when we notice and contemplate the dynamics associated with change—including the more subtle, covert dynamics—as they unfold over a period.

A **practice-based** view reinforces that leadership is grounded in learning-based interventions, rather than in a person. Focusing on practice reminds us that we need to work toward building our effectiveness in enacting learning-leadership. As we saw, a crucial aspect is the quality of our own thinking and awareness.

Another benefit of our learning-centered perspective on leadership stems from our differentiating leadership and management actions, the subject of Chapter 4.

We distinguished the management mode as action taken to deal with the explicit aspects of problems; the emphasis is on task achievement, with authority providing the legitimacy.

We considered that, in practice, management-oriented actions tend to overwhelm those reflecting a learning-leadership stance. Leadership can become almost totally eclipsed by management. Unless we can distinguish leadership- and management-mode actions we run the risk of espousing leadership but demonstrating primarily a management-mode orientation in practice. Such disconnection can fuel pessimism about the prospects for real change.

Differentiating management and leadership assists us to make choices about intervention options that are most suitable to particular situations; it enables us to consciously interweave the two in order to enhance the power of our interventions; and in assessing the relative attention we give to each over time, so that we may make remedial changes.

Enacting learning-leadership also requires the exercise of choice, the theme of Chapter 5. In particular, we looked at the nature of the choices involved in deciding whether to intervene in a problem situation from a leadership-mode or management-mode standpoint. We considered how the two modes can be used to different effects in two settings: one relating to dealing with so-called "underground rules," the other to do with responding to antagonistic behavior by others. Further shifts between the modes can be made as appropriate to deal with the problem most effectively. Also considered were three guidelines to support action in the leadership mode: work from observation, attribute reasonableness, and seek to act authentically. However, even when such guidelines are applied, the risks of undertaking leadership interventions need to be carefully appraised—and factored against the possible benefits.

Part 2 built on these foundations, introducing the ARIES framework to give the concepts a more practical face. The chapters in Part 2 contained a variety of tools including the Reflection Matrix, the inquiring framework, the expressing framework, and the transformational challenge. Yet, as we worked through these chapters, we saw that putting the practices into effect involves more than the skillful application of a set of techniques.

Attending, the subject of Chapter 6, requires that we step back, at least briefly, from our pursuit of task achievement, in order to pay close attention to those we are interacting with, to signals coming from the surrounding environment, and to our own self-talk. We also need to observe keenly. This means noticing, without leaping automatically to inference and conclusion. To do so implies a deeper quality of receptiveness than that of just "paying attention," which tends to have a definite achievement orientation, and is more clearly representative of the management mode. Critical to improving our attention is learning to center our awareness in the present moment. This is not something we can bring about by following a list of how-to points.

Reflecting was presented as the reciprocal of attending; this practice concerns making sense of that which is perceived. The discussion focused on using the Reflection Matrix tool. The tool is not sufficient by itself; even when applying the tool, a thoughtful and self-aware appraisal is still necessary. The reflecting process calls for us to attribute reasonableness to other stakeholders; yet, our minds are frequently full of unflattering attributions towards others. Using the Matrix process also requires that we name our own assumptions, interests, feelings, and knowledge and subject these to scrutiny. However, we must recognize that identifying and assessing elements that sit deep in our own mind is problematic, perhaps even more so than hypothesizing about these elements with respect to other stakeholders.

Inquiring, the subject of Chapter 8, was distinguished from result-oriented questioning, where the emphasis is on querying others to find solutions to problems. In contrast, leadership-mode inquiring involves asking questions with a view to enabling learning by all involved. To assist in identifying suitable questions for particular situations, a question-type framework was introduced. This framework emphasized the importance of "exploring" questions in learning-leadership work, and cautioned against over-reliance on "gathering and clarifying" questions, which are characteristic of result-oriented questioning.

Expressing, the practice examined in Chapter 9, refers to putting forward your views as one perspective on reality, rather than as "the" reality. The practice of expressing differs markedly from conventional concepts of advocacy, which emphasize prevailing over other views. In particular, expressing is about stating your views—and the assumptions, interests, thoughts, and feelings underpinning those views—in ways that indicate openness to other viewpoints and awareness of your own actions. A framework was introduced as an aid to help speakers prepare short verbal presentations. The tool will help you contextualize your remarks, achieve more perspective on what you say, and give voice to some elements that might ordinarily be left unspoken.

In Chapter 10, we saw that, when the management mode dominates, contention is often dealt with by a "rush to convergence," as people strive to reduce the tension, particularly through confining discussions to the explicit level. Yet, in our context, we see that more is to be gained by striving to establish shared meaning. This involves delving into, drawing out and integrating perspectives from the implicit as well as explicit levels. In this chapter, **synthesizing** is put forward as a collective term referring to four types of interventions: connecting interventions (which link together contributions to a conversation); integrating interventions (which combine two or more perspectives to bring about a new, different, or more complete way of framing the problem); transformational challenges (which draw our attention to the shift required to move from current reality to vision); and relational challenges (which identify areas in which shared understandings need to be developed in order to enable progress toward the vision).

Developing Your Own Learning-Leadership Capability

How might you go about developing your own practice in learning-centered leadership? A useful starting point might be to ask yourself some hard questions about the current reality of your own relationship to leadership. Think about those who have an interest in your leadership effectiveness—perhaps people who report to you, colleagues at your level, your manager, and external partners. Would they see you as enacting leadership at all? If so, to what extent? How would they describe the type of leadership you demonstrate? Would they see you more as someone who uses their authority to achieve desired results, as some-body who influences others towards goals, or perhaps as someone who practices the kind of learning-leadership we have been discussing? How could you test and validate your assessments?

Now, shift your attention to your future vision for your practice of leadership. How would you wish to regard—and have others regard—your leadership in, say, twelve to eighteen months? What kinds of new or different behaviors would you need to demonstrate? Does your vision represent an "achievable stretch" from your current reality? That is, to what extent is your vision desirably different from your present situation, yet also realistically achievable?

Once you have thought about vision and current reality with respect to your own leadership (and, desirably, also gained some feedback from others), you might consider expressing the implied shift as a transformational challenge. Try capturing the necessary movement "from" your current practice "to" your pre-ferred future leadership style in a few succinct sentences. This statement could serve as an ongoing reference point in reviewing—and perhaps rekindling—your practice.

To make the exercise more concrete, you could then set about defining a relational challenge. As we saw in Chapter 10, a relational challenge specifies an area where shared understanding is needed to support efforts to overcome a contentious problem. In relation to your own leadership, you might identify a critical aspect of a change issue where you need to establish a joint problem definition with another stakeholder. You might also consider how you might inquire into other people's views while also making it clear that your own views are open to inquiry.

Having defined a relational challenge, you need to act on it. Your practice of learning-leadership will only be actualized once you make your first intervention. This challenge of getting started should not be underestimated. It is easy to avoid beginning practice in this area, as we saw in Chapter 3, with Alice and the question of speaking with the principal of her school. There are usually plenty of other urgent tasks to attend to, and you may have fears about how your actions will be perceived. At some point, if your practice is to bear fruit, it is necessary to take the first step.

Once underway, maintaining your practice can be difficult as well, particularly if you experience early setbacks. One danger is that your "telling self" will want to take control. You will know this is happening when you hear your inner critic delivering messages to the effect that "I'm no good at this," or "this work is too difficult." If you become aware of this happening, allow yourself to observe quietly: ask what an invisible observer might notice and be careful to tease out observation from inference. A useful rule of thumb is, Question your practice, not your person.

Bringing to mind the three Chapter 5 guidelines—concerning observation, reasonableness, and authenticity—might also help you get back into a learning frame of mind, as may working with a skilled coach. (Information about coaching for learning-leadership is available at www.intheleadershipmode.com.) If you can get into such a mental state, the challenge is to focus on your next intervention—perhaps using the ARIES tools and frameworks. Remember, the intervention is the basic unit of learning-leadership. It is not a matter of whether or not you are a leader, or how good a leader you are. It is more productive to ask what you can learn from your last intervention so you can boost the prospect of the next one being even more productive.

Developing one's capability in learning-leadership is, in some ways, like traveling, where the emphasis is on discovery and experience, rather than reaching a certain point by a particular route. Your vision for your leadership represents the destination, but the journey is more than a straightforward trip from A to B. The route is neither clear at the outset, nor well signposted. You need to be prepared for some unexpected twists and turns—and perhaps some backtracking—along the way. Some might find this frustrating. But, the unforeseen experiences often bring learning and satisfactions of their own; they can be a large part of what makes the journey rewarding.

A Note on Developing Learning-Leadership Capability at Scale

While our focus has been on learning-leadership and its practice by individuals, I am frequently asked about how these capabilities can be developed on a larger scale, for an organization or other sizeable group.

We can also frame the work required here as a transformational challenge, as a movement "from" the present state of leadership "to" a vision for leadership achieved.

To articulate the first part of the challenge we must first become clear about the current reality of leadership and its development in the organization. This incorporates (among other aspects) perceptions and deep-seated assumptions, including those of top executives. Unless we articulate them openly, those perceptions and assumptions are likely to be unconsciously projected onto any efforts for change. A common belief, for instance, is that leadership development is for "others," rather than for the people at the top who are already designated as being "leaders."

For an executive group to become aware of its members' leadership-related assumptions, the group needs to be able to inquire into the meanings the members attach to leadership. Doing so is in itself an act of learning-leadership. So, in order to foster learning-leadership, a group must first be capable of demonstrating a degree of such leadership itself. For organizations in which management-mode thinking and behavior is dominant, this can be a considerable challenge. In such organizations, we might well hear rhetoric about leadership, but signs of actual practice are likely to be harder to find. Moreover, the group would need to gain assessments of current reality as seen by other employees (and possibly other stakeholders). How do employees interpret leadership? To what extent do they see it enacted at present? Such assessments could well be confronting to the top group.

One aspect of establishing current realities is to recognize that, because the management-mode orientation tends to predominate in most aspects of organizational life, it can also drive leadership development. Are we currently looking at leadership development through a management-mode lens?

Leadership development efforts in organizations commonly carry a management-oriented framing. The signs are that the accent is on "things" and tasks, with authority providing the underpinning. A typical effort centers on a program to develop a group of "high potentials" or "emerging leaders," for "leadership roles." Putting together and conducting the program might involve tasks like clarifying the capabilities needed, selecting providers, identifying high-potentials, designing the program, and evaluating results. Perhaps there is a steering group to oversee the program, as well as an executive sponsor. Although such an approach could be conceived of in many ways, it is not difficult to see that the emphasis is on tangibles (the program, a group of "high potentials"), tasks, and authority. Authority is implicit in both the program's governance arrangements, and in what the program is designed to produce (people capable of filling "leadership roles").

If an organization seeks to develop *both* a cadre of "future leaders" *and* learning-centered leadership capability more generally, then some attention to terminology may well be called for. In particular, it might be better to name the development of aspiring top executives as, say, "executive development," rather than "leadership development." Such nomenclature is consistent with a focus on developing people for higher-level roles while *concurrently* seeking to develop learning-centered leadership capability, in the sense of leadership dispersed throughout the organization and as involving specific kinds of behavior, rather than being restricted to particular people and/or roles.

The "to" component of the transformational challenge in our context implies the need for an executive group to clarify a shared future vision for leadership. This entails the executive group conversing about a preferred concept of leadership, including the kinds of leadership-related behaviors and attitudes they would like to see demonstrated. Leadership in such a vision might be viewed as a property of the system. We then see leadership as an approach to thinking and action, different from management, which potentially anyone, at any level, can apply in a manner in keeping with their role.

The kinds of behavior that give expression to the vision would need to be considered in the particular organizational or group context. However, examples of the types of features that might be considered include: people showing a willingness to float potentially controversial ideas, thoughts, and proposals; contention—difference of view—being regarded as healthy; an evident willingness to draw out and examine other perspectives, rather than stepping up to criticize them; people feeling able to inquire into the implicit territory of unspoken assumptions, interests, feelings, and knowledge; people actually testing out ideas in action, and reflecting on the experience gained.

As well as considering the kinds of practices that would indicate learning-leadership, consideration could be given to such matters as:

- How might leadership be expressed at different levels of the hierarchy? To what extent would desired behaviors be "expected," as distinct from encouraged?

- What are the drivers in the organization that currently sustain the predominance of management-mode behavior (insofar as it does dominate)?

- What kinds of factors could support movement towards the vision?

- How might learning-leadership be expressed and practiced at top executive levels?

There might also be scope to look at how management-oriented processes could support the development of learning-leadership. Possible examples include building references to leadership into job descriptions, promulgating statements of preferred behaviors, and structuring opportunities for groups to consider contentious problems.

Care should be taken not to romanticize an ideal organization were learning-centered leadership is prevalent. It would be naïve to think that such an organization would be free of the turf-wars, skirmishes, and inter-personal and inter-group conflicts that characterize most organizations. Nevertheless, thinking about and identifying preferred behaviors and attitudes can help to "light the way" for development efforts by indicating the kinds of practices to be encouraged. Such a set of preferred practices can also serve as a kind of "measuring stick," enabling assessment of the extent to which the organization is actually heading in this direction.

Harnessing the energy needed to support movement from the present state of leadership to the realized vision is another aspect requiring attention. This kind of deep change is not achieved by routine means, by merely developing and implementing a set of strategies, though this may be part of the picture. Rather, it requires relational work, and the sponsoring group needs to be directly involved. Such a group might begin by identifying a relational challenge for itself. One top group, for instance, set about re-inventing relations between itself and the managers at the next level down. Such an exercise may well bring complications, but it moves "leadership development" out of the HR department; the top group is now participating in it directly and experientially. When a top group reflects on, experiments with, and learns about its own leadership, it sets a powerful example of learning-leadership—and generates significant energy for change.

I have proposed three areas of potential benefits to be gained from pursuing a learning-centered approach to leadership: bringing the mental resources of a greater diversity of people to bear on dealing with contentious problems; allowing more of the available intelligence to be applied to such problems; and establishing a clearer focus on the real work of leadership (rather than using the language of leadership, but enacting management in practice).

To realize these benefits, we do not need to discard conventional leadership constructs. Rather, we need to re-imagine the "forest of leadership," from Chapter 1. The challenge becomes one of noticing the wood, with its variety of tall timbers, intermediate growth, and groundcovers. We need to recognize the different constructions of leadership, and consciously redirect our attention between them. Then, shifting our attention, we turn to face a different direction; we pull clear some vines obstructing the view, and there we see a distinctively different tree.

APPENDIX

More Untangling of the Vines of Leadership

This appendix extends the discussion in Chapter One on conventional approaches to leadership. Three topics are considered:

When Executives Decide on Contentious Matters
Drawing on ideas from chapters 2 and 4, as well as Chapter 1, we discuss the common tendency to confuse executive decision-making with "leadership," particularly when dealing with contentious problems. The proposition advanced here is that it is more useful to think of leadership as processes supporting joint sense-making. Decision-making, on the other hand, is a separate function, based in authority. (Authority is a defining feature of the management mode, rather than of the leadership mode, as we discussed in Chapter 4.)

Distributed Leadership: a cautionary tale
The argument here is that the approach sometimes referred to as "distributed leadership" is often, in implementation, simply a variant of conventional authority-based conceptions.

Leadership as Involving Mutual Influence
This discussion asks whether a mutual-influence perspective overcomes the limitations of influence-based concepts of leadership as discussed in Chapter 1, particularly in the context of transformational leadership.

When Executives Decide on Contentious Matters

The discussion on leadership and authority in Chapter 1 pointed to ways in which defensive behavior patterns tend to be reinforced in authority-based structures. In particular, I suggested that there were incentives for executives to assert their views strongly, and for the people reporting to them to suppress any disagreement with those views. These dynamics can inhibit the ability of groups to productively examine and work through contentious problems.

Sometimes, however, people do speak up, challenging the views of those in higher-ranked roles. When such disagreements occur, authority generally provides the resolution mechanism. Somebody in a position of authority makes a "call" as to what action to take. I have no difficulty with that. The difficulty arises when we think of such executive decision-making as representing the exercise of "leadership."

In Chapter 2, we examined learning-centered leadership, defining it (in terms of our "higher-level" view) as a process that involves people in jointly establishing current realities, clarifying preferred futures (purpose and vision), and harnessing energy for change. This form of leadership unleashes the potential for people to think together and work relationally, *across hierarchical levels*, to overcome contentious problems. What matters is people's expertise and interest relevant to the particular problem. This need not be a function of their rank.

Decision-making, on the other hand, is an authority-based function; ordinarily, decisions are made where responsibility and accountability sits. In Chapter 4, we advanced the proposition that authority is a defining feature of the management mode. Therefore, when we rely on our authority to get things done, including making decisions, we are likely to be acting from a management standpoint rather than a leadership one.

We have, in effect, two different functions. The first emphasizes people thinking and working together on contentious matters to achieve needed change; the second accentuates making decisions in response to the outputs of that process. We often think of the second of these functions as involving leadership. My proposition is that leadership—in our learning sense—is more properly attached to the first function, with its emphasis on joint sense-making. Conversely, making decisions as to what to actions to take is most usefully seen as a matter separate from leadership.

When we rely upon on authority to take care of *both* the thinking and deciding functions, we miss out—because we constrain our ability to use learning-leadership processes to sort out contentious problems. Unfortunately, this is often our default response when we are confronted with a contentious problem.

Now, recall the story in Chapter 1 of the executive team and managers at the next level down on their teambuilding retreat. The executive team believed they needed to handle the major issues, as that was their function as the "leadership team." Meanwhile, the middle managers complained that they were generally only consulted on minor matters. I propose that, in situations like this, there can be practical benefit in disentangling decision-making from leadership. Let us use the example of these two teams to explore the benefits of making that distinction.

If the teams were to adopt a learning-leadership approach, we might imagine the two groups working together in joint session—not necessarily without difficulties—to think together about the contentious problems their organization faces. The members of this combined group would be bringing their various perspectives—their intelligence, wisdom, and insight—to bear on these problems, thereby enriching the pool of resources they utilize with pertinent issues. I am envisioning here a leadership group in the sense of a group of practitioners applying learning-leadership processes to the problems facing their organization. This is, however, not a decision-making body.

In our example, the executive group would then be responsible for making decisions about the matters considered by the larger (executive plus middle manager) group. (To more accurately reflect their role, the top group might be advised to think of themselves as an "executive" team rather than a "leadership" team.)

In short, we will benefit from making this distinction, particularly through the application of a greater range of perspectives to making sense of the problem at hand. We need to build a stronger connection between leadership and joint thinking, while also loosening the attachment between leadership and decision-making.

Distributed Leadership—A Cautionary Tale

Reflecting dissatisfaction with conventional approaches to leadership, some authors have explored approaches that place less emphasis on the contribution of the individual leader.[1] A particular body of literature has focused on so-called *distributed* leadership. This form, which has attracted interest in the schools education sector, particularly in the UK, encompasses a range of approaches linked by the common aim of involving others beyond the school principal in contributing to school leadership.[2] This could be a good thing—perhaps.

A department head in one school observed that the implementation of distributed leadership could have unanticipated side effects. At her school, the school principal implemented this approach by allocating responsibility for a variety of functions to individuals on the staff. However, as the department head put it, so many responsibilities were assigned to so many people that no matter what she tried to do, she found herself treading on someone else's toes. The result was a kind of gridlock.

Distributed leadership, at least in the case of the school example mentioned here, is a construction that comes out of a leader- and authority-centered view of leadership. According to this view, the distribution of leadership entails enabling more people to exercise authority and, presumably, responsibility. To accomplish this, someone—most likely a person in a position of considerable authority—does the distributing. As such, it sounds similar to what others might describe as delegation. Thus, it still seems to reflect the assumption that leadership is a function of authority.

While devolving authority may be desirable in many instances, it is a long way from the learning-centered view of leadership discussed in this book.

Leadership as Involving Mutual Influence

In Chapter 1, our discussion of influence focused on leaders articulating a vision and mobilizing others toward it. It is important to acknowledge that some theorists have argued that influence is not a one-way street; others can wield influence as well.[3] Isn't it likely, for instance, that team members and colleagues—with different backgrounds, assumptions, and experience—can influence each other and the leader as well, thereby enriching the vision?

While this scenario is possible, one factor working against it concerns the distribution of influence in a group. We can expect that, as a rule, the person with the highest rank is the most influential. There may be situations where one or more individuals (perhaps with particularly imposing personalities, good connections, and/or control over some or other resources) are able to wield more influence than the person with the greater authority. However, authority tends to bring with it at least some power to offer reward—even if this is only a positive performance review—and to impose sanction. In such circumstances, individuals who in other circumstances might be influential, may elect to suppress some of what they believe, think, and know, rather than mount a challenge to authority. In this situation, multiple participants exert influence, but only one tends to pull the strings.

How does the mutual influence-based approach relate to transformational leadership? Bill Drath, from the Center for Creative Leadership in the U.S., has an interesting view on this question. In his book, *The Deep Blue Sea: Rethinking the Source of Leadership*, Drath argues that a mutual influence standpoint takes as given that the person with the most influence is able to encompass the diversity of other perspectives within their own.[4] As Drath puts it, "the leader understands and empathizes with the differing perspectives and needs of followers and becomes the holder, the repository of these differences."[5] This strategy might be workable so long as any differences in view are relatively minor. But, when others are operating from fundamentally differing assumptions or worldviews, the idea of the individual leader serving as the clearinghouse for all these different views becomes problematic.[6] The leader may sincerely believe that he or she understands these differing viewpoints, but this just may not be so. Other questions also arise, such as, How well can the leader evaluate these differing viewpoints? How can the leader establish that people are not engaging in self-protective strategies?

In Chapter 1 we discussed how transformational leadership, in its simpler form—a leader conceiving of a vision and attempting to influence others toward it—is complicated by the dynamics associated with authority relationships. These dynamics make it difficult for both leaders and followers to establish the authenticity of each other's viewpoints. When we add contention within the follower group as a factor, and the possibility of followers influencing each other as well as the leader, these authority-related dynamics still apply. The leader still has more influence. In effect, we are being asked to accept the assumption that the leader can fully comprehend and integrate the contention within the group, even though there may be incentives for group members to suppress at least some of their most relevant thoughts and feelings. Such an assumption is, at best, questionable.

NOTES

Introduction

1   Nor are the assumptions necessarily consistent with each other. If we define leaders as people who are regarded by others—and who regard themselves—in that way, the first assumption allows the possibility of leaders (and leadership) by people not in positions of formal authority. This possibility is precluded in the second assumption.

Chapter One

1   Wilford, JN 1994 "Australians find trees of dinosaur vintage," *The New York Times*, December 15, World News.

2   Personal interview of David Noble by Don Dunoon, 14 March 2007.

3   Information on the Wollemi Pine from: **http://www.rbgsyd.nsw.gov.au/information_about_plants/ wollemi_pine** (accessed 29 May 2007).

4   There is no intention to liken individual leaders to "vines in a forest." The vine reference is to concepts of the leader as being all-pervasive in discussions of leadership.

5   Rost, JC 1991 *Leadership for the Twenty-first Century*, Westport, Connecticut: Praeger, pp. 27, 43-44, 58, 134.

6   One leadership scholar who consciously sets about differentiating leaders and leadership is Linda Lambert, with her concept of "constructivist leadership." "Constructivist leadership separates leadership from leader and situates it in the patterns of relationships among participants." Lambert retains at least a concept of the "formal leader." In the next sentence she observes: "Reciprocity requires that the formal leader is growing and changing in concert with others." Lambert, L (and six colleagues) 2002 *The Constructivist Leader, Second Edition*, New York: Teachers College Press, pp. 39-40.

7   Peter Gronn refers to a "doctrine of 'exceptionalism'" which "assumes that leadership is the monopoly of individual role incumbents or, at best, a handful of strategically positioned actors in organizations." Gronn, P 2003 "Leadership: Who Needs It?" *School Leadership and Management*, Vol. 23, No. 3, pp. 267-290. See especially pp. 281-283.

8   Selznick, P 1957 *Leadership in Administration: a Sociological Interpretation*, Evanston, IL: Row, Peterson, p. 24, citied in Rost, *Leadership for the Twenty-first Century*, p. 130.

9   For another interpretation of the theme that leadership can come from anywhere in an organization, see Raelin, JA 2003 *Creating Leaderful Organizations*, San Francisco: Berrett-Koehler Publishers.

10 Morgan, G 1986 *Images of Organization*, Newbury Park: Sage, p. 176.

11 Yukl, G 2002 *Leadership in Organizations, Fifth Edition*, Upper Saddle River NJ: Prentice-Hall International, Inc.

12 Another scholar regarding influence as central to concepts of leadership is Joseph Rost. Commenting on leadership definitions in the 1980s, Rost observed: "If there are few other unifying elements to our collective thought about leadership, the notion of leadership as influence is one that clearly stands out." Rost, *Leadership for the Twenty-first Century*, p. 79.

13 For a wide-ranging review of transformational perspectives on leadership, see Avolio, BJ & Yammarino, FJ 2002 *Transformational and Charismatic Leadership: the Road Ahead, Monographs in Leadership and Management, Vol. 2*, Oxford: JAI (an imprint of Elsevier Science).

14 Edited extract from a video presentation by Dr Michael Deeley, former CEO of ICI Australia Ltd, included as curriculum material produced by Monash University for the (Australian) Industry Task Force on Leadership and Management Skills ("Enterprising Nation"), March 1996.

15 In a review of seven approaches to transformational leadership, Marshall Sashkin and Molly G. Sashkin found that vision (expressed as cognitive capability) was common to all seven approaches;

communication was a factor in six. Sashkin, M & Sashkin, MG 2003 *Leadership that Matters*, San Francisco: Berrett-Koehler Publishers, p. 183.

16 Kouzes, JM & Posner, BZ 2002 *The Leadership Challenge, Third Edition,* San Francisco CA: Jossey-Bass.

17 Kouzes & Posner, *The Leadership Challenge*, p. 112.

18 Kouzes & Posner, *The Leadership Challenge*, p. 112.

19 Kouzes & Posner, *The Leadership Challenge*, p. 143.

20 For a discussion of more self-serving forms of leadership, see Williams, D 2005 *Real Leadership: Helping People and Organizations Face Their Toughest Challenges*, San Francisco: Berrett-Koehler Publishers, pp. 13-18. Williams refers to "counterfeit leadership" which he describes as "putting a false set of tasks before the people"; 'false' meaning "any activity pursued by a group that has nothing to do with progress."

21 Such a leadership style has been termed "pace-setting." See Goleman, D, Boyatzis, R & McKee, A 2000 *The New Leaders: Transforming the Art of Leadership into the Science of Results*, London: TimeWarner Paperbacks, pp. 90-91.

Chapter Two

1 The term learning-centred leadership was used in my paper: Dunoon, D 2002 "Rethinking Leadership for the Public Sector," *Australian Journal of Public Administration*, 61(3): 3-18, September. Others have also used the term, notably in the schools education sector in the UK, but not necessarily with the same meanings as conveyed here.

2 It could be a cross-organizational group, an executive team, or a work group—even two people with differing perceptions on an issue they both care about.

3 Educational leadership theorist, Linda Lambert, and her colleagues, write of constructivism in learning and in leadership. Writing from a schools education perspective, they speak of "students constructing meaning from personal values, beliefs and experiences...The social nature of learning is emphasized: shared inquiry is a central activity." Lambert and colleagues define "constructivist leading" as a "reciprocal process among the adults in the school. Purposes and goals develop from among the participants, based on values, beliefs and individual and shared experiences...Shared inquiry is an important activity in problem identification and resolution." Lambert, L (and six colleagues) 2002 *The Constructivist Leader, Second Edition*, New York: Teachers College Press, p. 14.

4 Learning can also occur when group members become conscious of the nature of the differences between their views of the problem, without necessarily finding common ground.

5 Other group members could be demonstrating ambivalence or even opposition to this work, though this would presumably slow-down, if not curtail, the processes of building shared meaning.

6 Senge, PM 1990 *The Fifth Discipline*, New York: Doubleday/Currency, pp. 205-232.

7 As a graduate student in the late 1980s, I read Bill Torbert's book *Managing the Corporate Dream*. His concept of action inquiry was a key stimulus to my early thinking about how individuals could intervene, from a learning orientation, in contributing towards change. Torbert, W 1987 *Managing the Corporate Dream: Restructuring for Long-Term Success*, Homewood, IL: Dow Jones-Irwin. In a later book, *Action Inquiry*, Torbert defined the concept in these terms: "By action inquiry, we mean a kind of behavior that is simultaneously productive and self-assessing. Action inquiry is behavior that does several things at once. It listens into the developing situation. It accomplishes whatever tasks appear to have priority. And it invites a revisioning of the task (and of our own action!) if necessary." Torbert, Bill and Associates 2004 *Action Inquiry: The Secret of Timely and Transforming Leadership*, San Francisco: Berrett-Koehler, p. 13.

8 Argyris, C & Schön, DA 1996 *Organizational Learning 11: Theory, Method and Practice*, Reading, MA: Addison-Wesley. Argyris, C 1990 *Overcoming Organizational Defenses*, Boston: Allyn and Bacon.

9 Heifetz sees learning processes as critical in leadership for dealing with "adaptive" problems: "Because

making progress on adaptive problems requires learning, the task of leadership consists of choreographing and directing learning processes in an organization or community." Heifetz, RA 1994 *Leadership Without Easy Answers*, Cambridge, MA: Belknap Press of Harvard University Press, p. 187.

10 Lambert, *The Constructivist Leader, Second Edition*. (See earlier note, this chapter.)

11 In the context of a story of a piano company dealing with change, Wilfred Drath describes three distinct, though not mutually exclusive, principles for understanding leadership: Personal Dominance, Interpersonal Influence, and Relational Dialogue. Relational dialogue is closest to the concept of learning-centered leadership in the present book. But, as Drath acknowledges (p. 161) dialogue is both "relatively easy to do and quite difficult." Drath, W 2001 *The Deep Blue Sea: Rethinking the Source of Leadership*, San Francisco: Jossey-Bass and Center for Creative Leadership.

12 That framework is presented in Chapter 9.

13 French and Bell applied the iceberg image in the context of conceptualizing organizational development efforts. Our focus is broader; on contentious problems—including OD-related problems—where leadership is a consideration. They saw the explicit side of the iceberg—which they labeled as "Formal (Overt) Aspects" as including goals, technology, structure, policies and procedures, products and financial resources. The hidden or implicit side (terminology they used) was labeled "Informal (Covert) Aspects" and included beliefs and assumptions, perceptions, attitudes, feelings (anger, fear, liking, despair, etc.), values, informal interactions, and group norms. In our approach—as distinct from French and Bell's—the distinction between the explicit and implicit sides revolves around what is visible or observable. So, values, for example, would be on the explicit side inasmuch as they are stated or declared, and on the implicit side inasmuch as they can be inferred from actions. Similarly, feelings when named (as in "I am disappointed this report is late") would be on the explicit side, while they would be attributed to the implicit side inasmuch as they could be inferred from behaviors. French, WL and Bell, CH Jr 1984 *Organization Development: Behavioral Science Interventions for Organization Improvement, Third Edition*, Englewood Cliffs: Prentice-Hall, pp. 18-19.

14 Block, P 1993 *Stewardship: Choosing Service Over Self-Interest*, San Francisco: Berrett-Koehler, p. 10.

15 Drucker, P 1999 "Managing Oneself," *Harvard Business Review*, March-April.

16 This is a topic to be developed in Chapter 9, Expressing.

17 For an overview of several transformational leadership frameworks, see Sashkin and Sashkin 2003 *Leadership that Matters*.

18 Lambert, *The Constructivist Leader, Second Edition*.

19 A case in Chapter 8 illustrates leadership-mode interventions involving two people—a manager-direct report pairing.

20 Once a thorny issue has been put before a group, any of the group members who contribute on that issue—and do so relationally—can be regarded as intervening in the leadership mode. We do not need to establish that an individual group member holds an intention toward achieving change, just that they are contributing relationally in some fashion to the meaning-making process, even if that involves expressing disagreement with other views. This recognizes that in some situations—as with Bernardo's efforts in raising the innovation matter—learning-leadership will involve one individual taking the initiative in bringing a difficult problem before a group but with others—Linda in this case—contributing significantly in helping to make sense of the issue.

Chapter Three

1 "Juanita" is not a real person; she is an ideal, an imaginary prototype and an exemplar of the kind of coaching that is called for when one is learning to work in the leadership mode. Juanita has mastery of the practices and tools within the ARIES framework as well as the conceptual thinking behind the tools. She supports her clients in making informed and conscious choices about how best to respond to the opportunities and challenges they face. If the leadership mode is to become fully realized, skillful

coaching will be required. For more on coaching and the leadership mode, please refer to the book website: www.intheleadershipmode.com.

2   In Chapter 2, we viewed learning-centered leadership through two lenses. The "higher-level" view involves processes of establishing current realities, clarifying preferred futures, and harnessing energy for change. The "close-up" view refers to processes of making specific, relational interventions to further the work of learning-centered leadership. When we make such interventions we are functioning "in the leadership mode."

3   The idea of adopting a third-party standpoint to help gain perspective on a problem derives from the work of the **Harvard Negotiation Project**. See Fisher R, Kopelman, E and Kupfer Schneider, A 1994 **Beyond Machiavelli: Tools for Coping with Conflict**, Cambridge, Mass: Harvard University Press, p. 32. These authors, writing mainly in the context of international conflicts, propose asking what a conflict would look like to a "neutral third party," a "fly on the wall."

4   University of California psychiatrist, Arthur Deikman, distinguished between two modes of consciousness: "the object mode" ("functional, adapted to the need to act on the environment") and "the receptive mode" ("the intention [is] to receive from the environment rather than act on it"). Deikman, AJ 1982 **The Observing Self**, Boston: Beacon Press, pp. 70-75.

5   Bohm, D & Peat, FD 1987 **Science, Order, and Creativity**, New York: Bantam Books, p. 241. In Bohm and Peat's writing on dialogue we can see the kinds of qualities associated with relational working as described here: "In dialogue, however, a person may prefer a certain position but does not hold it nonnegotiably. He or she is ready to listen to others with sufficient sympathy and interest to understand the meaning of the other's position properly and is also ready to change his or her own point of view if there is good reason to do so." Bohm and Peat also contrast dialogue with discussion, in which "people usually hold relatively fixed positions and argue in favor of their views as they try to convince others to change." In terms of the framework in the present book, discussion could be seen as more associated with detached working. Since my first exposure to Bohm's ideas, my experience in teaching and practicing dialogue over several years, together with my reading and thinking about the subject, have helped shape the relational working/detached working construct as presented in this book.

6   In his book, **Dialogue and the Art of Thinking Together** (1999 New York: Currency, p. 270), William Isaacs writes of people in a dialogue "choosing to loosen their grip on their positions and take in a wider horizon." Isaacs suggests that there can be a crisis here for some people who hold their assumptions as "necessary." Coming through this is to understand that "though my positions may be right and well thought through, they are still not *who I am*. I can make space for other positions without jeopardizing my own inner stability."

7   Increasingly, a mindful orientation is being recognised as a core capability, both for individuals in relation to leadership and for organizations serious about improving their cultures and performance. For one perspective on mindfulness as it relates to leadership, see Daft, RL & Lengel, RH 1998 **Fusion Leadership**, San Francisco: Berrett-Koehler. See also Sinclair, A 2007 **Leadership for the Disillusioned**, Sydney: Allen and Unwin. For discussion of mindfulness in relation to organizational culture, see Weick, KE & Sutcliffe, KM 2001 **Managing the Unexpected**, San Francisco: Jossey-Bass.

8   Langer, E 1989 **Mindfulness**, Reading, Massachusetts: Addison-Wesley, pp. 61-79.

9   Langer, **Mindfulness**, p. 63. Langer used the heading "Creating new categories" whereas I have substituted "Being mindful of perceptions and language." (Langer's other features of mindfulness were "Welcoming new information," "More than one view," "Control over context," and "Process before outcome.")

10 Piderit, SK 2000 "Rethinking resistance and recognizing ambivalence," **Academy of Management Review**, 25 (4) pp. 783-794.

11 Langer, **Mindfulness**, p. 75.

12 An example of a specific system change with process implications might be the local education authority introducing a system of awards for innovative teaching practice, which has the effect of encouraging

innovation by teachers in Alice's school, including by those she has regarded as resistant to change.

13 Much of the key conceptual work on defensive practices in organizations has been done by Chris Argyris, though his many books are not always very accessible to the lay reader. A useful summary of an organizational defensive pattern, as Argyris found it to operate among the directors of a consulting firm, is presented in: Argyris, C 1993 *Knowledge for Action*, San Francisco: Jossey-Bass, pp. 98-99.

14 Patterson, K, Grenny, J, McMillan, R, & Switzler, A 2002 *Crucial Conversations: Tools for Talking When Stakes are High*, New York: McGraw-Hill, p. 47.

15 For an insightful account of applying the tortoise and the hare parable to matters of leadership, see Fullan, M 2001 *Leading in a Culture of Change*, San Francisco: Jossey-Bass, p. 121.

16 Gallwey, W Timothy 1997 *The Inner Game of Tennis*, Revised Edition, New York: Random House.

Chapter Four

1 A distinction between leadership and management as complementary systems of action was made by Harvard professor John Kotter in his 1990 book, *A Force for Change*, (New York: Free Press). Kotter saw management as involving, "Planning and budgeting," "Organizing and staffing," and "Controlling and problem solving." Leadership, in his view, involved: "Establishing direction," "Aligning people," and "Motivating and inspiring" (pp. 4-5). While Kotter's view of leadership was essentially influence-based, his idea of the two forms as sitting alongside one another, as largely distinct yet mutually reinforcing types of action, was an important source of inspiration for the leadership-management distinction in the present book.

2 These conventional assumptions are also discussed in the Introduction.

3 The relationship between leadership, management, and authority is also discussed in the Appendix.

4 Argyris & Schön, *Organizational Learning I I*, pp. 92-96, 117-120. Argyris and Schön's distinction between "Model I theory-in-use" and "Model II theory-in-use," (referring to underlying mindsets seen to drive individual action, as distinct from espoused theory of action), was undoubtedly the greatest single influence on my conceptualizing of the leadership and management modes and their relationship. (For a particularly clear overview of Argyris and Schön's concepts see, Frydman, B, Wilson, I, & Wyer, JA 2000 *The Power of Collaborative Leadership*, Boston: Butterworth Heinemann, pp. 47-61.)

5 Deikman, *The Observing Self*, pp. 70-73. Arthur Deikman's distinction between the object mode and the receptive mode (see endnote, Chapter 3) also informed the distinction between leadership and management presented here.

6 Kotter, *A Force for Change*, pp. 4-5. (See earlier endnote, this chapter.)

7 Quinn, RE *Beyond Rational Management*, San Francisco: Jossey-Bass, p. 86. Quinn's "Competing Values Framework" was an early but significant influence on my thinking about the processes of leadership and their relationship to management.

8 Rost, *Leadership for the Twenty-First Century*. (See later endnote, this chapter.)

9 Bennis, W 1989 *On Becoming a Leader*, Reading, Massachusetts: Addison-Wesley, p. 45.

10 Yukl, G 2002 *Leadership in Organizations*, Upper Saddle River, NJ: Prentice Hall, p. 5.

11 Some people will want to see influence as a critical feature of leadership. My position is not to deny the place of influence in leadership, but to regard learning as of prior importance (for the reasons advanced in chapters 1 and 2).

12 Marquardt, M 2005 *Leading with Questions*, San Francisco: Jossey-Bass, p. 91. (Marquardt used the extract to illustrate questioning processes; not in relation to the leadership-management relationship.)

13 Joseph Rost, in his 1991 book, *Leadership for the Twenty-first Century*, regarded management as involving "a relationship between manager and subordinates in which the distinguishing feature is authority." He defined authority as "a contractual (written, spoken or implied) relationship wherein people accept

superordinate or subordinate responsibilities in an organization" (p. 146). Rost's formal definition of management was: "1) Management is an authority relationship; 2) The people in this relationship include at least one manager and one subordinate; 3) The manager(s) and subordinate(s) coordinate their activities; 4) The manager(s) and subordinate(s) produce and sell particular goods and/or services" (p. 145).

14 Heifetz, *Leadership Without Easy Answers*, p. 57.

15 For such actions to reflect learning-leadership, the interventions need to be made relationally, with an intention by at least one of the parties toward deep-reaching change.

16 We would need to look more closely at the actual interventions made, to see whether they reflected a relational quality.

17 These interventions satisfy the three management-mode criteria: focusing on explicit aspects of a problem (e.g., improvement strategies), task action in relation to these explicit aspects (e.g., involving people in developing the strategies), and legitimization through formal authority (Alice's positional authority is what enabled her to pursue such actions).

18 The very lack of any sharp delineation between leadership and management can contribute to the belief that little is to be gained from trying to differentiate the two forms. This attitude appears to be expressed in the following quote from educational leadership and change theorist, Michael Fullan: "I have never been fond of distinguishing between leadership and management: they overlap and you need both qualities." (Fullan goes on to discuss "one difference that it makes sense to highlight: leadership is needed for problems that do not have easy answers.") Fullan, *Leading in a Culture of Change*, p. 2.

19 An example of an intervention where such ambiguity is evident is when one member of a group surfaces and questions another member's assumptions on a task/technical matter, saying: "I think you're assuming that we need to (do x) and that is incorrect…" The reference to surfacing assumptions is suggestive of leadership-mode work, insofar as the intervention delves into the implicit domain. Yet the task focus and lack of any relational quality points to the management mode.

20 The leadership-management distinction as framed here reflects a learning-based view of leadership. But my colleague, Iva Wilson, who contributed the Foreword, notes that other forms of leadership need to be kept in mind, particularly in crisis situations. Iva says that, for instance, if a building is burning down, what is needed is not learning-leadership as described in this book, but action-oriented leadership to deal with the crisis. Appropriate actions might be to ensure the fire is put out and perhaps to mobilize people to recover from the damage and restore operations. In terms of the model presented in this book, such actions could be seen as in the management mode (explicit aspects include the fire and operations, task aspects include putting the fire out and restoring operations, authority would that of the relevant executives or managers authorizing such actions). Iva makes the point that some people would describe actions like this as leadership—not learning-centered leadership, but leadership nonetheless. She applies the term, "leadership in the management mode" (personal communication).

21 If you work in a technical or specialist area, such as accounting, engineering, or machine operations, you may find it helpful to imagine a third circle added into the picture—representing technical/professional/ operational work—and connected with both the circles for leadership and management. This reflects the consideration that when people are practicing leadership-mode work, they need to set this not only against their management-oriented activities, but also against whatever technical, professional, or operational roles they might fulfill.

22 Joseph Rost in *Leadership for the Twenty-first Century* argues that "leadership was consistently viewed as excellent management in the 1980s." p. 141.

23 Warren Bennis and Burt Nanus in *Leaders: Strategies for Taking Charge* (1985, New York: Harper & Row, p. 21) said, "The problem with many organizations, and especially the ones that are failing, is that they tend to be over managed and under led." Similarly, John Kotter in *A Force for Change* (1990, p. 10) remarked that, "As a whole, the data strongly suggests that most firms today have insufficient leadership,

and that many corporations are 'over-managed' and 'under-led.'" More recently, Stephen Covey in **The 8th Habit** observed: …"it's become so evident to me that most organizations, families included, are vastly over managed and desperately under led." Covey, SR 2004 **The 8th Habit: From Effectiveness to Greatness**, New York: Free Press, p. 101.

24 Covey, SR 1989 **The Seven Habits of Highly Effective People**, New York: Fireside, Simon and Schuster, p. 151.

25 Interview on **Bush Telegraph** program, Radio National, Australia, October 12, 2005.

26 As with examples elsewhere in the book, these illustrations should be taken as representing possible scenarios rather than actual events. To keep the illustrations brief, you are asked to take as given that the interventions tagged as "leadership mode" and "management mode" are in keeping with the definitions of the two modes offered in this chapter. References to "management mode" or "leadership mode" actions with these interventions should be read as *mainly* management mode or leadership mode, allowing that some actions in the other mode may also be involved.

27 What makes this intervention management-mode is that it involves an explicit issue (the meeting structure), task action (reorganizing the meeting), and is done with authority (that of the executive team members with the chief executive as head).

Chapter Five

1 A definition of culture that I find useful, with its emphasis on dynamism and diversity, is by Joanne Martin. She refers to *manifestations* of culture such as dress codes, tasks, formal rules, informal codes of behavior, jargon, and insider jokes. Martin says: "When cultural members interpret the meanings of these manifestations, their perceptions, memories, beliefs, experiences and values will vary, so interpretations will differ—even of the same phenomenon. The patterns or configurations of these interpretations, and the ways they are enacted, constitute culture." Martin, J 1992 **Cultures in Organizations: Three Perspectives**, New York: Oxford University Press, p. 3.

2 The notion of underground rules as tacit understandings, as distinct from the values declared by the organization, is based on Edgar Schein's concepts of cultural assumptions and espoused values in organizations. Schein, E 2004 **Organizational Culture and Leadership: Third Edition**, San Francisco: Jossey-Bass.

3 Although his arguments are complex, Argyris suggests that defensive practices in organizations are, in part, a product of underlying values including staying in control, ensuring that people save face, and competing to win. Argyris, **Overcoming Organizational Defenses,** p. 13.

4 The management mode does not necessarily imply going along with underground rules rather than challenging them. A variety of strategies are possible in this mode. For example, someone in a position of sufficient authority could conceivably set about changing the "don't show your hand" underground rule by issuing a directive that active support for innovation is to be included as an element in managers' performance agreements in future (an explicit aspect is the new element in performance agreements; a task aspect is issuing the directive).

5 Uri, W 1991 **Getting Past No: Negotiating with Difficult People**, London: Business Books Ltd, p. 11.

6 Uri, **Getting Past No**, p. 17.

7 Bower and Bower present a model they call DESC: Describe (the behavior), Explain (your feelings about the behavior), Specify (a preferred, different behavior) and Consequences (rewards or sanctions from behaving in the way requested). Bower, SA and Bower, GH 1991 **Asserting Yourself**, Reading, Mass: Addison-Wesley, p. 90.

8 As we have seen, management-mode interventions can also be utilized in dealing with problems we recognize as contentious. But there our objectives are likely to be to control or limit the problem in some way, rather than to understand it jointly with others.

9   These guidelines are inspired particularly by the works of Chris Argyris and David Bohm. Argyris, *Overcoming Organizational Defenses*, pp. 104-107. Bohm & Peat, *Science, Order and Creativity*, pp. 241-242. I would like to acknowledge that particular inspiration for my thinking about reasonableness came from a workshop run in Melbourne in 1995 by Rick Ross, coauthor of *The Fifth Discipline Fieldbook:* Senge, P, Roberts, C, Ross, R, Smith, B, & Kleiner, A 1994, London: Nicholas Brealey Publishing.

10 Management-mode interventions can also be used to support safety. For instance, a convener or facilitator could work with members of a group to devise a set of behavioral indicators to govern the group's interactions. The convener/facilitator could possibly monitor the group's observance of the indicators or delegate these functions. (An explicit aspect is the behavioral indicators; task aspects include devising, monitoring, and delegating the indicators; authority comes from the role of convening or facilitating the group.) Note that the actions described in this scenario suggest a somewhat detached stance for the person in the convener/facilitator role. This is not a bad thing of itself; but challenges would include stepping into a more relational frame when exploring the substantive issues, and avoiding temptations to "protect" group members from difficult interactions.

11 The emphasis here is on holding open the reasonableness principle, not on trying artificially to make people feel better about themselves, such as by offering false complements. To do so would offend the "seek to act authentically" guideline.

12 Fullan, M 1993 *Change Forces: Probing the Depths of Educational Reform*, London: The Falmer Press, p. 24. Though Fullan is writing in an educational context, I would argue that his propositions about change are applicable in virtually any organizational setting.

PART TWO

Preamble to Part Two

1   Argyris, *Overcoming Organizational Defenses*, pp. 88-89.

2   Among many useful contributions in *The Fifth Discipline Fieldbook*, by Peter Senge and several colleagues, was a section entitled *Protocols for Balancing Advocacy and Inquiry* by Rick Ross and Charlotte Roberts (pp 253-259). The protocols were instrumental in shaping my thinking about how best to practice, and teach others to practice, expressing (my term) and inquiring. I subsequently came to think that more specific, structured frameworks were needed and that the protocols were overly geared to examining assumptions and reasoning. I wanted to give more attention to surfacing and exploring other hidden aspects including unspoken feelings, interests, and knowledge. That desire led me to developing the inquiring and expressing frameworks presented in chapters 8 and 9. Another influence was a framework presented in *Personal and Organizational Transformations*, a 1995 book by Dalmar Fisher and Bill Torbert. The authors outlined a categorization of four "types of speech": Framing, Advocating, Illustrating, and Inquiring. Torbert, WR & Fisher, D 1995 *Personal and Organizational Transformations*, London: McGraw-Hill, pp. 34-36. The model was elaborated in Torbert and his associates' 2004 book, *Action Inquiry*, pp. 24-37.

3   Bohm, D & Peat, FD *Science, Order, and Creativity*; Bohm, D 1996 *On Dialogue*, London: Routledge; Senge, P *The Fifth Discipline*; Senge, P, Roberts, C, Ross, R, Smith, B, & Kleiner, A *The Fifth Discipline Fieldbook*; Isaacs, D *Dialogue and the Art of Thinking Together*.

4   Checkland, P & Scholes, J 1990 *Soft Systems Methodology in Action*, Chichester: Wiley, pp. 33-35.

Chapter Six

1   Albom, M 1998 *Tuesdays with Morrie*, Sydney: Hodder Australia.

2   Albom, *Tuesdays with Morrie*, p. 135.

3   Some inferences may be at odds with others, pointing to a need for our inferences to be tested, a topic we consider in chapters 7 and 8.

4 Gallwey suggests that, during the actual game, players should focus on one aspect, whichever works for them, such as the seams of the ball. Gallwey, *The Inner Game of Tennis*, p. 85.

5 Sinclair, *Leadership for the Disillusioned*, p. 123.

6 Krishnamurti, J 1969 *Freedom from the Known*, New York: Harper & Row, p. 114. Krishnamurti, in this extract, was writing about meditation. He saw technique-based approaches such as those described as, in effect, masquerading as meditation. To him, meditation "is to be aware of every thought, of every feeling, never to say it is right or wrong but just to watch it and move with it. In that watching you begin to understand the whole movement of thought and feeling. And out of this awareness comes silence." pp. 115-116.

Chapter Seven

1 Reflecting on past experience is also important in relation to contentious problems. For instance, in the library change case story, it may pay Emily to think and learn more about why the library project has taken so long to get off the ground, and about what factors have caused it to stall. In the leadership mode, though, the primary focus of reflecting is on learning about the present realities of the various stakeholders.

2 Obviously, preparing a Reflection Matrix might not be a useful exercise if the parties are able to talk candidly and thoughtfully about their own assumptions, interests, feelings, and knowledge. But this is often not the case, in view of prevailing patterns of defensive behavior.

3 Note, though, that the Reflection Matrix can be used with as few as two stakeholders—the case owner and one other.

4 Drawing on the management-mode definition from Chapter 4, explicit aspects in this instance include the change management plan and agreements made; tasks include preparing the plan and gaining approval; and authority comes from Emily's role in managing the project, perhaps with endorsement from the council executive.

5 Emily would be unwise to attempt this exercise unless she is confident in her facilitation abilities. She should properly state that she has prepared her own version of the Matrix—if she has done so—but making this declaration does not oblige her to table that version. She should not show a Matrix prepared by one party to another party without the first party's permission.

6 Ideally, the analysis that Emily undertakes with the librarians would include the librarians' assessments of Emily's own implicit assumptions, interests, feelings, and knowledge. In practice, the level of threat likely to result would also need to be taken into account.

7 Donald Schön used the term reflection-in-action in *The Reflective Practitioner* (1984, NY: Basic Books).

Chapter Eight

1 If your intention in this instance is primarily to learn more about a problem yourself, your questions can still amount to leadership-mode interventions, as long as they are asked relationally with an intention toward deep-reaching change, and not simply as an exercise in personal or intellectual curiosity.

2 For discussion of the effects of having one's deeper assumptions challenged, see Mezirow, J 1991 *Transformative Dimensions of Adult Learning*, San Francisco: Jossey-Bass, pp. 167-168.

3 Brown, J with Isaacs, D and the World Café Community 2005 *The World Café: Shaping Our Futures Through Conversations that Matter*, San Francisco: Berrett-Koehler, p. 92.

Chapter Nine

1 Stone, D, Patton, B & Heen, S 2000 *Difficult Conversations*, New York: Penguin, p. 148.

2 The idea of stepping back to take a neutral or third party view in conflict situations has been proposed in books associated with the *Harvard Negotiation Project*, including Stone, Patton & Heen's *Difficult*

Conversations and Fisher, Kopelman and Kupfer Schneider's ***Beyond Machiavelli***.

3   You can also *combine* the elements, as long as each is covered in some form in your presentation outline. For instance, you might include an example (illuminating) as part of your structuring of your main propositions and evidence (asserting and supporting).

4   For a discussion of framing in the context of leadership action from a learning standpoint, see, Torbert, ***Action Inquiry***, p. 28. For a treatment of framing from an influence-based leadership perspective, see Fairhurst, GT and Sarr, RA 1996 ***The Art of Framing: Managing the Language of Leadership***, San Francisco: Jossey-Bass.

5   As a useful resource on story telling in the context of leadership, see Denning, S 2007 ***The Secret Language of Leadership***, San Francisco: Jossey-Bass.

Chapter Ten

1   A "contribution" refers to any verbal or non-verbal input to a conversation.

2   Connecting interventions, as with other synthesizing interventions, do not represent a distinct form of speech. They are specific applications utilizing the other four ARIES practices (attending, reflecting, inquiring, and expressing).

3   The contributions do not need to be opposed; they may be variations on a theme, differing expressions of similar ideas. Further, at least two contributions must each be held open as adding something to a reformulation of the problem. It is not sufficient that the speaker mentions the contributions but then effectively ignores them as she puts her own view.

4   The "from—to" format is an adaptation of the transformation framework of Peter Checkland and Jim Scholes: Checkland and Scholes, ***Soft Systems Methodology in Action***, pp. 33-34. Checkland and Scholes use the term "transformation" in the context of "some entity, the 'input,' being changed or transformed into some new form of that same entity, the 'output.'" They note that transformation can be "conceptualized according to different worldviews" and give examples of different perceptions of the transformation of a public library, including: "(from) a local population (to) a local population better informed;" "(from) local provision of education (to) that provision enhanced;" "(from) books and other materials on the shelves (to) books and other materials out in the local community." In the present book, the concept of the transformational challenge incorporates differing perceptions of current reality into one statement (the "from" component) and differing perceptions of the future vision (the "to" component, representing the vision achieved), into a second statement.

5   Care is needed in applying the term transformation as it carries other associations relating to leadership and change that are not intended here. One such association is transformation as makeover or renovation, as in "out with the old and in with the new." An urban neighborhood, for instance, might be said to be transformed when land no longer used for industrial purposes is redeveloped for purposes such as residential or recreational. Our concept of transformation does not imply disposing of what has existed; it may be more a matter of re-orienting existing resources. A second connotation concerns the term transformational leader. As noted in Chapter 1, this tag is sometimes attached to individuals seen to be capable of articulating compelling visions and inspiring others to pursue them. In that chapter, we noted and put to one side concepts of "the leader." In the same vein, let us set aside here ideas about the transformational leader—which is not to deny the contribution that people regarded in this way can potentially make.

Appendix

1   See, for example, the collection of essays on aspects of shared leadership in Pearce, CL & Conger, JA (Eds) 2003 ***Shared Leadership: Reframing the Hows and Whys of Leadership***. Thousand Oaks: Sage. Another framework that moves the spotlight away from the individual leader is Joseph Raelin's concept of "leaderful practice." Raelin, ***Creating Leaderful Organizations***.

2   John MacBeath, professor of educational leadership at Cambridge (UK) offers six models of distributed

leadership, from "formal" to "cultural." However, and as MacBeath observes, his sixth category is not really "distributed" leadership: "'Distribution' as a continuous process is no longer applicable because people exercise initiative spontaneously and collaboratively, with no necessary identification of leaders and followers." MacBeath, J 2005 "Leadership as Distributed: A Matter of Practice," *School Leadership and Management*, Vol. 25, No. 4, September pp. 349-366.

3 See, for example, Rost, *Leadership for the Twenty-first Century*.

4 Drath, *The Deep Blue Sea,* Refer Chapters 3 and 4. (Drath recognizes the shortcomings of a mutual-influence approach, and proposes a form of leadership based in "relational dialogue.")

5 Drath, *The Deep Blue Sea,* p. 81.

6 Mutual influence here requires that the leader, but not others, is able to step outside his or her worldview, or basic assumptions, in order to synthesize other views.

ABOUT THE AUTHOR

Don Dunoon spent the first nine years of his working life as a health services planner, after which he served as community affairs manager for Australia's national broadcasting organization, the ABC. In both of these environments, health service and broadcasting, Don became increasingly aware of the capacity of many ordinary people to exercise leadership. Whether these were operational health workers developing new service responses to emerging community health problems, or broadcasters stretching the envelope to get new programs funded and to air, there was leadership being conducted by people who had little or no formal authority. This observation led to a question that has shaped Don's work ever since: What knowledge and practices could enable the exercise of leadership at all levels of hierarchical organizations?

In the late 1980s, Don returned to academic studies, specializing in organizational behavior. In particular, he explored the interface between organizational learning and leadership. Since completing his graduate degree, Don has furthered this interest through his own consulting practice, New Futures —helping organizations and groups apply learning-leadership principles to deal with contentious problems more efficaciously. He also coaches individuals, contributes to academic programs, and conducts workshops and seminars on the subject of leadership.

Through the combination of his keen observation skills, academic training, and direct, applied experience, Don has developed a concept of leadership that is distinct from management, and deeply rooted in learning. Learning-centered leadership has truly been—and continues to be—Don's passion. Don lives in Sydney, Australia, with wife Jennifer and children Bridget and Liam.

INDEX

A

Action inquiry . . 34, 212 *note 7*
Advocacy 168
Albom, Mitch 120
Argyris, Chris . . . vi, 34, 215 *Ch3 note 13*, 76, 96, 115
ARIES: framework overview
. . . . 8–9, 113–115
  as practices and tools. . . . 114
Asserting and supporting,
  expressing practice . . 175–177
Assumptions, hidden . . 133–134
Attending:
  management mode and . . 118
  giving full attention and . . . . .
  120–122
  perceiving holistically and . . .
  122–123
  distinguishing between
  observation and inference . . .
  123–126
  to present moment . . 126–128
Attribution dynamic. 141
Authentic action. 103–104
Authority 3, 208
  learning-centered leadership
  and 5
  leadership as entwined with
  17-20
  as contextual factor with
  leadership 19
  leadership-management
  relationship and. 77
  management mode and . . . . .
  79–81
Avolio, BJ. . . . . 211 *note 13*

B

Beliefs 170
Bennis, Warren 76, 84

Block, Peter . . . . vi, 42
Bohm, David . . . . . . vi, 59, 115
Bower, GH 100
Bower, SA 100
Boyatzis, R . . . . 212 *note 21*
Breathing and attention . . . 127
Brown, Juanita 161

C

Case stories 9
  innovation 34–38
  school change. . . . .
  53–57, 59–62, 64–68, 70–72
  spatial imaging 95–98
  business unit review . . 98–101
  library change . . . .
  . . . . 119–20, 135–142
  golf club 167, 173–181
Categories, and mindful working
  64–65
Change:
  deep-reaching 32, 45–47
  surface-level. 45
Checking questions . . . 153–155
Checkland, Peter . . . .
  . . . . . . 115, 220 *Ch10 note 4*
"Close-up" lens, on learning-
  centered leadership . . . 31–32
Coaching and learning-centered
  leadership . . . . 213 *note 1*
Complementarity between
  leadership & management . . .
  82–84
Concentration 122
Conger, JA. . . . .
  . . . . 220 *Appendix note 1*
"Connecting" interventions . . . .
  186–189
Constructivism in learning and
  in leadership . . . . . 212 *note 3*
Constructivist leadership . . . . .

. . . . 211 *note 6*
Constructivist learning. 29
Consultation. 18, 57
Contention and management
  mode 184–185
Contentious problems . . . .
  . . . . 1, 4, 29
  explicit aspects 40
  implicit aspects 40–42
Conventional leadership
  assumptions. . . . .
  . . . . 2–4, 13–24, 76–78
Covey, Stephen 84
Creative synthesis 189
Culture, organizational . . . .
  . . . . 94, 217 *note 1*
Current realities 32–33
  jointly establishing . . . 38–42
  of own practice of leadership
  201
  of leadership in organization . .
  203
Curve Ball ride. 54–55, 169

D

Daft, RL. . . . . 214 *note 7*
Decision-making 207–209
Deeley, Michael . . . 211 *note 14*
Deep-reaching change . . . .
  . . . . 32, 45–47
Defensiveness 30, 42, 94,
  98–101, 215 *Ch3 note 13*
Deikman, Arthur . . . . vi, 59, 76
Denning, Stephen . . . .
  . . . . 220 *Ch9 note 5*
Detached working 56–57
  and management mode . . . 82
Developing learning-centered
  leadership capability:
  one's own 201
  at scale 203

Dialogue. . . . .
. . 115, 214 *note 5*, 214 *note 6*
Difficult behavior, intervening
with in leadership and man-
agement modes 99–101
Disclosing, expressing practice .
. 178–180
Distributed leadership . . . 209
Diversity programs 46
Donovan, Tony v
Drath, Wilfred (Bill) . . vi, 34, 210
Drucker, Peter 43
Dunoon, Don . . . 212 *note 1*, 223
Dynamic awareness 122

E

Employee engagement programs
. . . . 46
Energy for change . . . 32, 46–47
Evidence, expressing practice. .
. . . . 176
Executive group, challenges for
leadership development. . . 203
Explicit aspects of a problem . .
. . . . 1, 40
Exploring questions. . . 156–158
Expressing: relationally. 167
mindful working and 169–170
framework. 171–181
third-party perspective and. .
. . . . 174

F

Fairhurst, G. . . . 220 *Ch9 note 4*
Feedback and transformational
leadership 23
Feelings, hidden 133–134
Fisher, Dalmar. . . . .
. . . . 218 *Preamble note 2*
Fisher, R. . . . . 214 *note 3*
Framing. . . . . . . 220 *Ch9 note 4*
"From—to" form (transforma-
tional challenge) . . . .
. . . 190–191, 220 *Ch10 note 4*

Frydman, Bert . . . v, 215 *note 4*
Fullan, Michael . . . . .vi, 105,
215 *note 15*, 216 *note 18*
Futuring questions 160–161

G

Gallwey, W. Timothy. . . . .
. . . . vi, 69, 127, 171
Gathering and Clarifying
questions 155–156
Giving full attention . . . 120–122
Goleman, D . . . . . . 212 *note 21*
Golf club case story. . . . .
. . . . .167, 173–181
"Gorge" of leadership. 14
Grenny, J . . . . .215 *note 14*
Grid search. 149
Gronn, Peter. . . . . vi, 211 *note 7*
Guidelines for safer
intervention 101–105

H

Harnessing energy for change .
. . . . 32, 45–47
Harvard Negotiation Project . .
. . . . 169, 214 *note 3*
"Head of hidden intelligence". . 2
Heen, Sheila 169
Heifetz, Ronald. . . . . . . .vi, 34, 80
Hidden aspects of a problem. .
. 40–42
Hidden assumptions, interests,
feelings, and knowledge . . . . .
. 133–134
Hierarchy: and threat. . . . 18–19
and practice of leadership . 84
"Higher-level" view, learning-
centered leadership . . . 31–32

I

Iceberg metaphor 39–40
and hidden domains. . .133–134

Illuminating, expressing practice,
. 177–178
Implicit aspects of a problem . .
. . . . .1–2, 40–42
four domains 133–134
Implied authority 80–81
Inductive process 190
Influence:
as basis of leadership . . . .
. . . . 3–4, 20–24
leadership-management
relationship and 77
expressing practice and . . 168
mutual 209–210
Inner dimension of learning-
centered leadership 53
Inquiring: as a largely undeveloped practice 148
schools example 150
relational aspect 151
mindful working and. .151–152
process perspective 152
question-type framework . . .
. 152–161
preparation 161–162
safety in 162–164
"Integrating" interventions . . . .
. 189–190
Interests, hidden. 133–134
Interpretive lens,
and expressing practice . . 175
Intervention: in leadership
mode 32, 47–49
choices (leadership and
management modes) . . 97, 99
guidelines for safety . . . .
. 101–105
*see also Learning-centered
leadership, Leadership mode,
Management mode*
Interweaving leadership and
management, examples . . . . .
. . . . 89–91
Introducing, expressing practice
. . . . 174–175
"Invisible observer". . . 56,123,169
Inviting, expressing practice . . .
. 180–181

Involvement, meaningful . .46–47
Isaacs, David . . . 219 *Ch8 note 3*
Isaacs, William. . . . .
. . . . .vi l 15, 214 *note 6*

J

Janus-like character of
contentious problems l

K

Knowledge, hidden   133–134
Kopelman, E . . . . 214 *note 3*
Kotter, John. . . . . vi, 76, 84
Kouzes, JM 21–22
Krishnamurti, J 128
Kupfer Schneider, A . . . .
. . . . 214 *note 3*

L

Lambert, Linda . . . .
vi, 34, 46, 2 l l *note 6*, 212 *note 3*
Langer, Ellen . . . . vi, 64–65
Leaders:
  presumption of equivalence
  with leadership 3, 15–16
  focus on leaders as
  comforting 16
  problems of comparing with
  managers 16, 76–77
Leadership and authority
  see Authority
Leadership and influence
  see Influence
Leadership and leaders
  see Leaders
Leadership and management
  conventional assumptions . . .
  . . . . 4, 76–78
  relationship between
  (summary of). 82
  as complementary processes
  82–84

individual preferences. . . . 84
leadership in the shadow of
  management 84–87
"seeing" leadership in relation
  to management. 87–89
holding the two modes apart,
  .88–89
interweaving the two modes
  (examples of) 89–91
see also
Leadership mode
Management mode
Leadership development . . . . .
 203–205
Leadership mode. 5, 28, 32
  interventions in . . . .
  . . . . . 47–49, 97–98, 100–101
  in relation to management
  mode 82–83
  risks and opportunities. . . . . .
 105–108
  coaching and . . . . . 213 *note l*
see also
Learning-centered leadership
Leadership and management

Leadership, as espoused value,
  88
Leadership, constructivist . . . . .
  . . . . 211 *note 6*
Leadership, conventional
  assumptions. 2–4, 13–24
Leadership, counterfeit . . . .
  . . . . .212 *note 20*
Leadership, pace-setting . . . . . .
  . . . . 212 *note 21*
Learning–centered leadership .
  14
  characteristics 4–5
  benefits 5–6, 33, 197–198
  overview of concepts. .27–28
  interventions 28, 32
  learning processes 29
  viewed through two lenses . .
  .30–33
  starting propositions. 39
  differences from transformational leadership 49–50

inner dimension 53
risks and opportunities. . . . . .
 105–108
across hierarchical levels . 208
see also Leadership mode
Lengel, RH . . . . 214 *note 7*
Library change case story. . . . .
 119–20
  and Reflection Matrix. . . . . . .
 135–142
Listening 30
"Loose cannon" leaders . .19–20

M

MacBeath, John. . . . .
  . . . . . . 220 *Appendix note 2*
Management mode 4
  features of 78–82
  strategic aspects 81
  compared to leadership
  mode 82–83
  eclipsing leadership. . . .84–87
  reflecting and 132
  result-oriented questioning
  and 148–150
  advocacy and. 168
  expressing practice and . . 177
  contention and 184–185
  leadership development and .
 203
  interventions to support
  safety . . . . .218 *note 10*
Management skills 86
Marquardt, Michael 78
Martin, Joanne . . . . . . 217 *note l*
McKee, A . . . . 212 *note 21*
McMillan, R. . . . . . . .215 *note l 4*
Mezirow, J . . . . . 219 *Ch8 note 2*
Mindful working. 62–67
  perceptions and language . . .
  64–65
  process and 65–67
  inquiring practice and . . . . . .
  151–152
  expressing practice and . . . . .
  169–170

Mirror test 43
Morgan, Gareth . . . . vi, 20
Mutual influence 209–210

N

Nanus, Burt . . . . . . 216 *note 23*
National Parks and Wildlife
   Service, NSW 13
National Science and Technology
   Centre (Australian). . . . 54–55
Noble, David 13

O

O'Brien-Levin, JoAnne v
   see also Wyer, JoAnne
Observation and inference,
   distinguishing between . . . . . .
   123–126
Observation guideline. . . . .
  101–102
Openness in the moment . . . .
   121
Organizational defensive
   routines 96

P

Patterson, Kerry. 67
Patton, Bruce 169
Paying attention instrumentally
   118
Pearce, CL. . . . .
   . . . . 220 *Appendix note 1*
Peat, F, David 59
Perceiving holistically . .122–123
Peripheral perception 122
Piderit, SK. . . . . 214 *note 10*
Posner, BZ. 21–22
Power 18, 106
Powerlessness 87
Practice-basis 67–70
   expressing and 171
   developing one's own

learning-leadership capability
   202
Preparation, for undertaking
   interventions 106–107
Pressures favoring management
   activity over leadership. . . . . .
   84–87
Problems, types for which
   learning-leadership processes
   are intended 6–7
Process and change, mindful
   working 65–66
Process in-the-moment. . .66–67
Provisional language. 170
Purpose 31, 42–43
   of book 6
   expressing practice and . . 174

Q

Questacon 54–55
Questioning, result-oriented. . .
  148–150
Questions: well-crafted 147
   question-type framework . . .
  152–161
   Checking 153–155
   Gathering and Clarifying . . . .
  155–156
   Exploring 156–158
   Testing 158–160
   Futuring 160–161
   appropriate to the moment
   162
Quinn, Robert . . . . .vi, 76

R

Raelin, JA. . . . . . . 211 *note 9*, 220
   Appendix note 1
Reasonableness principle . . . . .
   102–103
Reflecting: relationship with
   attending 131
   in ARIES framework . 131–132
   close to the action . .143–145

social aspect 144
on past experience. . . . .
   . . . . 219 *Ch7 note 1*
Reflection Matrix: 133–143
   library change case story . . . .
  135–142
   value of 135
   stakeholders for inclusion 136
   completing the Matrix . . . . . .
  136–137
   reasonableness principle and
   137
   worked Matrix for library
   change case 138–139
   interpreting and utilizing
   completed Matrix. . .140–141
   testing Matrix content . . . 142
Reflection:
   usage of term 131
   in the management mode . . .
   132
Relational challenge. . .193–195
   in own practice of leadership
   201
   for an executive group. . . 205
Relational character of leadership-mode interventions . . . .
  47–49
Relational working. . . 30, 54–62
   as distinct from detached
   working 56–59
   in practice 59–62
   inquiring and 151
   expressing and 167
Resistance to change. . . .64–65
Result-oriented questioning . . .
  148–150
   management mode and. . 149
Risks and opportunities of
   learning-centered leadership
   . . . . 42, 105–108
Roberts, Charlotte . . . .
   . . . . 218 *Preamble note 2*
Ross, Rick. . 218 *Preamble note 2*
Rost, Joseph . . . .
   . . . vi, 15, 76, 211 *note 12*, 216
   note 22
"Rush to convergence" 184

S

Safer intervention, guidelines for,
. . . . 101–105
Safety 67
  in inquiring. 162–164
Sarr, RA. . . . . . . 220 *Ch9 note 4*
Sashkin, Marshall . . 211 *note 15*
Sashkin, Molly G. . . 211 *note 15*
Schein, Edgar . . . . vi, 217 *note 2*
Scholes, Jim. . . . .
      . . . . . . 115, 220 *Ch10 note 4*
Schön, Donald . . . .
      . . . . vi, 34, 76, 219 *note 7*
School change case story . . . . .
  53–57, 59–62, 64–68, 70–72
Schools, inquiring example . . . .
  150
Schools, student leadership as
  authority-based. 17–18
Schwartz, Morrie 120
"Seeing" leadership in relation to
  management 87–89
Selznick, Philip. 17
Senge, Peter . . . . vi, 33, 115
Service 42
Setbacks, dealing with 107
Shared leadership . . . .
      . . . . 220 *Appendix note 1*
Shared meaning 29, 47
Shared vision *see* Vision
Sinclair, Amanda . . . .
      . . . . 127, 214 *note 7*
Social construction of meanings
  29
Sound purpose *see* Purpose
Spatial imaging case story . . . . .
  95–98
Speaking provisionally 170
"Species" of leadership. 14
Stance, when expressing. . . 175
Stillness and attending. 126
Stone, Douglas. 169
Stories, expressing practice. . . .
  178

Supervisory authority . . . 79–80
Sutcliffe, KM . . . . 214 *note 7*
Switzler, A. . . . . 215 *note 14*
Symptomatic fixes 39
Synthesizing: interventions . . . .
  183–184
  management-mode responses,
  183–185
  "connecting" interventions, . . .
  186–189
  "integrating" interventions . . .
  189–190
  transformational challenge. . .
  190–193
  relational challenges . . . .
  193–195

T

Technical/professional authority
  80
Testing questions 158–160
Threat 30, 42, 94, 98–101
Torbert, William (Bill). . . . .
  . . . vi, 34, 115, 212 *note 7*, 220
  Ch9 note 4
Tortoise and hare. . . 215 *note 15*
Transformation. . . . .
  . . . . 220 *Ch10 note 4*,
  220 *Ch10 note 5*
Transformational challenge . . . .
  190–193
  one's own practice of leader-
  ship and 201
  leadership development at
  scale and 203
Transformational leadership . . .
  . . . . 3–4, 20–24, 33
  hazards of 22–24
  differences from learning-
  centered leadership . . . 49–50
Two lenses on leadership . . . . .
  30–33

U

Underground rules 95–96
Ury, William 99

V

"Vines" of leadership . . . .
  . . . . 14, 24, 75–77
Vision 31, 33
  transformational leadership
  and . . . . 20—24
  shared 43–45
  challenges of developing . . 44
  building and ARIES practices. .
  45
  transformational challenge
  and 191–192
  for own practice of leadership
  201
  for leadership in organization
  204

W

Weick, KE . . . . 214 *note 7*
Wilford, JN . . . . 211 *Ch1 note 1*
Williams, D . . . . 212 *note 20*
Wilson, Iva . . . .
  . . . v, 215 *note 4*, 216 *note 20*
Wollemi Pine 13
Worldviews 29
Wyer, JoAnne . . . . . . 215 *note 4*
  see *also*
  O'Brien–Levin, JoAnne

Y

Yammarino, FJ. . . . . 211 *note 13*
Yukl, Gary 20, 77

Printed in the United Kingdom by
Lightning Source UK Ltd., Milton Keynes
139080UK00001B/11/P